# ATLANTIS
*and the*
# COMING
# ICE AGE

---

"Once again Frank Joseph has shown that when it comes to Atlantis and related subjects, no one else knows as much. In this case he has taken on two very difficult subjects but has succeeded in extracting some of the most fascinating history anyone has seen in a long time."

J. DOUGLAS KENYON, EDITOR OF *FORBIDDEN HISTORY*
AND *ATLANTIS RISING* MAGAZINE

"Tracing the dispersal of Atlanteans and their knowledge, both prior to and after the destruction of their homeland, becomes extremely convincing because of the results of Joseph's scholarship and preciseness."

*NEW DAWN MAGAZINE*

# ATLANTIS
## *and the*
# COMING
# ICE AGE

## The Lost Civilization—
## A Mirror of Our World

## FRANK JOSEPH

Bear & Company
Rochester, Vermont • Toronto, Canada

Bear & Company
One Park Street
Rochester, Vermont 05767
www.BearandCompanyBooks.com

Bear & Company is a division of Inner Traditions International

Originally published in 2010 by Bear & Company under the title *Atlantis and 2012: The Science of the Lost Civilization and the Prophecies of the Maya*

**Library of Congress Cataloging-in-Publication Data**
Joseph, Frank.
  [Atlantis and 2012.]
  Atlantis and the coming ice age : the lost civilization, a mirror of our world / Frank Joseph.
      pages cm
  Includes bibliographical references and index.
  Summary: "Reveals the parallels between the rise and fall of Atlantis, cultures in ancient Mesoamerica, and our modern civilization" — Provided by publisher.
  ISBN 978-1-59143-204-3 (pbk.) — ISBN 978-1-59143-783-3 (e-book)
  1. Maya astronomy. 2. Atlantis (Legendary place) 3. Cayce, Edgar, 1877–1945—Prophecies. I. Title.
  F1435.3.C14J67 2015
  001.94—dc23
                                                                2014034601

Printed and bound in the United States by McNaughton & Gunn, Inc.

10  9  8  7  6  5  4  3  2  1

Text design and layout by Debbie Glogover
This book was typeset in Garamond Premier Pro with Gill Sans MT Pro, ITC Franklin Gothic, and New Aster LT Std as display fonts

Chapter 11 first appeared as "The Remarkable Inca Calendar," by Frank Joseph, in *Atlantis Rising* magazine 12, no. 72 (November/December 2008). It is republished here with permission.

Chapter 12 first appeared as "The Significance of the Number 11 in the 2012 Prophecy," by Frank Joseph, in *Mysteries* magazine, no. 23 (2009). It is republished here with permission.

To send correspondence to the author of this book, mail a first-class letter to the author c/o Inner Traditions • Bear & Company, One Park Street, Rochester, VT 05767, and we will forward the communication, or contact the author directly at **www.ancientamerican.com**.

# Contents

# Time Line of Significant Events

**9400 BCE** The Atlantean flood occurred, according to a literal reading of Plato's dialogues, *Timaeus* and *Kritias*.

**3814 BCE** The Age of Atlantis began with the zodiacal Age of Taurus.

**3114 BCE** The Mayan calendar's Long Count opened on 4-Ahau 3-Kankin (August 11), coinciding with the first of four global catastrophes. It was referred to by the Mēxihcah as 4-Ocelotl, or 4-Jaguar.

**2193 BCE** Earth's brush with Comet Encke resulted in a worldwide catastrophe, the Mēxihcah 4-Ehécatl, or 4-Windstorm.

**1628 BCE** The Mēxihcah 4-Quihuitl, or 4-Fire from Heaven, was aptly named for Comet Encke's return barrage of meteoric material, which generated a series of gigantic tsunamis to obliterate Lemuria.

**1198 BCE** The final destruction of Atlantis was associated with the Mēxihcah 4-Atl, or 4-Water.

**561 BCE** Solon returned to Athens from Egypt with the story of Atlantis.

**399 BCE** Plato composed his account of Atlantis based on Solon's copy.

**391 CE** The memorial column from which Solon had transcribed the history of Atlantis was lost when Christians demolished Egypt's Temple of Neith, where it had been preserved until that time.

**1514** Pope Leo X declared that the world would end five hundred years hence.

**1479** The Aztec Calendar Stone was erected atop Tenochtitlán's great pyramid.

**1521** Tenochtitlán fell to Spanish invaders on August 13.

**1790** Sewer workers in Mexico City accidentally excavated the Aztec Calendar Stone on December 17.

**1930** Serbian scientific genius Milutin Milanković discovered the relationship between recurring ices ages and variations in Earth's rotation.

**1945** The death of Edgar Cayce.

**1968** The Bimini Road was discovered.

**1972** The U.S. government launched Project Stargate.

**1973** Unaware of Nahui-Ollin, or 4-Ollin, Dennis and Terence McKenna calculated "the end of time" from the Chinese I Ching for December 22, 2012.

**2012** The Mayan calendar ended on the morning of the winter solstice, December 21, 2012, marking the beginning of a world transformation for better or for worse . . .

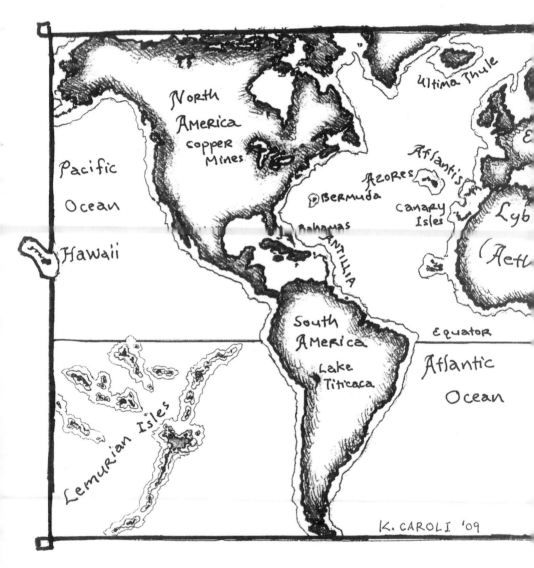

*Map of the ancient world showing the location of Atlantis*
*and the Lemurian Islands, drawn by Kenneth Caroli.*

# Rewinding the Mayan Calendar

Millions waited on the morning of December 21, 2012, to see if humanity would survive the next twenty-four hours. The much-ballyhooed Mayan calendar was poised to tick off its last moments after more than five millennia of marking time. The mystifying timekeeper had been set in motion 1,872,000 days earlier by the Long Count.

During the final years leading up to that terminal expectation, growing crowds of authors, magazine reporters, movie makers, and television producers foreshadowed doomsday with increasingly lurid imagery. Their dire prognostications were dismissed by scoffers, for whom 4-Ahau 3-Kankin, as the Maya referred to it, was simply the conclusion of an artificial cycle of time, nothing more. They claimed bragging rights when the proposed end date came and went with no perceptible change. But by limiting the Mayan calendar's final prediction to a single day, skeptics missed the point by a cosmic margin.

The Maya deliberately chose December 21, the shortest day followed by the longest night, as an allegory for decline and ignorance. It signifies an extended dark term—the figurative death of the sun—not a single cataclysmic twenty-four-hour period. They never intended 2012's winter solstice to be an event in and of itself, but instead meant it to delineate a shadow into which our world would begin to irreversibly move. Accordingly, the Mayan prophecy is right on target, as climate and civilization experience an accelerating "dissolution of forms" Friedrich Nietzsche himself predicted for humankind 150 years ago.[1] The quite observable imbalance of Earth's biosphere parallels political, economic, and cultural deterioration with unprecedented storm violence and record-breaking temperatures contrasting with popular mistrust of government, the collapse of long-established financial networks, and burgeoning illiteracy. Only in this broader sense can the Mayan calendar be properly understood as it was originally intended.

The morning of December 21, 2012, nonetheless presented a singular event in the heavens, with the southern end of our galaxy's Dark Rift forming a perfect alignment with the midpoint in the Milky Way. The Long Count began 5,126 years before, on August 11, 3114 BCE, with a celestial orientation as well, with the planet Venus transiting directly over the Pyramid of the Moon at Teotihuacán (meaning "where men become gods"), in the Valley of Mexico.* Although mainstream archaeologists date the Mesoamerican city no earlier than 200 CE, David Hatcher Childress, an author of alternative history, reports that "further radiocarbon tests gave a date of 1474 BCE (with a possible small error either way). A date of circa 1400 BCE is now widely accepted."[2] If the older date is correct, then it precedes the rise of the Maya by twelve hundred years and must, therefore, belong to an earlier, unknown people at least contemporaneous with the Olmec, who were Mesoamerica's earliest known civilizers, beginning around 1500 BCE.

Even with the older radiocarbon date, the time gap between the start of the Mayan calendar and the earliest evidence of occupation at Teotihuacán is quite large. We are left to speculate whether a sacred structure venerated before the present Pyramid of the Moon occupied the same position at the earlier date to align with the singular transit of Venus. Unique it certainly was, because the planet's appearance

---

*The transit of Venus over Teotihuacán's Pyramid of the Moon in the late fourth millennium BCE was discovered by astronomer Joseph Goodman in 1905.

directly over the Pyramid of the Moon (or a preexisting edifice) was a one-time orientation that never occurred before and will not happen again, just as the alignment between the Dark Rift and the midpoint in the Milky Way on December 21, 2012, was entirely novel. Although separated by fifty centuries, they nonetheless took place within six minutes of each other, at 11:05 a.m. and 11:11 a.m., respectively. Were the Maya and their unknown predecessors aware of the time synchronicity as well?

There are other cogent similarities: Their Long Count began with a universal catastrophe that Aztec high priests knew as 4-Atl, or 4-Water—with the number four signifying the cardinal directions, indicative of the disaster's global magnitude. The Long Count was likewise envisioned as terminating in a similarly worldwide cataclysm, a less specified Rebellion of Earth, suggesting—appropriately, in view of today's ecological concerns—trouble with our biosphere. The incredible astronomical precision with which the Maya and their forerunners delineated both the opening and closing of their calendar appears to have been a deliberate attempt at underscoring the accuracy of their predictions for global upheavals.

Scientists know, for example, that an acidity spike in Greenland's Camp Century ice core indicates a large and sudden increase of ash fall worldwide—a dust veil event around 3100 BCE—occasioned by the abrupt appearance of massive ash in the atmosphere. Evidence for this event is additionally recorded in tree rings in Ireland and England. It was caused by a comet or series of comets that rained down meteoric material around the Earth.[3] North-central Australia's five-hundred-foot-wide Henbury Crater is surviving testimony to that celestial barrage.

The Maya associated the planet Venus, the heavenly body connected to the beginning of the Long Count, with the Feathered Serpent, Kukulcan, their founding father from Patulan-Pa-Civan, far across the sea, "where the sun rises."[4] He was remembered as "the first after the flood," because he was the first to arrive after escaping from the former Land of Abundance when "a fiery rain fell, ashes fell, rocks and trees crashed to the ground. Then the waters rose in a terrible flood. The sky fell in, and the dry land sank into the sea."[5] Among the cultural gifts he bestowed on the indigenous peoples of Yucatán was a sacred almanac salvaged from lost Patulan-Pa-Civan, an heirloom they preserved and modified over successive generations. The almanac had been created in the Land of Abundance for chronicling significant human events by associating them with extraordinary natural phenomena, because both seemed connected through common cycles of time. As such, documenting these patterns supposedly allowed for predicting their recurrence in the related spheres of humankind and Nature.

The similarity between Kukulcan's story and the destruction of Atlantis is all too obvious. Indeed, that sunken realm and the Long Count seem inextricable; one illuminates the other. In my other books on the subject I relied mostly on science to argue a case for Atlantis, but here the drowned kingdom reappears in a psychic context, supported whenever possible by archaeology, geology, and comparative oral traditions. How could it be otherwise? Poseidon—the sea god whose colossus stood in an immense temple at the religious center of Atlantis—was himself a mythic embodiment of the link between the conscious and subconscious mind: while the ocean surface reflects one form of reality, just beneath, dynamic forces flourish unseen. With Poseidon as our guide, paranormal considerations are more than appropriate for this exploration.

*Atlantis and the Coming Ice Age* is divided into two sections. Part 1 covers the fate of Atlantis and the prophecies of calamity that have come down to us through the Mayan calendar, which is thought to have an Atlantean connection. Part 2 explores the visions of twentieth-century psychic Edgar Cayce regarding the island of legend. Together, these approaches shine a light on what may lie ahead for humans of the twenty-first century.

Chapter 1 recounts how Plato came to tell the story of Atlantis, although he is but one of many clues to the island. The ancient Egyptians also refer to a great island overwhelmed by the sea. Critics and naysayers abound, claiming Atlantis was either a figment of the imagination or an existing landmass that was misidentified, perhaps the island of Helike or Thera. The time of its existence is also a bone of contention, with dates ranging from three thousand to fourteen thousand years ago. Yet discovering our spiritual inheritance from Atlantis may be more important than pinning down the exact time and place of its existence. Chapters 2 and 3 discuss the esoteric energies associated with the island and the sacred numbers that went into its creation, from the six winged horses in the Temple of Poseidon to the ten kingdoms that made up the Atlantean Empire.

Chapters 4 and 5 shift our focus to Mesoamerican calendrics and their connection to the Atlantis of long ago, while chapter 6 discusses the end of the Mayan calendar on December 21, 2012, and presents the notion that 2012 represents merely the beginning of the end. We also explore what the figure associated with that end date—the Clenched Fist of Tonatiuh—might represent.

I became familiar with the Long Count during my first archaeological travels through Mexico in 1986, many years before the 2012 controversy became public. My sources indicate that the Maya did indeed anticipate a global catastrophe to close out the present age, just as a cataclysmic deluge—4-Atl, or 4-Water—began it more than five thousand years before. Although definite in their insistence on the occurrence of such a calamitous event, they were far less specific in describing it, hinting only that 4-Ahau 3-Kankin would usher in the Rebellion of Earth.

In searching for some disaster convincingly powerful enough to affect the entire world, or, at any rate, modern civilization, I ruled out the obvious suspects—asteroid collisions, germ warfare, nuclear or other weapons of mass destruction, viral epidemics, greenhouse gases, Planet X, gamma ray bursts, extraterrestrial invasions, overpopulation, and so forth. Most were at least theoretically possible to one degree or another, but unlikely. There are, however, several far more probable scenarios that fit the Mayan prophecy in terms of character and immediacy.

Foremost among them is not global warming nor climate change, but climate deterioration. As such, some professional climatologists wonder if Earth's Northern Hemisphere may have already entered another glacial era. Most believe we are at least overdue for a resumption of ice age conditions, which must set in, sooner or later. Could global warming trigger the next ice age? That theory and more about an impending deep freeze are discussed in chapter 7.

*Atlantis and 2012,* my first investigation of the Mayan calendar, explored a particular type of solar event known to science but hitherto unfamiliar to the general public: the electromagnetic pulse (EMP). It occurs in the form of a geomagnetic storm, when the shock wave of coronal mass ejections from the sun collides with Earth, compressing and transferring energy into our magnetosphere. The result is an extraordinary display of the aurora borealis in the heavens and worldwide power outages on the ground. The EMP interfaces with and shorts out everything electronic—from the Internet, telephone, television and radio networks, international power-grid systems, and avionics to refrigeration for food and medical supplies and pumping stations for gas and water. Since the publication of that volume, other researchers have delved deeper into the authentic menace of a coronal mass ejection, helping to establish and expand *Atlantis and 2012*'s original premise.[6] Chapter 7 presents the disaster that would ensue should we be struck by another super solar storm.

According to a study by Metatech Corporation, a storm with a strength comparable to a relatively minor EMP in 1921 that temporarily disrupted New York City transportation would destroy more than three hundred transformers and leave more than 130 million Americans without power, at a cost totaling several trillion dollars.[7] In June 2013 a joint venture from researchers at Lloyd's of London and Atmospheric and Environmental Research (AER) in the United States used data from a more powerful geomagnetic storm that occurred in 1859 to total the cost of a similar disaster and estimated it, conservatively, at $2.6 trillion. Damages would far more likely exceed this estimate to incur the ultimate cost, given our global civilization's economic decline, burgeoning crime, escalating international terrorism, and general pessimism for the future, resulting in the fulfillment of the Mayan calendar's most dire prognostications.[8]

The threat from our own star is not a once-in-a-millennium phenomenon. In July 2013, just weeks after Lloyd's of London issued its warning, global civilization had a brush with Armageddon. "The Earth barely missed taking a massive solar punch in the teeth two weeks ago," reports Paul Bedard in the *Washington Examiner*.[9]

Although astronomers are unable to determine when the next such incident will take place, they concur a coronal mass ejection at least as potent as 1859's Carrington Event is inevitable. That solar flare instantly severed communications across the United States, but fried wires were hastily restrung, burn-damaged telegraph stations quickly repaired, and everything was up and running in time for the Civil War. The same plasma surge today would utterly short out our electronically powered society, from Main Street to Wall Street. Virtually everything would go down at once, because America's electronic grid system is thoroughly interdependent, creating a "cascade effect" across the entire nation, just as all Quebec was blacked out in 1989 by a lesser, if similar coronal mass ejection.

While another ice age or Carrington Event could shake civilization to its core, both are minor incidents in comparison to the sea floor's immense stores of methane gas waiting for release from their eroding "cages" to cause the world's greatest extinction episode since the Permian Period, when more than 80 percent of life on Earth perished in an instant. This rapidly developing hazard warrants an entirely new discussion, one you'll find in chapter 9.

These doomsday scenarios are not alarmist conjectures but represent credible potentialities generated by actual phenomena and are, as such, plausible candidates for the Mayan calendar's lingering prophecy. Far from having been invalidated by the deceptively tranquil passage of 2012's winter solstice, that symbolic date simply marked the edge of a shadow into which our world descended. What may await us as it deepens is the subject of our story.

A world-changing moment of historic transformation, as embodied in the Mayan calendar, was anticipated by other, diverse cultures far beyond Mexico. Another prognosticating calendar followed by Hindu adepts of ancient India is remarkably similar to Mesoamerican versions. Could one have conceivably influenced the development of the other? Or were they separate but kindred legacies from an even older Atlantis? If independently invented, they tend to remarkably confirm the essential correctness of their shared conclusion; namely, that human civilization is scheduled to undergo its most decisive crisis during the twenty-first century. This global crossroads was additionally envisioned in the disparate folk traditions of North America's Hopi Indians, the Norse sagas of medieval Scandinavia, and Shang Dynasty China's I Ching, a predictive system more than three thousand years old, still in use today. Yet another non-Mayan calendar is described in chapter 10. A counterpart used by priests of the Inca Empire preserved the transformational highlights of their past, going back some thirty centuries. But it also foresaw an ultimate finality. Chapter 11 delves into the relationship between the Mayan and Incan calendars.

No conceivable scientific method could have enabled the Maya or their Atlantean predecessors to so accurately determine the one-time transit of Venus over Teotihuacán in 3114 BCE or the equally unique alignment between our galaxy's Dark Rift and the midpoint in the Milky Way in 2012. When conventional science reaches its limits, possibilities for remote viewing—projecting human consciousness beyond time and space—must be considered. Such is the topic of chapter 12. Chapter 13 delves into the question of how the Maya could have known the information revealed through their calendar.

No discussion concerning Atlantis is possible without including the Sleeping Prophet, America's greatest psychic of the twentieth century. Part 2 comprises nine chapters subjecting Edgar Cayce's subconscious insights about the lost empire to the most thorough scrutiny, aided by current scientific knowledge. The image that emerges is unusually vivid and human, with real-life men and women exerting limited control of their ultimately disastrous destiny.

Catastrophic choices form the core of the Mayan prophecy, and we find parallels with those predictions in ancient Atlantis, whose people were caught in a self-destructive pattern all too recognizable by humans living in the modern world. In endeavoring to clarify such awful comparisons, I begin by posing two questions: What did the Maya themselves really say about the end of their calendar? What are the most credible possibilities for its fulfillment?

## PART ONE

# The Prophecies

*Life beyond the Fifth Sun*

# 1

# Historical Atlantis

While neither the first nor the only one of its kind, Plato's account is the best-preserved description of Atlantis to have survived antiquity. It is, therefore, the most important document available to students of this sunken realm, made all the more valuable by the Greek philosopher's prestige among Western civilization's most influential thinkers.

He cites Atlantis in two dialogues—the *Timaeus* and *Kritias*—as an example illustrating the point he was attempting to make, that human societies begin to self-destruct when their citizens no longer honor organic relationships between the spiritual and the material spheres of existence. Imbalance in one, he states, sets up a deteriorating resonance in the other. Such a bond is unseen until the consequences of cosmic disharmony reveal themselves in physical destruction. This fact alone—that Plato used Atlantis to exemplify his argument—is sufficient evidence to verify the drowned kingdom's historical authenticity.

The account did not originate with him; he inherited it from Solon, the famous lawgiver who learned of the sunken civilization while visiting Egypt around 565 BCE. During his tour of a temple of the goddess Neith along the Nile Delta, a high priest translated the story of Atlantis, which had been recorded in hieroglyphic text on a monumental pillar.

The word *Atlantis* is a Greek alteration of the Egyptian word *Etelenty*. The name Etelenty appears in the Book of Coming Forth by

*Figure 1.1. Solon learned about Atlantis from a temple priest who translated an account of the lost city from a memorial column. In 561 BCE, the famous legislator returned to Athens, and the story was cited sixty-three years later in Plato's* Timaeus *and* Kritias.

Day (better known as the Book of the Dead), a compilation of Egyptian liturgical texts buried with the deceased to help the soul along its underworld journey through death to new life. *Etelenty,* according to Dr. Ramses Seleem's 2001 translation, means "the land that has been divided and submerged by water."

Variations of Atlantis as a flooded landscape occur often in ancient Egyptian literature. Thaut, the god of wisdom, also known as Thoth, was enraged by the decadence of an antediluvian humanity. "I am going to blot out everything which I have made," he declares in the Theban Recension of the Book of the Dead. "The Earth shall enter into the waters of the abyss of Nun [the sea god] by means of a raging flood, and will become even as it was in the primeval time!"[1] Thaut appears again in the Edfu texts, which locate the "Homeland of the Primeval Ones" on a great island overwhelmed by the sea with most of its inhabitants during Zep Tepi, or the First Time. Thaut escaped the deluge in the company of seven sages who brought their preflood technology to the Nile Delta, thereby sparking pharaonic civilization.[2]

After returning from Egypt with the story of Etelenty, Solon was preparing a Greek rendition when he passed away in 559 BCE. Plato's version presents most of the facts, but in a more straightforward form than the unfinished epic. Ignoring this documented pedigree, skeptics claim that Atlantis was unknown before Plato supposedly invented it. They fail to recognize, however, that Atlantis had already been memorialized in a public event conducted throughout ancient Greece.

During the Lesser Panathenaea female participants in the all-Athenian festival wore a garment caught at the shoulders and draped in folds to the waist. Known as a *peplum,* this garment was adorned with images "which showed how the Athenians, supported by Minerva [the Latin version of the Greek goddess Athena], had the advantage in the war with the Atlantes," according to the renowned nineteenth-century classical scholar Philipp August Böckh.[3] Because the Panathenaea was celebrated annually for centuries before Plato's birth, he could not have fabricated Atlantis, which was already well known to generations of Greeks. Furthermore, their long familiarity with the story underscores his purpose in using it as a veritable historical example for the philosophic argument he made in the *Timaeus* and *Kritias.*

Some skeptics claim he merely conflated a similar natural disaster that occurred during his own lifetime with a fictional Atlantis. They refer to Helike, located little more than a mile from the Gulf of Corinth. During major seismic activity, the large, important city and its immediate vicinity, with all its inhabitants, suddenly collapsed 1.25 miles beneath the surface of the earth. The sea rushed in, dragging down ten Spartan ships riding at anchor. There were no survivors. Over time, the sunken ruins of Helike were gradually silted over and lost until excavations brought them to light near the village of Rizomylos in the summer of 2001. Their archaeological discovery has since been added to the World Monument Fund's list of One Hundred Most Endangered Sites.

Yet Plato's account could not have been based on Helike's fate, because the Greek city was destroyed during the winter of 373 BCE, some twenty-five years *after* he wrote the Atlantis narrative, immediately following Socrates' suicide in 399 BCE. Moreover, Plato would have never succeeded at trying to pass off Helike as Atlantis, because the Achaean city's demise was an infamous affair that occurred during the lifetime of his contemporaries.

Other skeptics insist that the Aegean island of Thera was really Atlantis, but their arguments are no less flawed, and they unravel under scrutiny.* Suffice it to say here that Thera lies in the Mediterranean Sea, not the Atlantic Ocean, and additionally bears little in common with

---

*See Frank Joseph, *The Destruction of Atlantis,* Rochester, Vt.: Bear & Company, 2002, chapter 2, "Where Is Atlantis?"

Plato's description of Atlantis. None of the names cited in his account is found on Thera, which was too tiny for wars with Egypt, Italy, and Greece, as specified in the *Kritias*. Nor was Thera surrounded by a ring of mountains, populated by elephants, home to a mining or mineralogical center, in possession of three harbors, the site of an imperial city, or the capital of religious worship for the sea god Poseidon.

Attempts by conventional scholars to minimize or debunk Plato's account invariably fall on the facts he presents so clearly. He begins by telling us that Atlantis was a large island "greater than Libya and Asia combined."[4] His characterization has led some investigators to conclude that he was describing a massive continent. Yet the Libya and Asia of his time—2,400 years ago—made up only a fraction of the territories encompassed by those names as they are understood today. During the fourth century BCE, Libya was no more than a thin strip of North African coastline running from the western border of Egypt to perhaps Morocco, at most, while Asia meant Asia Minor, roughly the western third of what is now Turkey. Combined, these areas might result in an island as large as Portugal, but not anything approaching a true continent.

Atlantis lay in the Atlantic Ocean outside the Strait of Gibraltar, where it was almost entirely surrounded by a ring of high mountains, which opened on the south. A temperate climate allowed for two growing seasons, typical of other Atlantic islands, such as Madeira or the Canaries. The island was thickly forested, facilitating the construction of a large navy, which the Atlanteans used to pursue their imperialist agendas, and it was inhabited by scores of wild animals—most remarkably, the elephant. The appearance of this creature on an island in the middle of the Atlantic Ocean was a point used by skeptics to discredit Plato's account. In 1967, however, *Science* magazine reported the discovery of thousands of elephant teeth from forty different underwater locations along the Azores-Gibraltar Ridge. The recovery of these elephant remains validated Plato's account as few other finds have done in recent times.

The pachyderms evidently crossed from the shores of northwest

Africa over a former land bridge that extended into the eastern Atlantic. When the land bridge collapsed sometime within the past twenty-five thousand years, the elephants were stranded on the island of Atlantis. Standard translations of Plato's account perpetuate an error that, once corrected, suggests this former land bridge was used by the migrating elephants: "For in those days, the Atlantic was navigable."[5] Florida Atlantologist Kenneth Caroli states that "the original Greek word does not mean navigable. It means passable 'on foot.' It is their assumption of a maritime context that convinced scholars to twist the translation."[6]

From an aerial perspective, the city on the island resembled a target, laid out as it was in concentric circles of alternating moats and land rings. At the hub of the central artificial islet stood the holy of holies, a small golden shrine dedicated to the sacred marriage between a native woman, Kleito, and the sea god Poseidon. From their union sprang five sets of male children, the progenitors of a dynasty that ruled the Atlantean Empire. The island derived its name from the firstborn, Atlas; *Atlantis* means "daughter of Atlas."

*Figure 1.2. Fifth-century BCE relief statue of Atlas from the Athenian Parthenon (Elgin Marbles, British Museum).*

The city was surrounded by an extensive cultivated plain irrigated by an immense canal system fed by numerous rivers and freshwater springs of both cold and hot water, thermal sources typical of volcanically active islands. Approaching from the south, visitors would have seen three harbors, testimony to Atlantean sea power. Just beyond the broad marketplace, busy day and night with international commerce, reared a colossal wall of red tufa, white pumice, and black lava rock arranged in tricolor bands and sheeted with broad panels of polished bronze. Abutted by watchtowers, the great rampart entirely surrounded the city.

A single canal three hundred feet wide and one hundred feet deep ran from the outer wall to the coast, 5.5 miles away. A fully armed battleship was thus able to sail directly from the sea to the outer wall and through it to the first and largest moat on the other side. The other two moats were connected by four bridged canals five hundred feet across, guarded by towers and gates wherever the bulwarks touched solid ground. Vessels were able to pass under the bridges via these canals, which were cut straight through each land-ring, allowing the vessels to access the various moats.

At the perimeter of the outermost land-ring stood another wall of red, white, and black volcanic rock, plated with gleaming tin. Behind it was a racetrack that ran around the entire 1,800-foot-wide islet, which was otherwise given over to temples; priestly residences; gymnasia; separate public baths for men, women, and horses; stadiums; and public gardens.

The second, smaller land-ring, at 1,200 feet wide, was the seat of naval headquarters, with training facilities and marine barracks. The innermost and smallest islet was surrounded by a red, white, and black wall adorned with *orichalcum,* a high-grade copper. It enclosed the imperial palace, which was set in a large garden with an adjoining winery. Nearby was the monumental Temple of Poseidon, 600 feet long, half as wide, and 150 feet high.

The exterior of the structure, which resembled archaic Greek or early Etruscan sacred architecture, was covered in silver, save for, in the pediment over the entrance, golden figures signifying various deities.

Inside, a colossus of the sea god held his emblematic trident in his right hand while seizing with his left the reins to six winged horses that pulled the chariot in which he stood. The statue was so huge that its head almost brushed the ivory ceiling flecked with gold. Around the base of Poseidon were one hundred Nereids, nymphs riding dolphins, symbolizing initiates into the sea god's mystery cult.

The temple was a veritable hall for statuary, with figures of the original ten kings and their queens, "and many others dedicated by monarchs and private persons belonging to the city and its dominions," according to Plato.[7] They were grouped around a magnificent altar and holy pillar inscribed with the laws of the empire.

Adjacent to the temple was a bullpen from which a sacrifice was selected by the ten regents when they convened in the temple alternately every fifth or sixth year. They subdued the animal with nooses and clubs, then slit its throat with stone daggers to spill its blood over the sacred column. Thereafter, attendees pledged to uphold the laws and made toasts of wine mixed with bull's blood.

Not far from the Temple of Poseidon, at the midpoint of Atlantis itself, stood the small shrine dedicated to his primeval union with Kleito. This innermost islet was just three thousand feet across, although large enough to accommodate the imperial palace, great temple, and golden-walled holy of holies. Atlantis was a citadel and ceremonial center, not an urban setting. Its only permanent residents were imperial family members, their bodyguards, naval and army personnel, priests, and attendants. Rather than being a city where people lived, Atlantis was a public gathering place visited for entertainment and religious activities. The population resided in cities, in towns, or on farmsteads throughout the island. Its volcanic soil was highly fertile, allowing agriculture to flourish.

Atlantis was surrounded by a rectangular, uniformly flat plain nearly 350 miles long and 228 miles wide. This vast cultivated space was serviced by streams and rivers from adjacent mountains. The descending waters were conveyed into a gigantic irrigation canal 100 feet deep, 600 feet wide, and 1,118 miles long, circling the entire plain.

While this public works project may seem to some skeptics beyond the capabilities of any premodern civilization, archaeologists know that the Hohokam culture of the American Southwest, as long ago as the eleventh century, built a canal system that, if placed end to end, would have stretched more than one thousand miles, from Phoenix, Arizona, to well beyond the U.S. border with Canada. Plato describes the Atlanteans as extraordinary irrigationists. They created a network of river ways to float timber and produce to various parts of the island by boat—again reminiscent of the Hohokam, who identically employed their canal system. Such prodigious feats of agriculture were necessary to feed the 6,720,000 inhabitants of the island.

At the zenith of its power, Atlantis was the capital of an imperial enterprise that extended from "the opposite continent," as Plato referred to America, to Western Europe as far as Italy and across North Africa to the border of Egypt.[8] Names of the original ten kings listed by Plato suggest something of the empire's extent in that they correspond with certain geographical realms, mythical figures, or foreign peoples far removed from Plato's Greece. For example, Elasippos, Euaemon, Autochthon, and Azaes are the names of Atlantean kings cited by Plato. Lisbon was originally known as Elasippos, as the Portuguese capital was called even in late Roman times, while Cádiz, in southwestern Spain, was referred to as Gades, from the Atlantean king Gadeiros. Euaemon echoes Eremon, a royal flood hero who led other deluge survivors to the shores of pre-Keltic Ireland after the catastrophic inundation of his island kingdom. The Autochthones were described by Herodotus, Plato's fifth-century BCE predecessor, as Atlanteans dwelling along the western shores of Morocco, just as King Autochthon is cited in the *Kritias*. King Azaes appears to reference Plato's "opposite continent," where the Itzas were a Mayan people occupying coastal Yucatán.

While Ampheres (Joined or Fitted Together on Both Sides), Diaprepres (Bright Shining One), Mestor (Counselor), and Musaeus (Of the Muses) are less certainly associated with any particular people or place, flood stories featuring identifiable Atlantean themes were prevalent in Portugal, Spain, Ireland, North Africa, and Mexico, where most of Plato's Atlantean monarchs seem philologically connected. These holdings granted the Atlanteans fabulous wealth, particularly in the form of copper mines.

The emperor of Atlantis commanded the ancient world's most powerful armed forces, comprising 76,600 warriors. These included 14,400 archers, slingers, and heavily armed infantry, together with 10,000 chariots carrying 20,000 drivers and soldiers. There were also elite units, troops of royal bodyguards, officers, and an army of supply personnel.

Yet Atlantis was primarily a thalassocracy—a naval power—and its 1,200 warships were crewed by 14,400 sailors, marines, shipwrights, and dockhands. These impressive forces were augmented by the nine affiliated kingdoms that made up the Atlantean Empire. Although Plato does not provide their disposition of arms, together they formed a potent military phenomenon unequaled until the advent of Imperial Rome. Nor does he explain why Atlantis gathered its military might to launch an attempted conquest of the Mediterranean world. In any case, the Atlantean juggernaut seemed irrepressible, subjugating Western Europe as far as Italy and steamrolling across North Africa to penetrate the Egyptian frontier. The armies of pharaonic Egypt were crushed, and the entire kingdom tottered on the verge of surrender, when their Athenian allies scored a stunning victory against the invaders. Henceforward, the bloodied Atlanteans were progressively forced to relinquish their conquests in a series of defeats that eventually expelled them from the Mediterranean.

Sometime thereafter, widespread seismic upheavals swallowed up the Greek armies, and the island of Atlantis disappeared "during a single day and night" of catastrophic flooding.[9] The *Kritias* inexplicably breaks off just when Zeus, the supreme Olympian god, is about to condemn the Atlanteans for their degeneracy. The same kind of detailed description that brought their civilization to life would have doubtless painted the picture of its destruction. While some scholars speculate the dialogue was left incomplete for various unknown causes, the missing section was more likely finished but lost, like most classical literature.

*Figure 1.3. British artist Peter Bellingham's 1871 oil painting* Island Volcano *is a facsimile of the final destruction of Atlantis.*

More troubling is the only incredible anomaly in the entire account: Plato's repeated insistence that the Atlanto-Athenian War took place 11,400 years ago. The discrepancy between this remote period, when human society was only just emerging from the last ice age, and details of a typically thirteenth century BCE civilization portrayed by both the *Timaeus* and *Kritias* have compelled many investigators to dismiss the whole narrative as a work of fiction.

Plato's elaborate description of Atlantis unequivocally identifies it as a Late Bronze Age kingdom dating roughly from the sixteenth to thirteenth centuries BCE. Yet some seven thousand years earlier—when Plato says its forces invaded the Mediterranean Sea—neither Greek nor Egyptian civilization existed. Far from engineering any temple containing detailed records of Atlantis, Egyptians had invented nothing more technologically sophisticated than grindstones for making flour from wild grass seeds. The Athens portrayed by Plato as a victorious military power did not exist 114 centuries ago. In fact, the Greek peninsula was not even inhabited at the time.

Literalists who insist that Plato's ice age time frame must be upheld despite everything science understands about the period are obliged to explain how Atlantis could have flourished when the wheel had not yet been invented. There were no metal tools or weapons in 9400 BCE, no chariots, no irrigation projects, no urban centers, no large-scale agriculture, no monumental art, no ships, no written language, no armies—in short, nothing described by the dialogues. The temperate mid-ocean climate Atlantis is said to have enjoyed did not exist during the Late Pleistocene Epoch, as that postglacial period is known. It is an entirely impossible setting for Bronze Age Atlantis, no less outrageously erroneous than assigning U.S. history to the Middle Ages.

Literalists assume that their concept of time is identical to Plato's. As Caroli rightly observes, "the Greek system of numbers used throughout Roman times and after did not exist in Plato's day, let alone Solon's. The potential to confuse the earlier and later Greek systems is rarely considered. The older system was more decimal."[10] Moreover, the Nile Delta priests who supplied the original account were known to use a *lunar* calendar. Transposing Plato's 9400 BCE date from solar to lunar years brings Atlantis squarely into its proper temporal surroundings during the Late Bronze Age, circa 1200 BCE. It seems likely, then, that the ancient translator of the Egyptian text did not trouble himself with recalculating its lunar years into solar time but transcribed them, as he did all other information, verbatim from the inscription.

While his fidelity is an assumption, Plato's troublesome chronology might be more simply explained by what the British scholar Desmond Lee describes as the Greeks' "bad sense of time. . . . And though the Greeks, both philosophers and others, were interested in origins, they seem to have been curiously lacking in their sense of the time-dimension."[11] Perhaps nothing more than notorious Greek sloppiness concerning proper dating may be responsible for Bronze Age Atlantis's incongruous placement at the end of the Pleistocene Epoch. It is nonetheless curious that this period defined a major cultural surge known as the Mesolithic, or Middle

Stone Age, when northwestern Europe was resettled after the Last Glacial Maximum by extraordinarily creative invaders. These Upper Paleolithic people, known as the Magdalenians, were named after La Madeleine, a Vézère Valley rock shelter in the French Dordogne.

The Magdalenians first appeared on the shores of Normandy, as though arriving from the sea, then spread in all directions, from Portugal to Poland. Unlike their far less sophisticated predecessors, they dwelled in tents; manufactured superior flint tools; worked both utilitarian and aesthetic forms in bone, antler, and ivory; and sculpted stone figurines of passing skill. Their greatest surviving achievement is stupendous cave art, as preserved at such subterranean galleries as Lascaux in France and Altamira in Spain.

If the Magdalenians were not exactly Plato's Atlanteans, they may have been their Upper Paleolithic ancestors. Their appearance on the shores of Western Europe—when major coastal flooding occurred as a result of glaciers melting into rising sea levels—coincides with his Pleistocene time frame. Although less probable than the direct transcription of a lunar date, it is nonetheless conceivable that the 11,400 BP date Plato cites for Atlantis might refer after all to its Mesolithic roots. Atlantean beginnings around 9400 BCE may have been enough to satisfy him for the whole narration, given Greek indifference toward accurate chronologies of any kind.

Caroli brings out a more troubling possibility; namely, that the original Greek account was deliberately tampered with for religious reasons. He points out that not one of the earliest known versions

predates the ninth century, and most are no earlier than the twelfth or thirteenth. To equate the destruction of Atlantis with Noah's flood required reducing Plato's dates. But the oldest manuscripts assigned the Atlantean catastrophe to one thousand years before Solon's time. Later translators "corrected" it to match the then accepted figures from Plato. In many of the early texts of the *Timaeus*, it read 1,009, not 9,000 years. It was mainly monkish scribes doing the many copies of copies. But they expanded Plato's original chronology from 1,009 years in the *Timaeus* to 9,000 years, though the former is suspiciously precise, and so the more likely.[12]

While we may never satisfactorily reconcile a tenth-millennium BCE time frame for the events surrounding Atlantis, that curious period seems nevertheless to reflect on the sunken capital from the radically different perspectives of Magdalenian Europe or the Bronze Age. Perhaps both—separately or simultaneously—were meant, for whatever causes, to illuminate various aspects of the multifarious lost wellspring of civilization. If, as seems possible, Stone Age Magdalenians arrived on the Atlantic island during Late Paleolithic times, the impact of this artistically gifted people helped found and determine the early developmental course of civilization there. As such, their Bronze Age descendants, great artists in their own right, were the logical inheritors of a cultural richness going back to the very time specified by a literal reading of Plato's account.

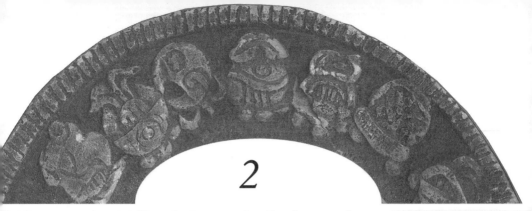

# 2

# Spiritual Atlantis

Chapter 1 defined the exoteric, or physical, reality of Atlantis. Yet its historical (prehistoric) existence was the material expression of esoteric energies that underpinned the lost civilization and drove its destiny. These esoteric expressions are of primary importance as we consider the forthcoming ice age.

Plato tells us that the Atlanteans were more interested in spiritual than material power.

> For many generations, as long as the divine nature lasted in them, they were obedient to the laws, and well-affectioned toward the gods, who were their kinsmen. They retained a certain greatness of mind, for they possessed true and in every way great spirits, practicing gentleness and wisdom in the various chances of life, and in their relationships with one another. They despised everything but virtue, not caring for their present state of life, and thinking lightly on the possession of gold and other property, which seemed only a burden to them. Neither were they intoxicated by luxury, nor did wealth deprive them of their self-control. By such reflection, and in the continuance in them of a divine nature, all that which we have described waxed and increased in them.[1]

His characterization of the Atlanteans as "kinsmen" of the gods

*Figure 2.1. Fifth-century BCE bronze colossus of Poseidon retrieved from the bottom of the Aegean Sea and currently at the National Museum of Archaeology, Athens, Greece. A monumental temple to the sea god stood near the center of Atlantis.*

was not merely a national myth, like Japan's pre–World War II belief in Emperor Hirohito's divinity. It was generated instead by a small shrine at the absolute midpoint of Atlantis, where a golden enclosure surrounded the holy of holies. It was here that Kleito, the mortal woman, entered into a *hieros gamos,* Greek for "temple marriage" or "holy union," with a god, Poseidon. The name Kleito, in fact, exemplifies the hieros gamos. "Kleito" derives from the Greek verb *kleito,* "to touch or titillate lasciviously, to be inclined to pleasure," according to sexologist Ian Kerner.[2]

Another writer, Joseph Wells, adds that Kleito is a diminutive of Kleitoris, from which the English word *clitoris* derived. He goes on to point out that Poseidon is partly formed from the Greek words *peos,* or *posthe,* meaning "penis," and *eidon,* meaning "idol."[3] The erect male and female sex organs are therefore represented in both names, symbolizing the Atlantean temple marriage between a mortal woman and an immortal deity cited in the *Kritias.* Poseidon's laws inscribed on a pillar ritually libated with bull's blood, as described in the dialogue, signifies the hieros gamos implicit in Kleito and Poseidon.

These observations contribute to Plato's fundamental veracity, for he could hardly have been expected to bother about such minute subtleties on behalf of mere fiction. They are, instead, part of the numerous details he included to affirm the historical reality of Atlantis.

As the sacred patron of all things pertaining to the sea, Poseidon esoterically personifies the subconscious. Water—particularly the ocean—is a metaphor for the mind: its surface (consciousness) reflects the phenomenal world, but just below the surface lies a darker, entirely contrary dimension of dynamic energy forms incessantly engaged in devouring each other. Kleito's holy union with such a mythic conception signifies an altered—or, more accurately stated, an *exalted*—state of consciousness.

The purpose of such a transformation lay in accessing human psychic potential for its application in the life of an already high, progressive civilization. Plato does not specify how this form of empowerment was achieved, probably because the knowledge was lost with the mystery cult that prevented such knowledge from being publicly disclosed. Plato himself was believed to have been an initiate in the Pythagorean Brotherhood. Followers who violated their oaths of secrecy forfeited their lives, including, it would appear, Pythagoras himself, who was stoned to death in a bean field for sharing his own principles with uninitiated outsiders. It may not have been coincidental that Pschonchis, the Nile Delta priest who translated the story of Atlantis from its hieroglyphic text on a temple column, bore the same name as one of Solon's Pythagorean teachers in Egypt.

Archaeobiologists believe adherents of the famed Eleusinian Mysteries were administered ergoline alkaloids from the fungus ergot, an early form of LSD, to expand their consciousness. During the mid-twentieth century, an important contributor to ethnobotany, R. Gordon Wasson, demonstrated that such hallucinogens were integral to virtually every spiritual discipline throughout the ancient Old World. These mystery cults were the mainspring of Near Eastern and European mysticism, with its emphasis on direct personal experience of the divine, as mythically dramatized by Kleito's hieros gamos. It was believed that such experience released psychic insights and powers endemic to, but otherwise dormant in, every human being. Psychoactive-ingesting practitioners of the Atlantean mystery cult were thus able to plumb the depths of subconscious potentiality—mythically personified by Poseidon fishing up choice catches on his trident—which granted them an otherworldly awareness.

This emblematic device—the trident—was symbolic of supreme spiritual power, topped as it was by three prongs. It is not unlike the three-pointed wand held by the Hindu master of creation, Shiva. The three-pronged weapon wielded by the Roman *retiarius* (gladiator), with his net of interdependent relationship ensnaring all things, made him a sacred impersonator of Uranus, the creator sky god. The Kelts worshipped their deities in groups of three and identified them with three heads or faces. The Hindu trinity of Brahma, Vishnu, and Shiva personify, respectively, *sat,* or being; *cit,* consciousness; and *ananda,* love—the components of godhood cyclically creating, maintaining, and destroying the universe. Height, breadth, and length are the preconditions for and define the limitations of the three dimensions of space or the three stages of matter, proceeding from solid to liquid to gaseous states—all elements of creation or creativity. Stylistically representing male genitalia, Poseidon's trident, grasped commandingly in his right hand, yet again underscores his role as divine bridegroom in the temple marriage, suggesting the tantric concept of sexual energy as a power to attain enlightenment.

The one hundred Nereids surrounding the base of his statue are yet another symbol of the transconsciousness associated with this deity. He was also honored by the Greeks for his creation of the horse, which they associated with virility and—when endowed with wings—spiritual illumination. Both of these qualities of hieros gamos are exemplified by the winged horses pulling his chariot in Atlantis's Temple of Poseidon. The number of these horses, however, is the key to the Atlantean mysteries, and sacred numbers interpenetrate, as described in the following chapter, the closure of epochs, such as the endings described by the Mayan calendar.

# 3

# Sacred Numbers

Plato reports in the *Kritias* that monarchs from across the empire assembled in Atlantis at the Temple of Poseidon "alternately every fifth and sixth year, thereby showing equal respect to both the odd and even numbers."[1] These regular meetings were not part of some formal religious convention but instead represented a pair of sacred numbers that incorporated the Atlanteans' entire civilization and determined the disposition of their daily lives.

Plato's Atlantis account is literally constructed with the numbers five and six and their multiples. Poseidon's colossus stood in a chariot drawn by six winged horses. The citadel itself embodied the number five in its three moats and two land-rings—or, simultaneously, the number six, including the central islet, which itself was five stades across. Atlantis's great canal ran fifty stades from the seacoast to the ceremonial city, and its outer wall was uniformly fifty stades from the largest land-ring.

An irrigation ditch surrounding the cultivated plain was ten thousand stades in length, and the Atlantean Empire itself comprised ten kingdoms. Allotments of land were parceled out in plots of ten square stades, with the total number of allotments at sixty thousand. Kleito bore five sets of twin boys, who formed the royal houses of Atlantis. Military leaders were obligated to provide a sixth part of the equipment for a war chariot. The Atlantean armed forces fielded ten thousand chariots, together with twelve hundred warships.

Why were five and six chosen as sacred numbers, with a preference for five? What did they mean to the Atlanteans?

Their numerical esotericism was carried by early colonizers from Atlantis to the Nile Delta, taught only in the Egyptian Mystery schools, until the sixth century BCE. Greek philosopher, Pythagoras, broke his oath of secrecy by going public with the holy system. It defined the progression of existence through associated numbers, beginning with "one" for the primal unity of the universe. Its division into pairs of opposites was "two." From this chaos arose the will of God in "three"—the reconciliation of unity and struggle, the Holy Trinity. The result of this divine rapprochement was harmony, itself epitomized in "four"—the four cardinal directions, etc. These preconditions allowed for the advent of God's co-creator in the material world. As such, five represents humankind, as signified by the five senses and five fingers to a hand: manual dexterity; solar, male energy; light and enlightenment. It stands for conscious action, acquisition, material achievement, technology, scientific inquiry, organization, civilization, militarism, conquest, justice, honor, duty, hard facts, self-control, and discernment. Five is the sacred center—symbolized by a circle enclosing a cross or a single point at the center—where the imperceptible is perceived (or where it manifests). The number six connotes female energy, because it is concerned with lunar cycles, nature, emotion, fecundity, liberty (always represented by a woman), instinct, premonition, creativity, peace, fairness, and forgiveness.

The Romanian mythologist Mircea Eliade states that six "is the number of mother-love. . . . It is an even number, which means it is female and passive . . . the number of marriage from the female point of view. . . . Six is essentially the number of the wife and mother."[2] Eliade cites an anonymous numerologist who observed that marriage license bureaus in the United States are forced to either work overtime or multiply their staffs to accommodate an increased number of applicants during six-year periods.

Six exemplifies the hieros gamos, the holy union between Father Sky and Mother Earth—the sacred bond between fertilizing force from above and innate potentiality from below, operating in the well-known principle of "as above, so below." The sixth tarot trump is known as the Lovers.

The significance of Plato's sacred numbers remarkably characterizes the lost culture, particularly its mysticism he described. The Atlantean dynamics of technology, organization, militarism, conquest, and imperialism resonate in the number five as the number is described above. This aggressive consciousness is contrasted with but complemented by six, the number of intuition, instinctiveness, nurturing consolidation, fertility, and creativity. These active and passive principles—solar-male and lunar-female energies—appear where they were wedded in the Temple of Poseidon, its exterior sheeted with gold and silver, the light of the sun and moon, each conveying its own set of mystical implications. Their holy union of the conscious and subconscious mind signifies a simultaneous florescence but deliberate control of psychic potential—the next step in human evolution.

The first son Kleito bore to Poseidon was Atlas. His pre-Greek name in Sanskrit means "the Upholder," or "He Who Supports, Holds Up," because he was envisioned in non-Platonic myth as a nude, bearded Titan down on one knee, bearing on his shoulders the sphere of the heavens or zodiac (not the world, as commonly mistaken in modern times). This figure was perceived in a tall peak far out at sea; when the sky was overcast, clouds concealed the summit, making the mountain appear to hold up the sky. Such imagery personified the disciplines of astronomy and astrology, both created by Atlas—in other words, their origins went back to Atlantis, meaning "daughter of Atlas." The island derived its name from the Titan—transformed by myth into a foremost mountain—as did the sea it dominated, the Atlantic Ocean.

Again, in non-Platonic tradition, the island of Atlas was home for him and his four daughters, the Hesperides, known by this name after their mother, Hespera, the Evening Star. She was associated with the distant west across the sea, where Atlas Island was located. Also referred to as the Western Maidens, the Daughters of Evening, Erythrai, and the Sunset Goddesses, the daughters Aegle, Arethusa, Erytheia, and Hesperia tended a garden, at the center of which stood the Tree of Life, another version of Poseidon's phallic pillar in his temple at the Atlantis acropolis.

Representing the four cardinal directions, the Hesperides surrounded their father, thereby rendering him the sacred fifth number as a midpoint. Clearly five was the Atlanteans' supreme holy number because they identified it with their eponymous first king, Atlas. They also revered him as the creator of astrology, which played a pivotal role in their society. The kingly sacrifice of a bull in the Temple of Poseidon was an entirely astrological ritual. Its victim was the astral bull whose slaughter meant the end of the Age of Taurus, something other Bronze Age peoples—such as the contemporary Trojans, Minoans of Crete, or Mycenaean Greeks—would have understood as a prelude to renewal. Taurus was similarly synonymous with rejuvenation and revival, which he engendered by having his own throat cut, thereby enabling plants and animals to spring from his blood. His myth was reenacted in a rite called the *taurobolium* to commemorate the death and resurrection of the hero Mithras, who personified the next age and baptized initiates into his cult.

Atlas was said to have invented astronomy and astrology simultaneously, because what later came to be known as two distinct disciplines was originally a single concept. Throughout the ancient world, astronomy was the precise observation of the heavens and documentation of their movement by astrologers for the accurate interpretation of cosmic influences on Earth. They believed that all physical phenomena were intrinsically connected to metaphysical actions and causes, that both were reciprocal and interactive. Therefore, one could be used to explain the other. After centuries of separation, scientists are gravitating back toward this ancient principle in their discovery that merely the physical presence of an experimenter influences the outcome of his experiment on a subtle yet critical level.

So, too, physicists understand that there are no fundamental differences between energy and matter, that the latter is but a subatomic variant, rearrangement, or recomposition of the former. Interchange of energy forms is again worthy of consideration, thereby allowing for infinite possibilities in which astrology or prophecies are no longer so easily dismissed, condemned, or ridiculed.

# 4

# The Calendar Stone

The form that Atlantean astrology or its predictive procedures took may, in fact, have best survived in the Mayan calendar and the Calendar Stone, or, more properly, Mesoamerican calendrics, which the Maya helped to create.

As mentioned in chapter 1, Azaes was listed by Plato as one of Kleito's sons who ruled a province of the Atlantean Empire. His name bears a striking resemblance to the Itza, a Mayan people who occupied coastal Yucatán, where they are most famously remembered for their impressive ceremonial city, Chichén Itzá. Its centerpiece is the pyramidal Temple of Kukulcan, the Feathered Serpent.

While the term *serpent* was often used as a title signifying power, the Maya were unable to grow facial hair and therefore possessed no word to describe Kukulcan's bearded appearance. They had to rely on their next closest adjective—*feathered*—to characterize the bearded founding father of Mesoamerican civilization. Had they not seen this foreigner from the ancient Old World with their own eyes, they would never have been able to dream up such a figure.

His conception as a bearded white man is by no means confined to pre-Columbian oral traditions. The walls inside a small masonry structure at the north end of Chichén Itzá's Great Ball Court are covered with bas-relief carvings clustered around the representation of Kukulcan as a male figure with a Semitic nose and long, full beard.

*Figure 4.1. This relief carving inside the Temple of the Bearded Man at Chichén Itzá's Great Ball Court represents the non-Indian profile of Kukulcan, the founding father of the Maya. We can compare this image with the ancient Greek conception of Atlas, the eponymous emperor of Atlantis, portrayed in a fifth-century BCE stone relief in chapter 1.*

This structure itself is known as the Temple of the Bearded Man.

He also makes an appearance nearby, atop the ninety-foot-high Kukulcan pyramid inside the walls of its shrine at the summit, among an identical quartet of bearded men holding up the Mayan glyph for "sky."

The Maya referred to these depictions of Atlas as Bacabs, twins representing the cardinal directions. So, too, Plato informs us that Kleito's sons from whom the royal houses of Atlantis descended were twins. Atlas was the creator of astrology, and each brother Bacab presided over one year in a four-year cycle, because they were deities of astrological time. They were believed to have come to Chichén Itzá just after a world-class deluge destroyed their capital across the sea. This lost homeland was described as the Red and Black Land, recalling Plato's description of the red tufa and black lava natural formations on the island of Atlantis.

The Itza were a Mayan people named after a variant of the Feathered Serpent, Itzamna. In the Mayan cosmology presented in the Books of Chilam Balam and in Juan Darreygosa's sixteenth-century *Historia de Zodzil,* Itzamna bears the title Serpent from the East and is described as "the first after the flood" that engulfed his island kingdom in the Atlantic Ocean.[1]

He arrived first at the island of Cozumel, off the Yucatán coast, where some temples dedicated to him still stand. Proceeding to the Mexican mainland, he built Chichén Itzá, or Mouth of the Well of Itza, and 149 other cities. In temple art, such as friezes at the Mayan ceremonial center of Tikal in Guatemala, he is portrayed as a long-nosed, bearded man rowing his boat across the sea from which he came. In the background of this sculpted frieze, running around the top exterior of the acropolis, is a volcanic island in the process of a major eruption while a stone city topples into the sea and a blond-haired man drowns in the foreground.

The identity of this scene could hardly be more obvious. When Teobert Maler, the Austrian archaeological photographer who found the frieze, saw it for the first time in 1915, he exclaimed, "until that moment, I dismissed Atlantis as a baseless myth. I knew at once that I had been mistaken."[2]

Itzamna's followers from the Red and Black Land of Tutulxiu, the Land of Abundance, or the Bountiful, far across the sea "where the sun rises," were the Ah-Auab: "foreigners to the land," "white men," or True

*Figure 4.2. Relief carving of a Bacab, or Atlantean figure, inside Chichén Itzá's shrine room at the Pyramid of the Feathered Serpent*

*Figure 4.3. Line-drawing impressions of Bacabs, or Atlantean figures, on the interior walls of the shrine atop Chichén Itzá's Pyramid of the Feathered Serpent*

Men.[3] On the twenty-seventh stele at Yaxchilan, on the eleventh stele at Piedras Negras, and on the Temple of Warriors at Chichén Itzá, they are portrayed as bearded, with long, thin noses, and European facial features.

The Books of Chilam Balam tell of life in the Red and Black Land as ideal for many centuries. One day, however, "a fiery rain fell, ashes fell, rocks and trees crashed to the ground. Then the waters rose in a terrible flood. The sky fell in, and the dry land sank into the sea."[4] This is doubtless the same event depicted on the acropolis at Tikal.

The Red and Black Land was also known as Tayasal and described in the Popol Vuh as "the lost homeland of the Ah-Auab, who came from the other part of the ocean, from where the sun rises, a place called Patulan-Pa-Civan."[5] These oceanic origins were naturally embedded in the very name of the people who built Chichén Itzá. It stems from the Mayan *itz,* for "magic," and *(h)á,* meaning "water," to form "magicians of (or from) the water (i.e., the sea)."

Given their city's abundantly Atlantean pedigree, evidence for the sacred numbers in its ceremonial architecture might be expected, such as in the Temple of Kukulcan's ten levels. Buried in the heart of the step pyramid, directly beneath the summit's Bacabs positioned at the cardinal directions on the four walls of its shrine, reposes a blue-eyed statue known as a *chac-mool,* which creates the sacred center and fifth number.

*Figure 4.4. Buried deep inside Chichén Itzá's Pyramid of the Feathered Serpent, in its own chamber, resides the blue-eyed statue of a reclining male figure known as a chac-mool.*

A few paces to the northwest, a sculpted panel in the Great Ball Court depicts a decapitated victim from whom six streams of blood drain and transform into serpents. Feathered serpents from Atlantis carried the technology and spirituality of their overseas homeland to establish a colony in Middle America at Yucatán—Plato's Azaes—from which their descendants, the Itza, derived their name and identity. As such, they were culture bearers who sparked Mesoamerican civilization, a synthesis of introduced Atlantean know-how and indigenous influences.

Among the most important gifts carried away from the island kingdom of Atlas was a scientific reckoning of time. Its original configuration was gradually eroded and eventually lost through the influence of successive native inflections, from the late fourth-millennium BCE Olmec and third-century BCE Maya, over the millennia to its last custodians, the Aztecs, in the early sixteenth century CE. Its core mechanism, however, remained intact, as cultural variations replaced one another. The better known of these are the Mayan calendar and the Aztec Calendar Stone.

The latter was accidentally dug up by sewer workers on December 17, 1790, before the large cathedral of Mexico City's El Zócalo, almost parallel to the front of the viceroy's palace. They pried the 24-ton disk from 2 feet below street level, then set it upright against the cathedral's eastern wall. Spectators were awestruck by the 13.5-foot-tall monolith sculpted from a single 4-foot-thick piece of gray black basalt still bearing traces of its original polychrome artwork.

Centuries earlier, the 50,000-pound slab had been hewn from quarries in the mountains south of today's Mexico City, near the floating gardens of Xochimilco. It was then transported somehow about thirty miles to the main square of Tenochtitlán and lifted more than halfway up the steep steps of the Great Pyramid. Lying flat on a broad landing, sculptors and artists undertook the complex task of carving and painting the bas-relief masterpiece during the reign of Emperor Axayacatl. Their labors were finished during the late fifteenth century, when the great disk was installed upright on its rim in a thronelike cradle. There the monumental symbol of eternity stood above the Aztec imperial capital for just forty years. It presided over the fall of Tenochtitlán on August 13, 1521, and the attendant collapse of Mesoamerican civilization.

The city had not even been envisioned by the Aztecs, who seized it from its original occupants after the Calendar Stone's completion in the late fifteenth century CE. Long before, Mēxihcah founders built Tenochtitlán on an island and patterned the capital, with its canals and causeways, after their ancestral homeland, Aztlán, a mountainous "white island" in the Atlantic Ocean.

In the process of converting the natives to Christianity by demonizing their culture, Catholic friars learned and recorded something of Mēxihcah origins in Aztlán but not much else from the few dwindling survivors of the disease epidemics unintentionally yet effectively introduced by the Spaniards. Prior to that catastrophic epidemic, Tenochtitlán was a sprawling urban center, with some 212,500 residents occupying a metropolitan landscape more than eight square miles in extent. The first Europeans to visit declared that its civil organization, sophistication, and beauty rivaled Paris, Seville, and Venice. "When we saw so many cities and villages built in the water and other great towns on dry land," remembered the veteran conquistador Bernal Diaz del Castillo, "we were amazed, and said that it was like an enchantment, on account of the great towers and boulevards and buildings rising from the water, and all built of masonry. And some of our soldiers even asked whether the things that we saw were not a dream. I do not know how to describe it, seeing things as we did that had never been heard of or seen before, not even dreamed about."[6]

Favorable first impressions did not prevent the conquistadors from systematically destroying the city and leveling it to the ground for mostly religious reasons. The Calendar Stone was dislodged from its cradle and sent careening down the front of the pyramid. It came to rest face downward in the dirt. Spanish Catholic friars cursed what they imagined was a demonic altar, then ordered it ritually buried. Something of their fanaticism survived into the late eighteenth century, when priests at the Cathedral Metropolitana informed parishioners they could gain heavenly grace by spitting on the freshly excavated disk and chipping off pieces with hand tools. To prevent its slow disintegration through vandalism, Mexico City authorities removed the Calendar Stone to an improvised shelter in Chapultepec Park, which eventually grew into the National Museum of Anthropology, where the artifact is now preserved.

At the bottom of the monolith are the ornately headdressed profiles of two male figures facing each other. The man on the left is Quetzalcoatl, an Aztec version of the Feathered Serpent, confronting his evil twin, Tezcatlipoca, or Smoking Mirror. The name refers to his talisman, a flint mirror he used to glimpse the future—appropriate enough, in view of the Calendar Stone's prognosticating features. In addition to his divine patronage of divination, he was also the god of enmity, discord, war, and strife, in opposition to the civilizing Feathered Serpent. Tezcatlipoca's appearance on the Calendar Stone demonstrates its pre-Aztec—probably even pre-Mēxihcah—origins. The Maya knew Smoking Mirror as K'awil, but a far older version was worshipped by the Olmec from the beginning of pre-Columbian civilization, thereby demonstrating the very ancient roots of Mesoamerican calendrics.

The bodies of both Quetzalcoatl and Tezcatlipoca are serpentine and divided into sections adorned with images of flames and jaguar limbs amounting to the fifty-two years in the Mēxihcah-Aztec century. The figures are, in fact, *xiuhcoatls,* or fire serpents, and therefore part of the overall catastrophic theme pervading the Aztec Calendar Stone. At the top of its rim, between the xiuhcoatl snake tails, is a square containing the date in which the Calendar Stone was completed—13-Acatl, meaning 13-Cane, or 1479 CE. The outer circle, interrupted at the top by this box and at the bottom by the sacred twins, is otherwise given over entirely to mathematical notations, as are the next four concentric rings. Even the smallest details, to the lone dot and a single diagonal line, signify arithmetical values.

For example, the squares at the outer perimeter contain representations of the maguey plant, whose leaves and stem each add up to one *xiuhmolpili,* a unit of 365 days, to complete one solar year. Square sections contain five dots, each representing weeks of as many days. Four larger indicators above four lesser pointers are, respectively, the major and minor cardinal directions. They simultaneously signify the eight divisions of the Mēxihcah-Aztec day from sunrise to sunset in eight intervals of three hours' duration each. All the data from the Calendar Stone can be used to accurately compute the solstices, equinoxes, and days of the zenith, which began or divided the Mēxihcah-Aztec year.

The innermost arrow atop a ring encircling the anthropomorphic image of the sun indicates the day when the sun rises to its highest point directly over Tenochtitlán. At celestial moments such as this one, small obelisks, known as *gnomon,* around the edge of the Calendar Stone cast shadows over different details of its sculpted face, pointing to the occurrence of solstices, equinoxes, and zeniths. The gnomon also marked the annual rotation of the circumpolar star groups and the apparent course of the sun each year.

The next ring features the twenty day signs of the Mēxihcah-Aztec month. Their original names and significance begin at the top right and go around to complete the circle: Xochitl (flower, life); Tecpatl (flint, violence); Olin (movement, potential); Cozcaquauhtli (vulture, disease); Cuauhtli (eagle, time); Ocelotl (jaguar, transformation); Acatl (cane, emptiness); Quihuitl (heavenly fire, judgment); Ozornatli (monkey, baser instincts); Itzcuintli (dog, loyalty); Malinalli (grass, peace); Atl (water, life); Tochtli (rabbit, alertness); Mazatl (deer, harmony); Miquiztli (skull, death); Coatl (serpent, wisdom); Cuetzpallin (lizard, dreams); Calli (house, preservation); Ehécatl (windstorm, travel); and Cipactli (alligator, Earth).

The Calendar Stone aided in the observation of important religious ceremonies each month. These include petitions to the rain god Tlaloc; Atlacualcaca, or Wants Water; and celebration of the Birth of Flowers during Tlaxochimaco in the spring. Military reviews paraded during Ochpaniz, the Month of Brooms, but the Atemoztli, Fall of Waters music festival, climaxed in the Izcalli mass sacrifice of tens of thousands of human victims taken from across the Aztec Empire.

At the center of the Calendar Stone is the ghastly face of Tonatiuh.

A flaming fire pot hangs over the sun god's forehead, or third eye, while his tongue lolls for bloody sacrifice. Flames sprout from his ears and nostrils, and the solar eagle's talons (in circles on either side of his face) grip human hearts.

The Aztecs and, presumably, their Mēxihcah predecessors revered Tonatiuh because he made mortal redemption possible when, at the beginning of the world, he threw himself into a fire. Rising from his own immolation, he took with him into heaven the souls of those who died heroically. All others descended into nine levels of hell before vanishing forever, like mist. Acceptably honorable deaths included falling in battle for men and expiring during childbirth for women. Voluntarily sacrificing their hearts to the flint knife, represented by Tonatiuh's greedy tongue, guaranteed paradise for both sexes.

He is surrounded at the center of the monolith by four squares repeating his calendrical title, 4-Ollin, or 4-Movement. It is also the name of the present epoch he personifies and the manner in which it will end. Like their Maya and Olmec precursors, the Mēxihcah believed that several defining cataclysms shook our planet in the ancient past. Each natural catastrophe was an event horizon delineating the end of a particular time period, or sun, in human history and the beginning of another. Those preceding 4-Ollin—which ended on sunrise of 2012's winter solstice—are symbolically represented in a quartet of boxes with Tonatiuh in the middle (see figure 4.5 on p. 44).

The most recent sun, appearing in the bottom-right square, is referred to as 4-Atl, or 4-Water, and depicts the world being destroyed by a great flood. The 4-Atl square frames the image of a pyramid sinking under a flood streaming from an overturned bucket, signifying the wrath of Chalchiuhtlicue.

The name Chalchiuhtlicue, or Our Lady of the Turquoise Skirt, graphically identifies her with swirling or stormy water. She was often represented in Aztec temple art as a goddess seated upon a throne surrounded by whirlpools of drowning men and women. It was her disaster that ended a former age of civilized greatness and ushered in a new one in Middle America with the arrival of survivors.

*Figure 4.5. Tonatiuh, the solar god of destruction, is portrayed at the center of the Aztec Calendar Stone.*

On her feast day, Chalchiuhtlicue was honored by priests, who collected reeds and ceremoniously placed them around her temple to signify her identification with the island home of Mēxihcah ancestors. Meaning literally "place in the water," Aztlán was also known by several other titles, including the Field of Reeds, synonymous with a place of great learning because reeds were used as writing instruments. As pointed out in the introduction to this text, ancient Egyptians half a world away identically referred to their ancestral homeland, Sekhet Aaru, as an island of high culture before it was engulfed by the Atlantic Ocean.

*Figure 4.6. This square (center of frame) at the central section of the Aztec Calendar Stone (restoration) symbolically represents the end of a former age, 4-Atl, with the figure of a pyramid inundated by water.*

The previous sun, at the bottom left of Tonatiuh, is 4-Quihuitl, or 4-Fire from Heaven. It too depicts an upturned bucket, but this one dumps flames on a burning pyramid. At the upper left, 4-Ehécatl, or 4-Windstorm, shows an eagle blowing on a pyramid while a dragonfly—synonymous with change—scoots away. The first and earliest sun is at the upper right, 4-Ocelotl, or 4-Jaguar, in which early humans and a race of giants were destroyed by wild animals. The 4-Ocelotl box is unique in that it is the only one that does not feature a pyramid, implying that this earliest sun took place before humans attained civilization. The number four—signifying the four cardinal directions—precedes each one of these cataclysms to indicate their worldwide effect.

The Calendar Stone's original identity is brightly illuminated by its incorporation of the sacred numbers of Atlantis. The disk design is made up of five alternating elements—six, if the central sun face of Tonatiuh is included—the same fundamental arrangement Plato described for the layout of "that sacred isle," Atlantis. On the Calendar Stone, the concentric ring just inside the outer circle carries square sections, each one containing five dots representing weeks of five days. Five more dots inside the circle signify intercalary days, making the system correspond to a solar year by bringing the total number to 365.

Groupings of the five were so frequent in and integral to the workings of the Calendar Stone that they were assigned their own designation as *nemontemi*. Two nemontemi of five dots surround each maguey plant on the monolith to represent one decade. It bears twenty such squares, plus two more squares on three sides, each with sixteen dots, for an additional six years.

Dots standing alone were referred to as *chalchiuhtlicue* after Our Lady of the Turquoise Skirt, the sea goddess who presided over the Atlantis-like destruction of 4-Atl, or 4-Water. Five chalchiuhtlicues are prominently positioned in the central hub around Tonatiuh's glaring sun face.

The third ring in from the outermost rim is composed of fifty-two *quincunxes* (squares containing four dots in each corner with one at the center). Although only forty are visible, the remaining twelve are obscured by the eight directional indicators. Fifty-two quincunxes total the 260-day count, harkening back to the earlier Mayan Tzol'kin. This was a sacred calendar used for divination purposes and for determining the time of religious or ceremonial events.

The Maya also operated a solar calendar, the Haab, comprising eighteen months of twenty days each, together with a five-day month at year's end known as the Wayeb, or Nameless Days. Mesoamerican civilizations before and after the Maya used a vigesimal, or base twenty numbering system, in conjunction with a base five numbering system.

The fifth number plays a pivotal role in the Mayan calendar, in that five *tun* cycles—groupings of 5,125-year periods—made up the Precessional Year, also known as the Great Zodiacal Year, comprising some 25,630 solar years and upon which the whole time-counting system was based.

Tezcatlipoca, who plays such a vital role in the Calendar Stone's symbolism, celebrated his main feast day during Toxcatl, the fifth month in the Mēxihcah calendar. After the last of the four cataclysms, they claimed the era in which they lived was the Fifth Sun (also known as the Fifth World), the last re-creation of the world, a time between the Great Flood and the next global catastrophe.

Arizona's Hopi Indians preserve the same belief, even to the use of identical terminology, stating that the Fifth Sun of our era ended with 2012's winter solstice, an indefinite period after which some unspecified global catastrophe will occur if the world is still in a condition of *Koyaanisqatsi,* meaning "life out of balance," or "life of moral corruption and turmoil."

It is clear, then, that the sacred numbers of Atlantis, particularly five—synonymous with civilization—are the Mayan calendar's fundamental denominators and found later expression in the Aztec Calendar Stone.

The name "Calendar Stone," however, is a misnomer in every respect. As already mentioned, the Aztecs appropriated astronomy and astrology from a previous people they conquered, the Mēxihcah. Nor was the stone a calendar; rather, it was a highly complex, sophisticated almanac—an astrological computer—for divination. It was known as the Aztec Calendar Stone only from the beginning of the twentieth century. The monolith's original name was Cuauhtlixicalli—House of the Eagle, or Eagle Bowl—but the Vessel of Time was closest to its real meaning. The eagle symbolized the sun, which in turn embodied the passage of time.

To the Mēxihcah and Aztecs, time was the supreme deity because it brings everything into existence, destroys everything, and brings new forms into being through a cycle of creation, destruction, and re-creation that nothing in the universe escapes. As we have discovered, they believed that Earth had been successively blasted by four cataclysms that wiped out society and pushed humanity to the brink of extinction. After generations of misery and hardship, the survivors and their descendants gradually repopulated the world and built new cultures. When humankind again forgot the past and grew corrupt, moral imbalance eventually upset cosmic law to call down another wholesale disaster. As before, a few were spared to start the long, painful ascent

*Figure 4.7. In this Aztec representation of their capital city, an eagle signifying the destructive aspect of time devours a snake (synonymous with Earth and physical existence) at the center of Tenochtitlán, where the Eagle Bowl, better known as the Aztec Calendar Stone, was located.*

back to civilization. The god of time is depicted in his most horribly ruinous aspect as Tonatiuh at the center of the Calendar Stone because he signifies the world disasters arrayed around him.

This cyclical pattern of human development alternating with global calamities convinced the Mesoamericans that they were required to behave within the observable laws of nature, as expressed in the time-tables of the heavens and the regular movements of celestial bodies. Each day the great disk gleaming from the steps of the Great Pyramid reminded the inhabitants of Tenochtitlán of the delicate balance between their behavior and cosmic judgment.

Zelia Nuttall, a renowned pioneer in Middle American archaeology for the Peabody Museum in Massachusetts, realized as long ago as the late nineteenth century that Mexico City's ancient sun stone had been "designed to control the actions of all the human beings of the state, bringing their communal life into accord with the periodic movements of the heavenly bodies."[7] She recognized how Mesoamerican awe of temporal cycles absolutely dominated the lives of the Aztecs and their forerunners for the previous forty-five centuries, going all the way back to the first Olmec.

At the moment of birth, the rest of the child's life was determined by his or her horoscope, and the day sign under which the infant was born arranged everything from the cradle to the grave. Each day was overseen by a different deity, whose glyph was a stylized portrait of its functions and character, which the mortal born on that day was obliged to assume in some way. Priests known as day keepers cast the horoscopes of all new babies and assigned them names from the days on which they were born. A case in point is a native mistress of the conquistador leader Hernán Cortés. He referred to her as La Malinche (Doña Marina), a corruption of her real name, Ce Malinalli, One-Grass, from the Aztec Calendar. Tezcatlipoca, its mythic figure whose dynamic actions kept the Vessel of Time filled with life-giving energies, was appropriately known as Ipalnemoani, He by Whom We Live, and Titlacauan, We Who Are His Slaves.

Marriages were contracted, travels undertaken, rituals enacted, wars declared, treaties ratified, buildings erected, business deals concluded, sexual activity allowed or forbidden—in fact, virtually all human activities were regulated by an astrological regimen monumentalized in the multicolored Cuauhtlixicalli glowering from atop its pyramid over the people of Tenochtitlán.

Far from being the first of its kind, the Aztec Calendar Stone may actually be a monument to a type of sacred device, some portable instrument used to compute significant astronomical data. The sculpture is perhaps a faithful reproduction of a much smaller original device probably no larger than two or three feet in diameter. The sculpted monolith plainly shows five or six disks within its shallow bowl and superimposed one atop another like stacked plates, as though they were meant to turn either clockwise or counterclockwise, independently of each other, aligning with certain figures to obtain desired coordinates.

The Cuauhtlixicalli's eight pointers, or indicators, may have been affixed to different rings of a smaller instrument after which the sun stone was modeled. Turning the rings to a different position would move its arrow to the desired numerical value, thereby arriving at a particular computation.

The Eagle Bowl's real identity as an apparatus is additionally suggested by the notches and gears that make up its outer circles. When they and their various meshing parts are highlighted separately, they resemble the internal mechanism of a working instrument. If this is indeed the case, there was probably more than one—so many, in fact, every high priest may have possessed an astrological calculator, and the Aztec Calendar Stone memorialized a standardized type.

That it was, in fact, reproduced on a smaller scale was reported firsthand by Bernal Diaz del Castillo in 1521, when he and his fellow conquistadors were approached by *caciques,* or imperial representatives of Moctezuma II, the Aztec emperor, bearing goodwill gifts. These included "a wheel like a sun, as big as a cart-wheel, with many sorts of pictures on it, the whole of fine gold, and a wonderful thing to behold, which those who afterward weighed it said was worth more than ten thousand *reales.* Then another wheel of greater size made of silver of great brilliancy in imitation of the moon with other figures shown on it, and this was of great value, and very heavy."[8]

Because such important though nonetheless perishable devices were commonly associated with the priesthood, its members had a permanent testimonial to their craft erected in a prominent position of authority atop the capital's Great Pyramid, where it overlooked central Tenochtitlán.

While the Eagle Bowl's function as a monument to some kind of sacred computer operated by influential holy men is unproved, its identity as an astrological almanac is more certain. Atlantean origins likewise begin to emerge with the Cuauhtlixicalli's incorporation of the sacred numbers five and six—especially five—which Plato tells us were the mystical common denominators of Atlantis.

# 5

# Four Global Catastrophes of the Atlanto-Mayan Calendar

The numerous connections with Atlantis are graphically multiplied by the quartet of squares surrounding the Calendar Stone's central hub. They match the four global catastrophes that punctuated Atlantean history and ended it. A consensus of scientific opinion at Britain's Fitzwilliam College, in Cambridge, during the summer of 1997, found that our planet had been subjected to a set of celestial bombardments beginning somewhat more than five thousand years ago.

In 1984, archaeoastronomer Marc Davis, paleogeologist Piet Hut, and climatologist Richard A. Muller suggested "extinction of species by periodic comet showers."[1] Their controversial article in the journal *Nature* eventually led to an international symposium of scientists convening under the banner "Natural Catastrophes during Bronze Age Civilizations: Archaeological, Geological, Astronomical and Cultural Perspectives." Pooling their multidisciplinary expertise in 1997, they concluded that a recurring comet or comets narrowly missed Earth on four separate occasions—circa 3100 BCE, 2200 BCE, 1600 BCE, and 1200 BCE. Each close pass showered Earth's Northern Hemisphere with meteoric material, resulting in cataclysms on a worldwide scale.[2]

Further, the four catastrophes correspond to global event horizons in the early history of civilization: the rise of high cultures in Mesopotamia, the Nile Valley, and the Valley of Mexico at the turn of the fourth millennium BCE; the collapse of Egypt's Old Kingdom and Mesopotamia's Akkadian Empire and the rise of China's first dynasty (the Xia) around 2200 BCE; the end of Europe's Old Bronze Age, the implosion of the Hittite Old Kingdom, and the sudden termination of China's Xia Dynasty about 1600 BCE; and the close of the Late Bronze Age, the abandonment of Britain's Stonehenge after eighteen centuries of continuous occupation, and the beginning of the decline of pharaonic Egypt (from which it never recovered) circa 1200 BCE.

All these and numerous other related circumstances were preceded by or accompanied by natural disasters of historically unprecedented magnitude and destructiveness. The late fourth millennium BCE witnessed violent volcanic outbursts from Iceland to Mount Saint Helens and planetwide flooding from the Amazon River, which swelled into a gigantic lake, to the Dead Sea, where water levels rose three hundred feet.

In 2200 BCE, an extensive land bridge connecting Malta to a nearby island fell into the Mediterranean Sea, causing tsunamis that flooded the entire archipelago, while virtually all of Europe's peat bogs burst into flames. The volcanic island of Thera detonated in the Aegean Sea during 1628 BCE with the equivalent force of ten thousand 50-megaton atomic bombs, just as an eruption of comparable magnitude took place in New Zealand. In 1198 BCE, Earth suffered a severe climate regression when several thousand cubic miles of ash were ejected into the atmosphere by global volcanism combined with meteor strikes from the eastern Atlantic Ocean and North America to Australia.

Each of these four natural catastrophes coincided with the close passage of Comet Encke, named after the German astronomer who first calculated its orbit in 1822, Johann Franz Encke. Their parallel to the quartet of worldwide cataclysms cited on the Aztec Calendar Stone is not unique. To the south, among the Andes, Incan priests told of four successive waves of overseas mass migration to coastal Peru undertaken by the pioneering Ayar-manco-topa, the wandering Ayar-chaki, the civilizing Wiracocha, and the warlike Ayar-aucca—all separated by several centuries and set in motion by their own natural cataclysms.

The Hopi Indians of the American Southwest believe that the world has been destroyed four times over. Followers of Zoroastrianism's Zurvanite predecessor, Plato's contemporaries in Persia during the fourth century BCE contended that four previous world ages had each been brought to a violent end through the recurring visitation in Earth skies of Tistrya. Although identified as a star, Tistrya generally signified an unspecified bright light in the heavens. Tistrya's Zoroastrian version, Ahriman, is more specifically described as a comet or meteor shower "attacking the axis and deranging the heavens, thereby causing the catastrophes," in the words of Florida Atlantologist Kenneth Caroli.[3]

The ancient Greeks recalled the great floods of Ogygea, Phoroneus, Deucalian, and, of course, Atlantis. While Plato does not describe the destruction of Atlantis, he does state in the *Timaeus*:

> There have been and will be many different calamities to destroy mankind, the greatest of them by fire and water, lesser ones by countless other means. Your own story of how Phaethon, child of the Sun, harnessed his father's chariot, but was unable to guide it along his father's course, and so burnt up things on the Earth, and was himself destroyed by a thunderbolt, is a mythical version of the truth that there is at long intervals a variation in the course of the heavenly bodies, and a consequent widespread destruction by fire of things on the Earth.[4]

Plato provides remarkable evidence demonstrating that the Atlanteans were not only aware of these cataclysms but structured their most important religious ritual around them. His detailed description of a bull sacrifice undertaken by the ten kings in the Temple of Poseidon every fifth or sixth year was, as mentioned previously, an astrological ceremony commemorating the Age of Taurus.[5] According to Max Heindel (1865–1919), the renowned Danish authority on the zodiac, it ended in 1658 BCE.[6]

This calculation coincides with the third worldwide catastrophe occasioned by the close passage of Comet Encke, which triggered the nuclear-like eruption of Thera's volcanic mountain in the Aegean Sea and the penultimate destruction of Atlantis. Neither Heindel nor Plato could have known that the end of the Age of Taurus was an almost perfect template for the global cataclysms of 1628 BCE. The kings of Atlantis ritually sacrificed a bull to commemorate the close of this zodiacal age while they prayed to Poseidon to protect them from another such disaster. A thirty-year discrepancy between the geophysical date for Thera's detonation, with its attendant upheavals around the world, and the end of the Age of Taurus suggests that the calculations of either the geologists or Max Heindel, or both, are off the mark by an insignificant trifle. Yet the kings' celebration of their bull sacrifice throws an extraordinarily revealing light on their time parameters, because it at once removes Plato's Atlantis from some impossibly incongruent setting during postglacial times to a period squarely in the Bronze Age, at the close of the Age of Taurus, after 1628 BCE.

If, as it would appear, the Age of Taurus corresponded with the Age of Atlantis—at least until the end of the Middle Bronze Age—then Taurus and Atlantis must have shared a common beginning. According to Heindel, the Age of Taurus began in 3814 BCE. This date, too, is a remarkable fit, suggesting the likely birth of Atlantean civilization. It would have required several centuries of development before Atlantean society reached cultural levels high enough to begin influencing the outside world by the end of the fourth millennium BCE.

The Aztec Calendar Stone obviously refers to a worldwide memory of global cataclysms so traumatic they became defining moments in ancient human prehistory and our reckoning of time. These cataclysms appear in the squares clustering around the hub of the Calendar Stone, beginning particularly with the most recent catastrophe, the great deluge, a clear reference to the destruction of Atlantis in every respect.

Evidence of the deluge is found in the second day sign of the Aztec Calendar Stone: Mazatl. It represented the Mēxihcah deer god and goddess, who "raised a great mountain," called Place Where the Heaven

Stood, in the middle of the Atlantic Ocean.[7] Their offspring were pairs of twin sons, who built glittering palaces and shrines until they were mostly killed by a massive flood that sank Place Where the Heaven Stood to the bottom of the sea. One pair of royal deer twins survived the calamity, however, by sailing to the shores of Middle America, where they built the first postdeluge kingdom.

Comparisons are too obvious between Place Where the Heaven Stood, "a great mountain," and Mount Atlas; the inundation that overwhelmed the locations; and Mazatl's and Kleito's pairs of twin princes, both of which built glittering palaces and shrines.

The famous Argentine author Jorge Luis Borges, director of Buenas Aires' Biblioteca Nacional (National Public Library), cited a North African correspondence to the Mēxihcah myth of Mazatl. He wrote that Jakob Ben Chaim, a sixteenth-century rabbi in Fez, quoted a fragment from the Sibyl of Erythraea on an obscure Moroccan tribe who "had their original dwelling in Atlantis, and are half-deer."[8] The Erythraean Sibyl was Herophile, a Chaldean prophetess from Babylonia who presided over Apollo's oracle at the Ionian town of Erythrae during the Late Bronze Age, just when Atlantis was destroyed.

Plato's description of Atlantis inundated "during a single day and night" is seconded by the Mayan Chimalpopca Codex, which reported that their ancestral island came to a bad end "in one day of deluge. Even the mountains sank into the water."[9]

The Maya legend of the Four Suns recounts how death came to their overseas' ancestors from out of the sky: "It rained fire upon them. They were swallowed by the waters."[10] This was the Unuycit, when an ancestral homeland, Patulan-Pa-Civan, perished with all but a handful of survivors, who sailed to the shores of Yucatán during the remote past. Mentioned in the Dresden Codex, the Haiyococab was the Water over the Earth, from which the "Earth-upholding gods fled when the world was destroyed by the Deluge."[11]

The Popol Vuh, or Book of Counsel, a cosmological collection of the fundamental historical and spiritual beliefs of the Maya, describes the Hun yecil—the Drowning of the Trees—when the U Mamae, or

Old Men, survivors of an Atlantic cataclysm, built their first postdeluge temple near the banks of the Huehuhuetan River in thanks to the gods for their escape.[12]

Tulan, yet another name for the Feathered Serpent's homeland, was smothered by

a resinous thickness descended from heaven. The face of the Earth was obscured, and a heavy, darkening rain commenced; rain by day, and rain by night. There was heard a great noise above their heads, as if produced by fire. Then were seen men running, pushing each other, filled with despair. They wished to climb upon their houses. And the houses, tumbling down, fell to the ground. They wished to climb upon the trees, and the trees shook them off. They wished to enter into the grottoes, and the grottoes closed before them. Water and fire contributed to the universal ruin at that time of the last great cataclysm which preceded the Fourth Creation.[13]

Out of these violent upheavals, the last migrations arrived in what is now Guatemala: "Those who gazed at the rising of the sun had but one language. This occurred after they had arrived at New Tulan, before going west. Here the language of the tribes had changed. Then speech became different. All that they had heard or understood when departing from (Old) Tulan had become incomprehensible to them."[14] Reflecting the quartet of natural disasters that struck during Atlantean times, four different Tulans appear in the Cakchiquel Manuscript: "It is where the sun set that we came to (New) Tulan from the other side of the sea, and it is there that we were conceived and begotten by our mothers and fathers."[15]

These accounts preserved by the Maya in their most sacred documents unquestionably reflect the destruction of Atlantis. Even 4-Atl's translation as 4-Water shares its meaning with the Sanskrit *atl*, because both "support."

The previous event horizon, 4-Quihuitl, or 4-Fire from Heaven, graphically describes the effect of Comet Encke's disastrous brush with

Earth in 1628 BCE. Its earlier near miss during 2193 BCE is known as 4-Ehécatl, or 4-Windstorm, which is similar to the description put forth by Swedish geologists Lars Franzen and Thomas B. Larrson, whose material evidence for a major natural catastrophe at that time reveals "indications of strongly increased atmospheric circulation in rhythmically appearing periods" caused by numerous midair bursts of meteors and asteroids, resulting in, literally, worldwide windstorms.[16]

More of this second global event came to light in spring 2013, when researchers were surprised to discover how the ancestral European population goes back little more than four thousand years. Prior to the late third millennium BCE, our Cro-Magnon ancestors underwent some thirty-five centuries of uninterrupted progress after entering the European continent, where their descendants eventually emerged as modern humans. But findings disclose that this steady development was derailed when Europe's original population was radically supplanted by another.

"What is intriguing," states Alan Cooper, coauthor of the study, "is that the genetic markers of this first pan-European culture, which was clearly very successful, were then suddenly replaced around forty-five hundred years ago, and we don't know why."[17] In an April 23 edition of the scientific journal *Nature Communications,* he explains how his team at the University of Adelaide Australian Center for Ancient DNA analyzed mitochondrial DNA from thirty-seven skeletal remains; they belonged to men and women who lived in Germany and Italy more than four thousand years ago. Mitochondrial DNA lies in the energy-making structures of human cells and is passed on through the maternal line. Cooper and his colleagues concentrated their investigation on haplogroup h, specific DNA from a certain genetic group widely dispersed throughout Europe but rare elsewhere.

Results "established that the genetic foundations for modern Europe were only established in the Mid-Neolithic, after this major genetic transition around four thousand years ago," according to team member Wolfgang Haak.[18] "The genetic profile changes radically, suggesting that some mysterious event led to a huge turnover in the population that made up Europe," comments a science reporter for *Fox News.*[19]

"Something major happened," Cooper says, "and the hunt is now on to find out what that was."[20]

Geologists know that sometime before 2100 BCE, a 359-megaton asteroid exploded over Argentina, leaving a series of impact craters across the Rio Cuarto area. During this same period, according to Maltese researcher Anton Mifsud, a large land bridge between Malta and the nearby island of Filfla cataclysmically collapsed, generating giant waves that flooded the whole archipelago and brought about the end of Neolithic civilization on Malta.[21] Traces of major faulting in the submarine Pantelleria Rift upon which both islands sit have been dated to 2200 BCE.[22]

Swedish geologists Lars Franzen and Thomas B. Larrson found in their geologic material "indications of strongly increased atmospheric circulation in rhythmically appearing periods" throughout the Bronze Age, with a high peak in the late third millennium BCE. Ash fall from the Icelandic volcano Hekla-4 dates a major eruption to about 2290 BCE.[23]

In March 1998, a specialist in paleoclimatology, Harvey Weiss, professor of Near Eastern archaeology at Yale, showed that the Habur Plains of northern Syria represented a highly productive agricultural and metropolitan region until all its farmlands and cities were rapidly abandoned. A prolonged, extreme drought forced mass evacuations. Ancient ocean sediments from the Gulf of Oman dated the sudden deterioration of what had been a stable climate to circa 2200 BCE.[24] Weiss's conclusion was substantiated by Peter DeMenocal at Columbia University's Lamont-Doherty Earth Observatory, in New York. He found that chemical signals from the Greenland Ice Sheet Project 2 coincided with the Syrian drought.[25]

Four years before DeMenocal's confirmation, a researcher at the Swiss Technical University in Zurich analyzed sediment cores from the bottom of Lake Van, because it lies near the headwaters of the Tigris and Euphrates Rivers in eastern Turkey. Gerry Lemcke determined that the lake's volume of water declined radically at the same time, with catastrophic effects for the rural and urban populations of Mesopotamia.

Meanwhile, glaciers renewed their advance in Lapland, northernmost Sweden, and the Himalayas.[26]

Franzen uncovered "spherules" similar to specimens reported in Syria. He made "a comparison of certain rare minerals found in the burned layers of the bogs, possibly cosmic dust, with the site of the Tunguska blast of 1908."[27] The small, spherical trace evidence from the Syrian and Siberian sites showed how the organic disposition of both locations had been violently altered by a celestial impact of cataclysmic proportions.

Irish oak chronologies display evidence of an extraordinary "narrowest ring" event in 2345 BCE, which, Baillie believes, "could have a cometary relationship."[28] At the same time, major flooding took place at Lough Neagh, the largest lake in the northern part of Ireland, and radiocarbon dating of floodplain deposits in central England's Ripple Brook catchment evidenced drastic increases of sediment deposition.[29] The World Chronicle section of the Irish *Annals of Clonmacnois*, which record events in Ireland from prehistory to 1408 CE, describes "lakes breaking out" all over the country at this time and causing nationwide panic.[30]

The height of Egyptian civilization in the Old Kingdom simultaneously collapsed with the fall of its last dynasty, the sixth, in 2181 BCE. A Coptic account in the *Abou Hormeis* papyrus tells of a fiery danger that appeared just then from "the heart of the Lion," the Constellation Leo, near the star Regulus.[31] Accompanied by loud thundering in the sky, a rain of burning stones shattered Egypt in "the first minute of Cancer," followed immediately by the Great Flood.[32] Caroli states that the report "could refer to a period when the summer solstice left Leo for Cancer, circa 2200 BCE. The papyrus sets the catastrophe for three hundred ninety-nine years after a prophetic dream, which resulted in building the Great Pyramid. If so, the event occurred sometime after 2254 BCE."[33]

A mysterious mass death, including widespread fires, occurred concurrently at the Egyptian port city of Mendes, which was abandoned until the advent of the New Kingdom.[34]

According to Bruce Masse, an environmental archaeologist at the Los

Alamos National Laboratory in New Mexico, evidence for widespread destruction in Palestine after the start of the twenty-second century BCE "suggests that a cosmic impact may have been a factor, a date which fits well with the estimate of 2188 BCE for the Sodom and Gomorah impact."[35] Just then, the Akkadian Empire collapsed when Ur-III came to a sudden close, circa 2160 BCE. The Agade Empire died with its last king, Shu Durul, in 2139 BCE. A contemporary epic, *The Curse of Akkad,* tells of "heavy clouds that did not rain," "large fields which produce no grain," and "flaming potsherds that fall from the sky."[36]

Contemporaneous Chinese told of ten "suns" falling from the sky, and nine years of cataclysmic floods followed the reigns of the emperors Kuan and Yu. Caroli believes "both were connected to sky-dragons, probably comets."[37] Using royal chronologies, he dates the "ten suns" incident to circa 2141 BCE. Emperor Shun wrote of a large meteor he saw fall from the sky and strike Earth around 2240 BCE, followed by the Great Flood: "The whole world was submerged and all the world was an endless ocean. People floated on the treacherous waters, searching out caves and trees on high mountains. The crops were ruined and survivors vied with fierce birds for places to live. Thousands died each day."[38]

The Archbishop of Armagh, James Ussher, author of the King James Bible, deduced through internal evidence of the Old Testament that Noah's flood occurred in 2349 BCE. He was followed by one of the seventeenth century's great scientists, William Whiston, successor to Isaac Newton at Cambridge, who concluded that the cataclysm had been brought about by the near miss of a large comet.

In the *Laws,* Plato states that "the famous Deluge" of Ogyges took place less than two thousand years before his time, or circa 2300 BCE.[39] Varo, the Roman scholar, wrote that it occurred around 2136 BCE. In classical Greek tradition, the Ogygean flood was accompanied by nine months of darkness (ash fall).[40]

The *Oera Linda Book,* a compilation of ancient North German oral histories transcribed in 1256 CE, known in Old Frisian as *Thet Oera Linda Bok,* tells how the ancestors of the Frisian people fled from Atland—an ancestral island in the Atlantic Ocean. The precise year cited by the *Oera Linda Book* for that calamity is 2193 BCE, which pinpoints the destruction of Atlantis, a catastrophe that sent its refugees to populate other areas of the world. This conclusion has only now been confirmed by University of Adeliade scientists. They have identified a late third millennium BCE disturbance in our genetic ancestry that violently separated the beginnings of modern humans from our Atlantean origins. Mythic, historic, and geologic references combine with these new DNA discoveries to demonstrate that the near miss of a large comet around 2200 BCE catastrophically affected the Middle Bronze Age, killing off sizeable proportions of its populations and radically displacing others. The event horizon was of such a magnitude as to fundamentally alter the human genetics of the European continent forever afterward.

Although 4-Ocelotl, or 4-Jaguar—the first of the four global cataclysms, involving the near annihilation of humanity by wild beasts—seems less clearly associated with the upheavals of 3100 BCE, its celestial character survived in the Aztec version, which told that the evil Tezcatlipoca turned himself into another sun a very long time ago. To save Earth from being burned by twice as much heat, Quetzalcoatl knocked Smoking Mirror (Tezcatlipoca) out of the sky, but as he fell, Tezcatlipoca transformed himself into a monstrous jaguar and took out his frustration on men and women by attacking them everywhere. He was prevented from utterly devouring humankind when Quetzalcoatl again intervened to drive him off, thereby inaugurating a new age, or sun, for the world. Tezcatlipoca eventually returned to blow the Feathered Serpent high into the sky with a powerful wind that devastated the whole Earth (4-Ehécatl, or 4-Windstorm).

While wandering among the stars, Quetzalcoatl collected a sufficient number of heavenly flames to hurl them down at his enemy, forcing him yet again from power, but setting the entire planet on fire in the process (4-Quihuitl, or 4-Fire from Heaven). The water goddess Chalchiuhtlicue, Our Lady of the Turquoise Skirt, finally doused the conflagration with a global flood, from which a few humans survived to begin life over again (4-Atl, or 4-Water).

# 6

# Mayan
# Astronomy and Gods

Because time repeats itself, the Maya believed, they should be able to predict the future. This was the fundamental tenet upon which their calendar was based: coming events were foreshadowed in the past. From this supposition, Mayan astronomers developed a complex system of timekeeping based on the scientific inheritance of their U Mamae ancestors, the Old Men who carried the principles of celestial mechanics from doomed Aztlán-Atlantis to the shores of Yucatán. There they evolved the Tzol'kin, a 260-day calendar, and the Haab, a 365-day calendar, along with the Calendar Round—a synchronized cycle of the Tzol'kin and Haab that lasts for fifty-two Haab.

These intricate organizations of time were not intuited by shamans during altered states of consciousness, nor were they the religious hallucinations of controlling priests presuming to speak for the gods. They were, on the contrary, the exclusive results of close and accurate observations of natural phenomena faithfully documented over the course of numerous generations. For example, the Tzol'kin's 260 days derived from the 260-day period covering the length of human pregnancy, leading some archaeologists to conclude that the calendar was developed by midwives to predict the arrival of newborn infants.

Because the solar circumambulation of Venus is 1.6 times faster than that undertaken by our planet, its thirteen revolutions around the sun require eight Earth-years to complete. Proof that the Maya were aware of this 13:8 ratio is expressed by the numbers they used to identify Venus and calculate its movements—thirteen and eight. In fact, their calculations of the Venus cycle were accurate within a two-hour margin of error.

Particularly amazing was their knowledge of an event at the heart of our investigation. On the morning of December 21, 2012, the winter solstice sun was, in fact, aligned with the galactic equator, the central line of our galaxy as it appears from Earth. This orientation included dark areas at the galactic core created by interstellar dust extending along the Milky Way from the galactic center beyond the constellation Aquila, the Eagle (perhaps the Aztec Calendar Stone's Eagle Bowl). Remarkably, neither the Dark Rift nor 2012's alignment were known to modern science until the mid-twentieth century. How the Maya or their Atlantean predecessors could have learned about either astronomical phenomenon without the use of deep-space telescopes and super computers is a mystery. But the fact that the Maya *were* aware of these orientations powerfully underscores the credibility of their statements regarding the controversial winter solstice.

Predictions for this date appeared in their Long Count of 1,872,000 days beginning on August 11, 3114 BCE and terminating 5,125 solar-years later on December 21, 2012. The Long Count began with the destruction of the Fourth World, and the Fifth World ended with the rising sun on 2012's winter solstice. Mēxihcah calendrics were usurped by the Aztecs, and the Maya obtained much of theirs from the Izapa. Inhabiting a ceremonial capital likewise known as Izapa, near Mexico's Pacific coastal plains of Chiapas, close to the modern border with Guatemala, the Izapa were a transitional people connected with Mesoamerica's first civilization. More likely, they were the Olmec themselves, or, at least, their last remnants, known to possess the Long Count, which they passed on to the Maya.

"There are no specific markings or statements about the year 2012 on the archaeological artifacts at Izapa," observes John Van Auken of Virginia's Association for Research and Enlightenment. "But there are numerous images at Izapa that portray a rare celestial alignment that appears in the skies in the years around 2012. This galactic alignment marks the rebirth of the December solstice and the rebirth of the Sun Lord over Seven Macaw's attempts to replace him. The Sun Lord rises through the Dark Rift in the Milky Way, located between Sagittarius and Scorpio."[1] The celestial alignment Van Auken refers to is depicted on a late preclassical (circa 600 BCE) stela at Izapa.

In the Mayan Popol Vuh and, presumably, in Izapa myth, Vucub Caquix, or 7-Macaw, was a demonic bird that tried to take over the sun and moon in a twilight zone between the Fourth and Fifth Worlds. Although his complex story is not entirely comprehensible, he was doubtless intended to signify an evil influence, given the nature of his sons, Cabracan and Zipacna. They were the instigators of earthquakes, implying 4-Ollin's Earth movement set to end our present world. "4-Ollin" was an Aztec term for the beginning of the Fifth Sun, that period of time stretching from the late fourth millennium BCE to the early twenty-first century CE.

The Maya's earliest known written reference to their earlier version of 4-Ollin was found in the former Izapa-Olmec realm of Chiapas at Tortuguero, site of a classic Mayan city (200 to 700 CE) north of the better-known ceremonial center at Palenque. The incomplete, partially legible inscription on Tortuguero's Monument 6 has been translated by Mayan epigrapher David Stuart: "At the end of 13 Baktuns, on 4 Ahau 3 Kankin, 13.0.0.0.0; [something] occurs when Bolon Yokte descends."[2] The recently concluded Fifth Sun comprised 13 Baktuns, each one containing 144,000 days. The date 4-Ahau 3-Kankin, 13.0.0.0.0, was December 21, 2012.

Archaeologists Nikolai Grube, Simon Martin, and Mark Zender (University of Texas) offered a complementary translation: "'It will happen' (*utom*), [effaced section], 'and he will descend' (*yem*). They involve the 'coming down' of B'olon 'Ok, or Bolon yokte K'uh. The Thirteenth Bak'tun will be finished [on] Four Ahaw, the Third of K'ank'in.' [Effaced] will occur. '[It will be] the descent [?] of the Nine Support [?] God(s) to the' [effaced]."[3]

*Figure 6.1. At the ceremonial center of Copán, in Honduras, stone representations portraying the god of the underworld threaten to destroy humankind at the end of the Mayan calendar, "when Bolon Yokte descends" on the world after December 21, 2012.*

Bolon Yokte, who is depicted as well as mentioned on the Izapa stela, was the terrible lord of the underworld, leader of all the forces of destruction, the personification of triumphant chaos and conflict. His spotted jaguar pelt signifying the starry night sky identifies him with his place of origin in the heavens, while "the mouth of the jaguar represents the Underworld Portal, which is seen in the sky as the Dark Rift in the Milky Way," according to researcher John Major Jenkins.[4]

The descent of the Nine Support Gods indicates as many levels of hell will descend upon Earth some unspecified time after 2012's winter solstice. Interestingly, the words describing exactly what will take place "when Bolon Yokte descends" have been lost, probably due to weathering over the course of time—or they may have been intentionally effaced by someone who could understand them long before modern archaeologists were able to translate the inscription on Monument 6. Perhaps a literate Maya reading it was so horrified by the prediction that he deliberately blotted out all words identifying the precise nature of the coming event in a magical effort to prevent its occurrence. In any case, there can be no doubt that the Maya—from their Olmec predecessors at Izapa to their Aztec inheritors in Tenochtitlán—consistently regarded 4-Ahau 3-Kankin, the close of the Fifth World, as an all-encompassing catastrophe unrivaled for its destructiveness.

The coming of a Sixth World is neither mentioned nor implied anywhere, because humanity is not supposed to survive "when Bolon Yokte descends" after the close of 13-Baktun. Twenty-first-century scholars endeavor to put a positive spin on the Mayan prophecy, arguing that it merely refers to a transition from one age to another. The passage may be accompanied by a natural upheaval here or there, and social disruption may shake up a few cities, but humankind is supposed to survive. More than that, some modern interpreters claim 2012's winter solstice signaled a new golden age of renewal for all the peoples of our planet. The world will be purged of its mistakes so that humanity may at last dispense with all the inequalities that have so far hampered indefinite progress.

These Pollyanna prophecies are largely baseless. Researchers who instead confine their investigations to the Mesoamerican source materials come away with entirely opposite conclusions. Bolon Yokte may appear once in temple art beside the Tree of Life, but such a single uncertain reference cannot make the God of Creation out of the Lord of Hell. Nor do edifying versions of 4-Ahau 3-Kankin square with the Mēxihcah's own term for the nature of the Fifth Sun's closure: Macuilli-Tonatiuh, literally, the Clenched Fist of Tonatiuh.

Readers will recall Tonatiuh's bug-eyed portrayal at the center of the Aztec Calendar Stone, where his blood-spattered tongue drips with human hearts, while others are held in the grasp of his pitiless talons. His forehead is adorned with a pot spilling flames. Fire blazes from his nose and ears. As such, Tonatiuh is disappointing as the messenger of a new era characterized by international peace and human renewal.

*Figure 6.2. A relief sculpture from the Aztec capital, Tenochtitlán, depicting Macuilli-Tonatiuh, Clenched Fist of Tonatiuh, a vengeful god who will bring chaos to the world sometime following the close of the Fifth Sun, which terminated with 2012's winter solstice.*

In fact, he embodies the end of thirteen Baktuns in the Nahui-Ollin, or 4-Ollin. This period is, moreover, ruled by Xolotl, the dark and malevolent aspect of the Evening Star, the planet Venus, which plays such a vital role in Mesoamerican calendrics. For example, 2012's winter solstice was transited by Venus, according to the Maya, and the Long Count was set in motion 5,125 years before by Kukulcan, the Feathered Serpent and beneficent incarnation of Venus.

As this planet's evil incarnation, Xolotl was the Mēxihcah death god, who conveyed souls to Mictlán. It was into this underworld that the sun disappeared each night under Xolotl's control. Depicted in sacred art as a skeleton, he was additionally the god of misfortune and fire. All these dire characterizations tell us far more about the real nature of 4-Ollin than all the good-natured spin put on it by today's upbeat interpretations.

Yet for everything the Maya and those who came after them had to say about the calamitous end of the Fifth World, the precise nature of its closure was never spelled out. The Mēxihcah originally told their Spanish inquisitors in the early sixteenth century that 4-Ollin meant simply "movement." Other native informants elaborated slightly, indicating more specifically that 4-Ollin signified "Earth movement," which Catholic friars presumed must have signified an earthquake.

Of the more than six million mixed descendants of the Maya living today across Guatemala, Mexico, and Belize, the Lacandones are the most direct linear descendants of the Maya, and they still preserve the authentic meaning of 4-Ollin: the Rebellion of Earth. They refer to themselves as the Hach Winik, or True People, for their devotion to the original principles of the Maya, a claim emphasized by their residency near the ancient ruins of Bonampak, with its vibrantly polychrome frescoes painted during 790 CE.

Hach Winik pilgrims still conduct religious activities at this famous ceremonial center in Chiapas, where the Olmec ruins of Izapa and its nearby surviving inscription of the Mayan prophecy may be found. Perhaps five hundred of these True People still survive in a single village, Lacanja Chansayab, close to the border with Guatemala. Their ancient calendar appears to have chronicled the four natural catastrophes that struck our planet during the Bronze Age, and it correctly predicted 2012's winter solstice alignment with the galactic center.

How accurate were ancient Mesoamerican projections for 4-Ollin? At least some degree of their accuracy may be gleaned from the Aztec Calendar Stone's success rate in anticipating historically verifiable events. For example, it warned of the Feathered Serpent's disastrous return on Reed-1, or 1519 CE. The prophecy came true when Hernán Cortés first set foot on the shores of Mexico that very year at Veracruz, at the same location where Quetzalcoatl made his Mesoamerican debut long before. His fair-complected physical resemblance to their ancient cultural hero and the superior technology both figures possessed, combined with the Spaniard's fortuitous appearance at the prehistoric flood survivor's same landing site just when the Calendar Stone specified it would happen,

*Figure 6.3. A sculpted monolith at the Honduras National Museum from the Mayan ceremonial city of Copán depicts the underworld god, Bolon Yokte, who they believed would unleash destructive forces on the world after the last day of their calendar.*

convinced the Aztecs that Cortés was himself the returned Feathered Serpent. It was because of this tragic mistaken identity that an empire of millions was caught off-balance and subdued by five hundred conquistadors with thirteen horses and a small number of cannons.

Atop the Calendar Stone appears Reed-13, a box enclosing the image of a maguey plant and surrounded on three sides by thirteen dots, each representing thirteen heavens, which made up a single sun. The glyph signifies the end of a World, or major epoch, corresponding to the year 1479 CE. Precisely thirteen years later, Christopher Columbus dropped anchor off the island of San Salvador in the Bahamas, opening up the New World to European colonization and bringing about the subsequent eradication of Mesoamerican civilization.

Appropriately, Reed-13 occupies the top position of the Calendar Stone, where arrowheads touch it on either side and the uppermost indicator points at its underside, as though all the elements of the Eagle Bowl culminated in this particular sign. As such, Reed-13 represents the supreme date of the entire object and suggests that the Cuauhtlixicalli was made just then, because the astrologer-priests determined that 1479 to 1492 would simultaneously encapsulate the year of its creation and that of their society's downfall in units of thirteen.

Apparently, the Vessel of Time was created and erected over the residents of Tenochtitlán primarily to announce this impending doom. To them, it was a monstrous timepiece winding down the last years of the Aztec Empire, reminding its subjects to brace themselves for the inevitable end of their world.

Only this dire prediction can account for the numerous graphic references circling in concentric rings around the horrid face of Tonatiuh, the personification of time in its thoroughly destructive aspect.

# 7

# The Great Winter

Whether the Rebellion of Earth predicted by ancient Mesoamerican ancestors and calculated for the near future heralds a global renewal, as some twenty-first-century investigators predict, or a worldwide catastrophe as suggested by the Maya themselves remains to be seen. Its very name—the Rebellion of Earth—does, however, suggest an ecological catastrophe of the kind conservationists have been warning against and Hollywood producers have been making movies about since the late twentieth century. To be sure, the Rebellion of Earth seems to anticipate the disastrous consequences of environmental abuse some observers believe have been accumulating in Earth's biosphere since the onset of the Industrial Revolution. If, or especially *when,* such a calamity takes place is cogent to the impending 4-Ollin.

More certain, however, than debatable scenarios for some abrupt adversity sparked by a polluting global economy are prospects for a coming ice age. The last one ended around 9500 BCE, which means that another is due just now, according to paleoclimatologists. Their study of the geologic record shows that ice ages begin and end about every one hundred thousand years, punctuated by less cold, geologically briefer intervals every twelve thousand years. Some researchers conclude that the past dozen millennia more likely represent a warm interlude in an ice age that is still in progress. If so, the resumption of far colder conditions worldwide is not only unavoidable but due to snap back with a suddenness that can paralyze most life on Earth.

*Pravda's* online website caused an international stir in early 2009 when it headlined "Earth on the Brink of an Ice Age." The article by science writer Gregory F. Fegel tells of a growing consensus among climatologists concerning "the very real threat of the approaching and inevitable Ice Age, which will render large parts of the Northern Hemisphere uninhabitable. . . . The data from paleoclimatology, including ice cores, sea sediments, geology, paleobotany and zoology, indicate that we are on the verge of entering another Ice Age, and the data also shows that severe and lasting climate change can occur within only a few years."[1]

Fegel refers to recent studies by Dr. Oleg Sorokhtin, a staff researcher with the Oceanology Institute at the Russian Academy of Natural Sciences in Moscow. Sorokhtin and his colleagues found that their research of Earth climate change over the past one hundred thousand years "strongly indicates the imminent climax of the Holocene [our present geological epoch] and its sudden replacement by a new glacial age during the first half of the present century."[2]

Other Russian climate experts concur. "By the mid-21st century the planet will face another little ice age similar to the Maunder Minimum [the previous little ice age]," according to Khabibullo Abdusamatov, head of the Russian space research laboratory. It must come, he states, "because the amount of solar radiation hitting the earth has been constantly decreasing since the 1990s and will reach its minimum approximately in 2041."[3]

Most of Abdusamatov's colleagues disagree only with his relatively moderate assessment of the coming glaciation. They anticipate something far colder and enduring than the Maunder Minimum. Fegel reports:

> The Earth is now on the brink of entering another Ice Age, according to a large and compelling body of evidence from within the field of climate science. Many sources of data which provide our knowledge base of long-term climate change indicate that the warm,

twelve-thousand-year-long Holocene period will rather soon be coming to an end, and then the earth will return to Ice Age conditions for the next 100,000 years.[4]

Russian scientists are not alone in predicting a new ice age for our immediate future. Climatologists of the Western Institute for Study of the Environment Colloquium (a nonprofit collaboration of environmental scientists, practitioners, and the interested public in Lebanon, Oregon) agree that the Northern Hemisphere is in immediate danger of "an imminent transition to ice."[5] In their institute article "An Urgent Signal for the Coming Ice Age," Peter Harris and John Faraday point out how "the geological record shows that the transitions are sudden, long term and extreme."[6]

Scientific awareness of ice age causation and its cyclical return is not new. As long ago as 1842, the French mathematician Joseph Alphonse Adhemar first proposed that our planet's glacial episodes result from regular alterations in its angular relationship with the sun.[7] Although contemporary scholars rejected Adhemar's theory, it was taken up and elaborated thirty-three years later in Scotland by James Croll, an elected fellow of the Royal Society and correspondent of Charles Darwin. In *Climate and Time in Their Geological Relations,* Croll cites variations of Earth's orbit on climate cycles. He was the first scientist to identify the ability of ice-albedo to magnify solar feedback (*albedo* is the reflecting power of a surface). During periods of high orbital eccentricity, he argues, ice ages take place in regular cycles.[8]

Building on the ideas of Adhemar and Croll during 1930, a geophysicist genius in the Balkans, Milutin Milanković, demonstrated a correlation between glacial activity and Earth's gradually alternating angles toward the sun. Earlier he revised the Julian calendar for the Serbian Orthodox Church. Wikipedia declares, "His calendar is, in fact, the most accurate calendar in the world today."[9]

Milanković found that ices ages correlate to the tilt of our planet over a forty-one-thousand-year time span; the shape of its orbit, which alters during a one-hundred-thousand-year period; and the precession of the equinoxes, or "wobble," gradually rotating in the direction of Earth's axis every twenty-six thousand years. These cycles affect the amount of solar radiation reaching our planet and combine to produce the alternating ice age maximums and warm interglacials.

Milanković's discoveries were greeted with uncertainty by other scientists, then gradually dismissed as improvable until the late twentieth century. In early 1968, Wallace S. Broecker, the Columbia geophysicist who coined the term *global warming* seven years later, found that the Milanković hypothesis was "supported by precise dating of coral reefs and deep-sea sediments."[10] According to Harris and Faraday, "When paleoclimatologists met in 1972 to discuss how and when the present warm climate would end, it was expected that rapid cooling would lead to the coming ice age."[11] Satellite monitoring of the biosphere then confirmed Milanković's solar-glacial cycles. "These data sets may be used to serve as a signal for the coming ice age," Harris and Faraday suggest.[12]

Four years later *Science* magazine published a virtual validation of Milanković's work in "Variations in the Earth's Orbit: Pacemaker of the Ice Ages." Authors John Imbrie, James Hays, and Nicholas Shackleton announced a correlation they uncovered between climate data obtained from ocean sediment cores and Milanković's Earth-sun relationship. Combined, "the results indicate that the long-term trend over the next 20,000 years is towards extensive Northern Hemisphere glaciation and cooler climate."[13]

Today, Milanković's explanation is, as *Pravda* asserts, "the predominant theory to account for Ice Age causation among climate scientists."[14] Their reconsideration of his proposals in the 1970s was prompted by growing concern for climate deterioration generally and an understanding of its mechanism. A 1974 issue of *Time* magazine reported that "38 ships and 13 aircraft, carrying scientists from almost 70 nations, are now assembling in the Atlantic and elsewhere for a massive 100-day study of the effects of the tropical seas and atmosphere on worldwide weather."[15]

Observers from various scientific fields participating in the Global Atmospheric Research Program (GARP) found that a mere 1 percent decrease in the amount of sunlight striking the surface of Earth could tip the climatic balance sufficiently to cool temperatures and precipitate an ice age in a very short time. They learned, too, that temperatures have been as high as they are now only about 5 percent of the past seven hundred thousand years; in other words, our climate has been enjoying an anomalous warm phase that cannot last much longer.[16]

While GARP researchers were endeavoring to determine just when the next glaciation might take place, others at CLIMAP (Climate: Long range Investigation Mapping, and Prediction) hauled up deep-sea core drillings going back over the last half million years to discover that the coming and going of ice ages closely follows Milanković's cycles of precession, orbital shape, and rotational wobble. The ocean-bottom cores also showed that glaciation sometimes began and ended with great suddenness.

The Younger Dryas stadial, also referred to as the Big Freeze, was a brief thirteen-hundred-year cold snap that afflicted the world about twelve thousand years ago. (A stadial is a period of lower temperatures during an interglacial, or warm period, of an ice age.) Within a single decade, temperatures plummeted worldwide. Increased snowfall blanketed every mountain range on Earth, all of Scandinavia's forests were reduced to tundra, and drought overcame the Levant. In North America, numerous animal species went extinct, while the Clovis culture—an early society of Paleo-Indians—entered a steep decline from which it would never recover.

The respected editor of *New Scientist* magazine, Nigel Calder, was sufficiently alarmed by these disclosures to declare in the July 1975 issue of *International Wildlife* magazine, "The facts have emerged in recent years and months from research into past ice ages. They imply that the threat of a new ice age must now stand alongside nuclear war as a likely source of wholesale death and misery for mankind."[17]

Climate research in the following decades confirmed and deepened the worst suspicions about glaciation. The Greenland Ice Core Project of 1987 sent an improved drilling apparatus nearly two miles beneath Earth's surface to retrieve samples formed over the past quarter-of-a-million years. The specimens revealed that every ice age within that time parameter began abruptly.

The British scientific journal *Nature* reported in 1999 that Antarctic ice cores collected at Lake Vostok demonstrated how glacial maximums alternate with warm periods known as interstadials in recognizable patterns, yet again confirming Milanković's hypothesis. The Lake Vostok cores showed that "today we are near to the end of a warm interglacial," according to *Pravda,* "and the Earth is now due to enter the next Ice Age."[18]

Its expected arrival seems at odds with concerns for global warming caused by industrial pollution. While debate still rages over civilization's effect on the natural environment, any questions regarding climate deterioration due to interference by modern humans may be knocked into a cocked hat by Earth's own rotational cycles, which are responsible for initiating glaciation in recurring patterns. Some scientific observers argue, however, that human meddling in the biosphere does play a direct role in fostering ice-age conditions.

Reid A. Bryson at the University of Wisconsin–Madison and other climatologists point out that dust and other particles released into the atmosphere as a result of farming and fuel burning block more and more sunlight from reaching and heating the surface of Earth, fostering cooler, wetter conditions that allow for ice ages. His conclusions prompted geologists Gillford H. Miller and Anne Vernal to ask, in a 1992 issue of *Nature,* "Will Greenhouse warming lead to Northern Hemisphere ice-sheet growth?"[19] They were answered that same year by climatologists Ken Caldera and James Kasting, who revealed the "susceptibility of the early Earth to irreversible glaciation caused by carbon dioxide clouds."[20]

At his death in June 2008, Bryson was widely recognized as "a towering figure in climatology and interdisciplinary studies of climate, people and the environment."[21] According to his obituary by Terry Devit, he "pioneered the use of computer models in climate science . . . was among the first to explore the influence of climate on humans and human culture and, in turn, some of the human impacts on climate. He was an early developer of simple computer models to study the causes of past climate change, comparing those simulations with records of paleo-climate and human culture."[22]

John Kutzbach, University of Wisconsin–Madison professor emeritus of atmospheric and oceanic sciences, said of Bryson, "His interdisciplinary interests and knowledge of these topics allowed him to see connections that others missed and to initiate studies that are still at the cutting edge of climate research."[23] Given his recognition as the pioneer of climatology, Bryson's belief in human contribution to prospects for a new ice age deserves serious consideration. He was, however, less a proponent of either global warming or cooling than of climate destabilization, in which extremes of both increasingly hot and cold conditions irregularly alternate with each other.

"The principal weather change likely to accompany the cooling trend is increased variability—alternating extremes of temperature and precipitation in any given area," science writer John H. Douglas explains in *Science News* magazine.[24] He continues:

> The cause of this increased variability can best be seen by examining upper atmosphere wind patterns that accompany cooler climate. During warm periods, a "zonal circulation" predominates, in which the prevailing westerly winds of the temperate zones are swept over long distances by a few powerful high and low pressure centers. The result is a more evenly distributed pattern of weather, varying relatively little from month to month or season to season. During colder climate periods, however, the high-altitude winds are broken up into irregular cells by weaker and more plentiful pressure cells, causing formation of a "meridional circulation" pattern. These small, weak cells may stagnate over vast areas for many months, bringing unseasonably cold weather on one side and unseasonably warm weather on the other. . . . Thus, while the hemisphere as a whole is cooler, individual areas may alternately break temperature and precipitation records at both extremes.[25]

The distorted meteorological mechanism Douglas describes has been borne out by events that came to pass nearly forty years after Nigel Calder's prescient 1975 article was published. In late February 2012, temperatures in southeastern Minnesota briefly shot up to 80 degrees Fahrenheit, far above anything ever documented there in midwinter. One year later the season's greatest blizzard struck the same region on May 3. Never before in recorded memory had a major snowstorm struck the southern section of the state so late in spring. It was no fluke, but part of an unusually cold system with below-freezing temperatures that preceded it by months and persisted into the end of July, when record low temperatures in the forties dominated the Upper Midwest.

Climatologists explained that the jet stream was dipping abnormally southward, bringing lower temperatures. The jet stream is a narrow current of air flowing at high speed from west to east between levels of the atmosphere where temperatures decrease or increase with altitude. What the weather experts neglected to mention was the cause for its atypical behavior. With the atmosphere's continuous accumulation of industrial output, winds driven by Earth's rotational spin spiral carbon dioxide toward the polar regions, raising temperatures, which depress the jet stream southward. In other words, global warming is to blame for below-average temperatures in the Upper Midwest.

Generations of unremitting industrial pollution have gathered around the Arctic, where particulates are heating the northern polar region, thereby pushing the jet stream farther south. This displaced cold air is compressing and distorting Northern Hemisphere weather patterns, bringing unseasonably below-normal temperatures to some areas and excessively high temperatures elsewhere. The contrasting temperatures result in more frequent abnormally violent weather as a precursor to an artificially induced return to glacial conditions: "Scientists at the National Aeronautics and Space Administration [NASA] believe more air pollution could trigger another disastrous ice age, NASA administrator James Fletcher says."[26]

This is no idle speculation. "Carbon dioxide in atmosphere reaches landmark level," announces Erin Wayman in a spring 2013 article in *Science News* magazine.[27] "On May 9, the atmosphere above Hawaii's

Mauna Loa volcano reached a milestone: For the first time since record keeping began there in 1958, the daily mean carbon dioxide concentration reached 400 parts per million," Wayman writes.[28] The Mauna Loa Observatory is the world's oldest continuous monitoring station of carbon dioxide. "At 400 parts per million," she explains, "greenhouse gas concentration is now higher than it has been for millions of years."[29] Wayman continues:

> In spring of 2012, Alaska, Canada and several other Arctic locations surpassed the 400 ppm benchmark. Parts of the Southern Hemisphere should top 400 ppm within the next few years. And by 2016, scientists at the National Oceanic and Atmospheric Administration expect global average concentrations of the greenhouse gas to hit 400 ppm. The last time Earth's global $CO_2$ concentrations were that high was during the Pliocene epoch, 5.3 million to 2.6 million years ago, when summers in the Arctic were 8 degrees Celsius warmer than they are today. $CO_2$ levels have been rising sharply with the increase in fossil-fuel burning since the Industrial Revolution, when the global average was 280 ppm. The rise of $CO_2$ has accelerated in recent decades. In the late 1950s, $CO_2$ concentrations increased about 0.7 ppm per year. In the last ten years, that rate jumped to 2.1 ppm per year.[30]

These conditions began coming to a head during a fortnight in early July 2013, as temperatures rose 2 to 5 degrees Fahrenheit above average over much of the Arctic Ocean. On July 13, a webcam stationed at the North Pole revealed that snow and ice were being rapidly replaced by a growing meltwater pond. By month's end it had expanded into a foot-deep aquamarine lake. Meltwater ponds now account for more than half of the Arctic's sea ice. They link up across the smooth surface of the ice, creating a network that traps heat from the sun.[31]

By the end of July, Anchorage, Alaska, broke its record for the most consecutive days of temperatures above 70 degrees Fahrenheit. Fairbanks, too, surpassed all previous heat levels when temperatures soared above 80 degrees for more than a month.³² Warming at the Arctic region is forcing the jet stream farther south, bringing much colder, extreme, and violent weather to the contiguous United States in a pattern consistent with the onset of a glacial epoch. The ice age–like identity of these effects is defined by the disappearance of ice from the North Pole, an unprecedented occurrence that dramatically demonstrates a radical deterioration of the climate.

"The last time that scientists can say confidently that the Arctic was free of summertime ice was 175,000 years ago," according to the National Snow and Ice Data Center, "during the height of the last major interglacial period, known as the Eemian. Temperatures in the Arctic were warmer than now and sea level was also four to six meters [thirteen to twenty feet] higher than it is today, because the Greenland and Antarctic Ice Sheets had partly melted."³³ In other words, today's industrial warming and melting of the northern polar region is artificially causing ice age conditions that were similarly, if naturally, brought about during the height of the last major interglacial period, 125,000 years ago.

In fact, southeastern Minnesota's unseasonable blizzard of 2013 was just the most obvious forerunner of a new ice age that may already be upon us. It joins another harbinger of just two years before, when the United States suffered the highest number of tornadoes in its history. From April 25 to 28, 2011, 358 tornadoes killed 349 people and inflicted widespread damage, tripling the prior record for tornadoes during that month and breaking the overall record for tornadoes in a single month. The widest tornado on record—2.6 miles across at its peak—struck El Reno, Oklahoma, on May 31, 2013. The previous year the lowest pressure ever recorded at Earth's surface when adjusted to sea level was generated by a tornado near Manchester, South Dakota, which dropped to 850 millibars in less than one minute. Such precedent setters have all been concentrated within the early years of the present century.

They join numerous other examples of radical climate change, so many and so often that they are regarded as commonplace. One year's record-low or record-high temperatures are broken by the following year's extremes, which will be inevitably surpassed in the coming months and years. Meanwhile, other storms and hurricanes of previously unknown violence, floods of biblical proportions—sometimes in areas never before affected—and western wildfires more frequent and broadly destructive than anything in living memory are now part of the American landscape.

On June 29, 2013, Philadelphia International Airport was drenched by 8.02 inches of rain that fell in just 4.5 hours. By way of comparison, the previous record holder, 1999's Hurricane Floyd, required 20 hours of rainfall to discharge 6.63 inches on the city. Nothing approaching such a cataclysmic downpour has been documented in Philadelphia since detailed weather records were first kept in 1872.[34] Leading up to the Philadelphia deluge, Douglas tells how "a survey of nine American cities showed increased rainfall ranging from 9.0 to 27.0 percent. The severity of these storms is also affected. Near Houston, Texas, hailstorms were found to increase by 430 percent. The most detailed of these studies is under way in the St. Louis area, where an urban-related 25 percent increase of thunderstorms was found to affect some 1,000 to 2,000 square miles of the surrounding area."[35]

Beginning in the final two decades of the past century, Earth's climate deterioration has been punctuated by monster hailstorms, the likes of which have never before been recorded in meteorological history. In Europe's most catastrophic event of this kind, baseball-size hail fell during July 12, 1984, on Munich, Germany, injuring four hundred people and causing more than $2 billion damage to seventy thousand homes, plus nearly two hundred aircraft. In North America, $1.6 billion worth of damages (adjusted to current dollars) was inflicted along the Front Range of Colorado between Colorado Springs and Fort Collins on July 11, 1990. It was surpassed five years later when a hailstorm that struck the Dallas–Fort Worth, Texas, metro area on May 5, 1995, caused more than $2 billion in losses. Yet more destructive was a barrage of 3½-inch hailstones that blasted the Sydney, Australia, area on April 14, 1999, for less than one hour. Some twenty thousand structures, together with forty thousand vehicles worth $3 billion (in U.S. currency) were damaged in Australia's most expensive natural disaster, and, so far, the single costliest hailstorm in world history.

North America's most expensive hailstorm occurred on April 10, 2001, as it racked up $2.4 billion in damages along the Interstate-70 corridor from eastern Kansas to the St. Louis area then crossed the Mississippi River into southwestern Illinois. Worse befell China the following year, when twenty-five people were killed and thousands more injured by falling hail in Henan Province on July 19.

A foot-high accumulation of hailstones in Clayton, New Mexico, was swept into a draw by five inches of rainfall on August 13, 2004. A culvert in the draw became clogged by the flow, allowing the hail to pile up to fifteen feet deep behind it.

The largest officially recognized hailstone in the United States fell near Vivian, South Dakota, on July 23, 2010. More like a meteorite, it originally measured at least ten inches in diameter and twenty inches in circumference and weighed more than two pounds.

In 2013 Earth experienced greater record-breaking hailstorm activity than any previous year. On June 25, Singapore was hit with its first-ever hailstorm, and its one-inch stones panicked residents. "Singapore rests at sea level just one degree latitude north of the equator," explains meteorologist Christopher Burt. "It is extremely rare for hail, let alone large hail, to fall in the tropics at sea level.[36]

Foot-high accumulations of hail piled up within thirty minutes during the evening of July 3 that same year in the town of Santa Rosa, New Mexico, where the bizarre sight of snowplows clearing the streets in midsummer was without precedent. Three days later, other foot-high accumulations formed a white streak two miles wide and ten miles long between the towns of Airdie and Irricana in southwestern Alberta, Canada. Yet another singular hailstorm struck the Hawaiian island of Oahu on the following July 14. "Not only is it highly unusual for hail to fall over Hawaii," says Tom Birchard, senior meteorologist for the National Weather Service in Honolulu, "but some stones that measured as large as three inches are likely record-breaking."[37]

The accelerating development of these unprecedented hailstorms belongs to an increasingly unhinged climate characterizing the onset of another ice age. The chief difference between it and all previous glacial eras lies in human contribution to the process of change by heating the atmosphere, speeding up the geologic timetable, and intensifying conditions.

Like virtually all of his colleagues, Bryson concluded that the present Holocene Epoch of mild temperatures that have characterized Earth's climate over the past five thousand or more years is about to end soon. Just when is a question scientists are beginning to answer with growing certainty. "The fact is that ice ages recur in a dependable, predictable cycle that's about to repeat itself," according to Robert W. Felix, author of *Not By Fire, But By Ice.* "The next ice age could begin in our lifetimes."[38]

"If the earth's recent history is any clue, says marine geologist Cesare Emiliani of the University of Miami, a new ice age could become a reality," wrote *Time* magazine in 1972.[39] One of the greatest geologists and micropaleontologists of the twentieth century, Emiliani (1922–1995) was the founder of paleoceanography. "The world could be as little as fifty or sixty years away from a disastrous new ice age," a leading atmospheric scientist, Dr. S. I. Rasool of the National Aeronautics and Space Administration and Columbia University, told the *New York Times* a year before Emiliani made his statement.[40] Interestingly, Rasool's prediction appears to have accurately prefigured the abnormal cold periods experienced across North America's Upper Midwest beginning in 2012.

In 2008, Dr. Oleg Sorokhtin told the RIA Novosti Press Agency, "Earth has passed the peak of its warmer period, and a fairly cold spell will set in quite soon. Real cold will come when solar activity reaches its minimum by 2041."[41]

"The frequency of 90 degree days in the U.S. has been plummeting for eighty years," observes Steven Goddard in *Real Science,* "and 2014 has had the lowest frequency of 90 degree days through July 23 on record. The only other year which came close was 1992, and that was due to dust in the atmosphere from Mt Pinatubo."[42]

Abdusamatov's statement that "a fairly cold spell will set in quite soon" ominously coincides with the Maya's dire prophecy. They did not indicate that the Fifth Sun would terminate in a glacial event, although the abundant astronomical and solar imagery surrounding 4-Ollin is associated with Earth's rotational cycles, which are responsible for recurring ice ages. The sudden onset of catastrophically frigid conditions may not result in the extinction of humankind, but civilization would not fare as well.

With at least the entire upper third of the Northern Hemisphere buried under ice, the stresses of mass migrations in the direction of warmer southern areas, coupled with the loss of farmlands and the unbearable overloading of every form of energy production, would cause famine and strife on a monumental scale. If the next ice age is comparable to the last one, all of New England down to its southeastern quadrant would be covered by fifteen-story-high glaciers. They would additionally cover the entire Great Lakes region down to the tip of southern Illinois, the northern half of Missouri, eastern Nebraska and South Dakota, most of North Dakota, plus the northern regions of Montana, Idaho, and Washington. All of Canada and Russia would be uninhabitable. In Europe, Scandinavia, the British Isles, Poland, the Baltics, most of Germany, and the northern Balkans would be covered by ice.

Population displacement alone could shatter the foundations and framework of organized society. Those fleeing beyond the reach of the ice would not be spared its consequences, however. With all but some of the Northern Hemisphere's crop regions lost, a crippled agriculture would not be able to feed 7 billion people suddenly confined to less than two-thirds of their previous living space. Merely being able to breathe would become increasingly difficult, because the oxygen-producing forests of the north would have disappeared. These projections are based on the most recent glaciation, which was far milder and spread over much less territory than previous ice ages.

"According to the academy report on climate, we may be approaching the end of a major interglacial cycle, with the approach of a full-blown 10,000-year ice age a real possibility," Douglas writes. "Again, this transition would involve only a small change of global temperature—two or three degrees—but the impact on civilization would be catastrophic."[43]

The glaciation that accompanied or immediately followed the extinction of the dinosaurs about 65.5 million years ago was at least twice as ravaging and appears to have been a truly global affair. "The evidence is now abundantly clear," Bryson states, "that the climate of the Earth is changing in a direction that is not promising in terms of our ability to feed the world."[44] He is referring to colder, drier conditions resulting in global crop failures and the subsequent effect on human life, "like a billion people dying."[45]

Challenges presented by the next ice age, regardless of its relative severity, will inevitably be sorted out in the way humans invariably respond to social dislocation; namely, through war and other forms of population control. Bolon Yokte will reign over Earth for the next one hundred thousand years, until Xolotl shall have conveyed most of humankind—perhaps all of it—into the bowels of Mictlán, never to return.

None of this should come as a surprise. We like to think of ourselves as immortal in at least some respects, but the biological history of Earth is an unbroken chronicle of extinction. The Cretaceous-Tertiary event is famous for its annihilation of the dinosaurs, when 65 percent of all life on Earth fell victim to sudden mortality. Previous downsizings of this kind were sometimes responsible for much greater death rates. The Ordovician-Silurian, Late Devonian, Permian-Triassic, and Triassic-Jurassic events exterminated virtually every kind of creature in the world. There are far more species that have flourished and forever winked out of existence than are alive today.

We ourselves have already lost innumerable members of the human genus—Neanderthals, *Homo habilis, Homo erectus,* and others. Modern humans, such as the ancient Egyptians, Sumerians, Babylonians, Etruscans, Trojans, Olmecs, Aztecs, Anasazi, Inca—not to mention the Atlanteans—and many other peoples are no longer with us. In consideration of their passing, we early-twenty-first-century Earthlings must not imagine that our admittedly fragile civilization is immune to the same forces—historical or natural—that purged them and our nonhuman predecessors from the planet.

If an impending ice age is the next agent of extinction, what might be its connection to the Mayan calendar? Felix concludes that glaciation's geological trip mechanism is Earth's magnetic field because it "holds tectonic forces in check. But when the field weakens during a reversal, that balance disappears. Suddenly unleashed, underwater volcanoes heat the seas and excess moisture rises into the sky. Then the moisture condenses and falls to the Earth as giant snowstorms and great floods."[46] He believes that underwater volcanism triggered by a geomagnetic flip is responsible for ice age conditions, not Earth's rotational wobble. In any case, glaciation is invariably accompanied by such polar reversals.

Does our planet's magnetic field actually have some bearing on tectonics, glaciation, and recurring extinction patterns? According to Dr. David E. Loper, professor emeritus of geological sciences at Florida State University, "There is evidence that climate, volcanism, and magnetic reversals may all be correlated."[47] He is seconded by professor of Earth and environmental sciences at Columbia University, James D. Hays: "The possibility that here is some connection between reversals, climate change, and extinctions cannot be ruled out."[48]

As long ago as 1964, Australian archaeobiologist I. K. Crain suggested a "possible direct causal relation between geomagnetic reversals and biological extinctions."[49] Building on his research ten years later, climatologists C. G. A. Harrison and J. M. Prospero detected "reversals of the Earth's magnetic field and climate changes."[50] Their colleagues, Thomas J. Crowley and Gerald R. North, went further in 1988 to find evidence for "abrupt climate change and extinction events in Earth history."[51] They are seconded by David M. Raup, who writes in the journal *Nature* of "magnetic reversals and mass extinctions."[52]

It would appear the Maya left no opening for escape from 4-Ollin and its terminal consequences. They did not mention a Sixth Sun nor promise any future cycles of destruction and renewal. All we are told is that the descending Clenched Fist of Tonatiuh will precipitate the Rebellion of Earth sometime after the winter solstice of 2012.

Even so, the Maya indirectly offered a faint glimmer of hope to late–Fifth Sun humankind. They insisted that existence rested upon balance and that all forms of energy were not only interchangeable but actually nothing more than variations of the same impulse. In this, they prefigured modern physics by at least two thousand years.

Imbalance anywhere, they reasoned, must invariably generate exponentially amplifying distortion and physical consequences all along the energy spectrum. The human victims of Earth's previous four catastrophes—4-Ocelotl, 4-Ehécatl, 4-Quihuitl, and 4-Atl—deserved their fate because they had tampered with the cosmic equilibrium of their world. The imbalance they created through unnatural lifestyles, attitudes, and behavior set up a swelling frequency around the universe that recoiled on them ten-thousandfold. They could have escaped the cataclysmic verdict that fell upon them, however, if the imbalance they were responsible for setting in motion had been corrected in time to sufficiently damp down its gathering resonance, thereby removing its vibrational destructiveness. That, in essence, is what the ancient Mayan cosmologists would probably most want us to understand. They, the great masters of calendrics, might warn us that there is still time, although admittedly precious little, to mitigate, if not to altogether avoid, the worst of 4-Ollin by a revision of human behavior as universal as it is radical.

At the last conceivable moment we can swerve to narrowly miss a collision with fate through an ethical about-face. To sidestep a global calamity we require no less than a global reorientation with regard to our fundamental relationship with nature. If, as a species, we do not sufficiently alter our self-destructive conduct, what might we expect? The arrival of a new ice age—or a dramatic resumption of the Pleistocene Epoch that never really left us—seems to offer the most likely scenario.

That most recent glacial period began gently approximately one hundred thousand years ago, although it soon after lapsed into violent change. Geologist Geneviève Woillard at the Université Catholique de Louvain tells how a warm phase (the Eemian Period) immediately preceding the last ice age ended "in less than twenty years."[53] Her European colleagues at the Greenland Ice Core Project further conclude from contemporary samples they retrieved nearly two miles beneath the surface of Earth's largest island that the latest glaciation began "catastrophically."[54] W. F. Ruddiman and A. McIntyre wonder about the "severity and speed of Northern Hemisphere glaciation pulses" in the 1982 *Geological Society of America Bulletin*.[55]

"Scientists once thought the onset of an ice age would be very gradual, with glaciers slowly pushing down from the North," Douglas observes, "but recent studies of cored material taken from the sea bottom and remaining glaciers indicate the transition can be rather sudden—a matter of centuries—with ice packs building up relatively quickly from local snowfall that ceases to melt from winter to winter. Major changes in vegetation can occur even more quickly, with a forest becoming a prairie in less than a century, and a savannah turning into a desert in a few decades."[56]

In fact, the onset of glacial conditions could occur much faster, as they did in the past. Felix mentions that "worldwide temperatures plummeted twenty degrees Fahrenheit almost overnight."[57] Summarizing the environmental transition revealed by the Greenland ice cores, science reporters for the *American Journal of Science* explain, "It was as though the climate of Nome, Alaska, suddenly descended on San Francisco."[58]

The 2004 movie *The Day After Tomorrow* dramatized sudden glaciation sweeping across the Northern Hemisphere within a matter of days but is such a rapid change likely to happen again? "When we looked at the records of past temperate intervals," Woillard writes, "we found abrupt shifts in forest composition at the end of all previous interglacials."[59] While not all climatologists may agree with Felix's conclusion that "every ice age began fast," geological upheaval appears to have punctuated at least the early stages of glaciation whenever it took place. We might expect the next ice age to begin no less violently.

Would the Maya have placed such emphasis on the demise of the Fifth World and surrounded it with such apocalyptic imagery merely to mark the end of one calendrical era and the start of another, as some observers insist? Or did they know something we are only beginning to suspect?

# 8

# A Super Solar Storm

While the onslaught of a new ice age might coincide with the end of the Mayan calendar, another natural event offers perhaps an even more likely possibility.

In January 2009, geophysicists at the U.S. National Academy of Sciences (NAS) announced that a super solar storm could catastrophically affect our world before midcentury, when sunspots will become particularly numerous and active. Although the dotlike phenomena appear as mere "spots" from our perspective 93 million miles away, they are not benign blemishes on the photosphere but roiling hurricanes of incomprehensible size. During early 2008, astronomers observed two sunspots, each one as large as the planet Jupiter, or 318 times larger than Earth. Concentrations of intense magnetic activity, sunspots eject far into space enormous clouds of superheated plasma thousands of miles long, together with coronal masses of plasma, or charged high-energy particles.

How vulnerable has our electronic technology, which we rely on more every day, become to exceptionally powerful solar flares? This was the question that concerned members of the NAS in May 2008. Funded by NASA, their paper tells how "the workshop brought together representatives of industry, the government, and academia to consider both direct and collateral effects of severe space weather events and contemporary society's vulnerability to space weather."[1]

They found that global civilization is at a higher risk for solar storms than at any other time in its history because modern society runs on electricity. A billion-ton plasma fireball striking our planet's atmosphere would violently distort its magnetic field, thereby injecting tremendous surges of current into the entire electrical power grids of the Northern Hemisphere. As Michael Brooks explains in *New Scientist* magazine, "The greatest danger is at the step-up and step-down transformers used to convert power from its transport voltage to domestically useful voltage. The increased DC current creates strong magnetic fields that saturate a transformer's magnetic core. The result is runaway current in the transformer's copper wiring, which rapidly heats up and melts."[2]

Incapable of absorbing such a sudden and colossal burst of electricity, the entire power grid overloads and fries. The transformers are shorted because all of them are strung together like extension cords plugged one into the other: Californians receive their electricity from Oregon, Floridians get theirs from Pennsylvania, and so forth.

Former Central Intelligence Agency (CIA) director James Woolsey states that knocking out just twenty of the two thousand to three thousand transformers in the United States would shut down electricity to large areas of the nation "for a long time."[3] He points out that getting them back online would take years, because transformers are no longer made in the United States. Until early this century they were built entirely in northern Europe, but their manufacture has been increasingly entrusted to cheaper, less quality-driven private companies in South Korea. Each transformer averages one-and-a-half years to complete, and transporting the exceptionally heavy equipment to North America and setting it up require additional months. Should a dozen or so transformers go down, repairing them with alacrity is not possible because, according to Woolsey, they only have about 5 percent of the replacement parts.

NAS scientists stress that the effects of a solar-generated electromagnet pulse on our interconnected network are *not* theoretical, and they point to historical examples. In March 1989, an only slightly stronger than usual gust of solar wind generated an electromagnetic surge across Quebec, superheating and melting its power lines to plunge six million Canadians into darkness for nine hours at the cost of $2 billion in damages and business losses. Had the EMP instead struck New York or Washington, D.C., only several hundred miles south, damages would had tallied in the trillions.

Canada's late-twentieth-century incident was nothing compared to the Carrington Event of 130 years earlier, which struck just before noon on September 1, 1859. In a sun storm lasting eight days, "the entire Earth was engulfed in a gigantic cloud of seething gas, and a blood-red aurora erupted across the planet from the poles to the tropics," according to Stuart Clark, a British writer for the European Space Agency. "Around the world, telegraph systems crashed, machines burst into flames, and electric shocks rendered operators unconscious. Compasses and other sensitive instruments reeled as if struck by a massive magnetic fist."[4]

For the first time in recorded history, people throughout the Caribbean were treated to spectacular displays of the aurora borealis. Its glow was so brilliant across the Rocky Mountains that gold miners, assuming that morning had already come, awoke to prepare breakfast. This remarkable phenomenon was named after English amateur astronomer Richard Christopher Carrington (1826–1875), who discovered that a solar disruption caused these events. Its effects were relatively harmless, owing to electricity's low level of application in the mid-nineteenth century, but if a super sun storm of equivalent magnitude were to occur today, its impact would be far more serious.

"In 1859, the technology was quite low in comparison to today's technology," says Bruce Tsurutani of NASA's Jet Propulsion Laboratory.[5] The telegraph had been invented just fifteen years before. "However," Tsurutani continues, "the technology that we rely on today is much more vulnerable."[6] According to the NAS paper, "Electric power is modern society's cornerstone technology on which virtually all other infrastructures and services depend."[7] It goes on to report that within ninety seconds after three hundred key transformers overload and melt down, a cascade effect will surge through the grid network to which they are all connected, cutting power to 130 million Americans. Europe, Russia, China, and Japan would be likewise affected.[8]

John Kappenmann, a power industry analyst with California's Metatech Corporation, says that water distribution will be affected "within several hours; perishable foods and medications lost in twelve to twenty-four hours; loss of heating/air conditioning, sewage disposal, phone service, fuel re-supply and so on."[9]

Quite literally, the whole infrastructure of the United States and the rest of the industrialized world depends entirely on electricity. If power is cut off, everything from national defense to sewer sanitation stops. Agriculture is especially vulnerable, and not only because the country's food supply cannot operate without water or transportation. Today, Americans depend on a mere 2 percent of the U.S. population who are farmers for their food, compared to around 90 percent little more than one hundred years ago. In a potential crisis of the magnitude posed by a Carrington Event, local self-sufficiency in at least feeding themselves would not exist.

While lights go out around the Northern Hemisphere, water taps will run dry for anyone residing in high-rise apartment buildings, because electrically powered pumps will cease to function. People living at ground level can count on enough water left in the pipes for another twelve hours, but nothing thereafter. Subways and every form of electrically powered public transportation will cease to operate. With no electricity for fuel pumps, private cars and delivery trucks will be limited by how much gas they happen to still have in their tanks. Should an EMP on the scale of 1859's burst occur, fuel availability will not be an issue, because all automotive and computer electrical systems will be shorted out.

All Internet systems will go down, and many computers unfortunate enough to be operating at the moment the sun storm hits our magnetosphere will fry. Every bank and most businesses—certainly the larger corporations—will stop operating, together with the elevators in their office buildings. We will not be able to access automated teller machines (ATMs), which rely on orbiting relay stations. The economic foundations of the United States—already badly cracked by a chronic recession and the collapse of its financial institutions—will totter to a fall.

Aircraft in flight at the time will be especially vulnerable, because they navigate largely by avionics. Many will simply lose all power and crash. Only the lucky ones will be able to force land at the earliest opportunity. Televisions and radios will fall dark and silent; our telecommunications satellites will be knocked out by the solar storm. Backup generators will be able to keep vital services going only until the fuel to run them expires. Hospitals strictly limiting themselves to essential care would be able to function for seventy-two hours, according to the NAS report, but not thereafter. Pharmaceuticals would be among the first industries to collapse as perishable medications succumb to production, storage, and distribution shutdowns, dooming many individuals—especially the elderly and diabetics—who depend on drugs to keep them alive. Kappenmann points out, "In the U.S. alone, there are a million people with diabetes," and all will die without insulin.[10] Even wider health hazards will arise when the nation's sewer treatment facilities are terminated.

After supermarkets have been emptied, food will become increasingly scarce because the trucks that supply them will be out of gas. Any food that happens to be on hand in our refrigerators will spoil within the first week.

Save for those who have adequate working fireplaces and large stores of wood to see them through the winter, Americans will not be able to heat their homes because most natural gas and fuel pipelines need electricity to function. Nuclear power stations will not be dependable because they are programmed to shut down when the grid is overloaded, and they cannot be restarted until it is operating again.

With all hydrants inoperable, conflagrations everywhere will rage out of control, reducing fire fighters to little more than monitors. Even more disturbing—especially for urban residents—will be the drastically reduced capabilities of law enforcement agencies. Hampered by a massive communications shutdown and rapidly dwindling fuel reserves, police officers will find their normally onerous duties virtually impossible to fulfill. America's rising crime rate will skyrocket, as street criminals take advantage of the situation, just as they did in New Orleans during Hurricane Katrina. That natural disaster caused damages of $125 billion.

"If a Carrington Event happened now," concludes Paul Kintner, a plasma scientist at New York's Cornell University, "it would be like a hurricane Katrina, but 10 times worse."[11] NAS geophysicists argue that a severe geomagnetic storm could result in $2 trillion worth of damages. Further, given the federal authorities' infamously incompetent response to the crisis in New Orleans after the hurricane struck in 2005, the scope of chaos to ensue would be beyond our present comprehension. "A contemporary repetition of the Carrington Event would cause . . . extensive social and economic disruptions," the NAS report warns.[12]

According to the Uniform Crime Reports of the Federal Bureau of Investigation for January 2009, no less that one hundred thousand "known" gang members infest the United States. The real number is estimated to be higher by approximately twenty thousand armed criminals. The reports go on to point out that, given consistent trends since the early 1990s, these figures could double by midcentury.[13] In comparison, the mighty German Sixth Army that surrendered at the Battle of Stalingrad in 1943 numbered ninety thousand men. America's more than one hundred thousand gang members can be counted upon to avail themselves of the social disruption caused by a major solar event. How a largely unarmed, unprotected populace would cope with such a threat suggests a potential for social implosion in a kind of civil war that, by comparison, would make the mid-nineteenth-century Civil War seem like a calm affair.

Clearly, replacement transformers would be most urgently needed before conditions reached that stage. The NAS paper puts recovery time at four to ten *years*. The chaos that would reign during such a period could preclude all attempts at reconstruction. Brooks tells *New Scientist* magazine, "It is questionable whether the U.S. would ever bounce back."[14]

To be sure, recovery would not only be a matter of building and setting up new transformers but also of trying to do so in the midst of extreme economic and social chaos. Just the demographic nightmare of many millions of people escaping on foot from colder regions of the north for warmer southern climes would radically reconfigure the continental United States, imperiling its political existence. The collision of mass migrations with settled populations already stressed by disintegrating conditions might lead to the kind of violence that topples civilization.

These postulated results for another Carrington Event are not alarmist fantasy. "I don't think the NAS report is scare-mongering," says Mike Hapgood, chair of the European Space Agency's weather team.[15] "Scientists are conservative by nature, and this group is really thoughtful," states James Green, head of NASA's planetary division, adding, "This is a fair and balanced report."[16] "We're moving closer and closer to the edge of a possible disaster," according to Daniel Baker, the University of Colorado's space weather expert at Boulder and chair of the NAS committee that issued the controversial paper.[17] "It could conceivably be the worst natural disaster possible," Kappenmann adds.[18] "If it happens anytime soon," observes science writer Robert Roy Britt, "we won't know exactly what to expect until it's over, and by then some modern communication systems could be like beachfront houses after a hurricane."[19]

Since the late twentieth century, directors at NASA have wanted to replace the inadequate and aging sun-monitoring satellites that form our planet's only advance warning system for solar storms. Their proposal won approval during the George W. Bush administration but was put on hold after Barack Obama entered the White House. In 2009, prospects for actually materializing the new observatory seemed uncertain, especially when the United States suffered its disastrous economic downturn that removed such endeavors from further consideration.

The potential for cataclysmic damage inflicted on modern society by a super solar storm was taken so seriously by NASA that it budgeted $850 million to launch a sophisticated probe of our sun on February 11,

2010. The Solar Dynamic Observatory (SDO) was blasted into space by an *Atlas V* rocket and took up station in a geosynchronous orbit that allows for constant contact with a pair of radio dishes in New Mexico. These receive 1.5 terabytes of data about the sun every day from a trio of SDO instruments, equivalent to about 380 full-length feature films shot aboard the probe and transmitted every second.

Most important, this information contains the direction and velocity of solar winds and is able to warn of any highly charged particles heading our way. The window of opportunity that it offers power companies, however, seems impractically narrow. That an alert sounded by a satellite from outer space could filter down to Earth through the electric companies' chain of command in time to disengage the nation's transformers before a plasma bombardment strikes our magnetosphere seems too much to ask. A coronal mass ejected from the solar photosphere normally requires three or four days to reach Earth, allowing at least some time to sound a warning. But 1859's Carrington Event took just seventeen hours and forty minutes to cover the ninety-three million miles from the sun. "It arrived faster than anything we can do," says Hapgood, an expert on global geography and astronomy.[20]

Yet even if the SDO does sound an advance alarm, there is no one on Earth to really do much about it. The U.S. Department of Energy would be nominally in charge of acting on any such warning but has a small staff with little time or resources for anything more than gathering statistics for local research. The larger Federal Energy Regulatory Commission has only limited authority for dealing mostly with potential, so far entirely theoretical, terrorist threats against transformers but is more concentrated on cost considerations. The North American Electrical Liability Corporation is a private concern hired by the federal government for general security issues pertaining to the country's electrical network, among numerous other infrastructures. These three entities, far from pooling their information, do not even communicate with each other and would, in a solar storm crisis, undoubtedly work at cross purposes.

"Nobody is really in charge of security for the grid," declared

Woolsey in late July 2013, "and no intelligence group with a staff that is planning how to deal with these threats, as they come up, is in place. There is actually no structure to the electrical grid's management. Consequently, as variabilities come about . . . we are not in a position to respond at all, much less promptly."[21]

Given the U.S. government's appalling track record when attempting to cope with far lesser natural catastrophes, such as Hurricane Katrina or, more recently, Hurricane Sandy, federal authorities and their bungling bureaucrats can hardly be depended on to act with well-oiled efficiency. Nor can the governments of Canada, Mexico, and Europe be expected to act with alacrity. The very nature of democratic systems, for all their "globalization," prevents them from applying the kind of immediate, unilateral response required to disengage all electrical power networks before the super solar storm arrives. Russia and China, in addition to Third World countries such as India, will, of course, be left in the dark, quite literally, by these events. Even if the United States responds in time and properly, other nations of the Northern Hemisphere would not. The collapse of their electronically based infrastructure would precipitate a worldwide calamity no one would escape, given the current fragility and interdependency of our world economy.

While politicians are unable to make proper use of the scientific genius that went into America's SDO, the probe's true Achilles' heel is its geosynchronous orbit. Twice each year, for three weeks near the equinox, the satellite moves into a position in which views of the sun are blocked by our planet for a period of time each day. If a super solar storm were to erupt toward Earth during those biannual moments, it would overtake us with complete surprise. Moreover, an incoming solar flare on the order of the Carrington Event might saturate and roast all sensors carried by SDO before it had an opportunity to fire off a single signal. For all the probe's state-of-the-art technology, either it or the political chain of command required to make it function utterly failed during mid-July 2013's near miss—as described in the introduction to this book—with an electromagnetic pulse from the sun of similar magnitude to its immense 1859 predecessor.

How likely is another Carrington Event to occur? According to *Scientific American,* "ice cores suggest that such a blast of solar particles happens only once every five hundred years."[22] Other astrophysicists conclude that these incidents are twice as rare. That should give us about another 350 to 800 years to make suitable preparations. But geophysicists point out that ice-core dating reveals no discernible pattern of a five-hundred- or one-thousand-year cycle for super solar storms, which are, in any case, generated perhaps by the sun's imperfectly understood gravitational mechanisms. In fact, the early-twenty-first-century repetition demonstrates that scientists had miscalculated. The mid-nineteenth-century Carrington Event and its 2013 near miss were separated by a mere 154 years. Tsurutani believes Earth's next super solar storm "could very well be even more intense than what transpired in 1859. As for when, we simply do not know."[23]

Sunspots vent the sun's internal stress, and clusters of them result in relatively weak, harmless storms as they disperse thermodynamic pressures. Their occasional disappearance altogether means that these pressures are not being relieved. Instead, sunspots accumulate stored energy that must eventually burst to the surface in a single plasma event. The longer sunspots are absent, the more powerful a resulting coronal mass ejection.

Beginning in 2009, observers were surprised to find no blemish on the face of our star. Its clear complexion persisted into March 2012, when the largest tornado ever seen began to dance across the sun. This solar prominence was, in the words of *National Geographic* magazine, "big enough to swallow a hundred Earths."[24] According to Xing Li, an astronomer at Aberystwyth University in Wales, the solar tornado was 124,000 miles tall. "The structure is huge," he explains, "and the velocity of the material is several tens to hundreds of thousands of kilometers per hour. . . . A sun tornado starts when a huge injection of plasma—charged, superheated gas—happens to shoot up one of the structure's legs. The plasma is guided along the heliacal shape of the structure's magnetic field, giving rise to a coherent rotation of material."[25]

The monster solar tornado of 2012 suggests a particularly violent phase the sun has entered, with potential for solar flares on a similarly unprecedented magnitude. As such, possibilities are optimum for another Carrington Event during the current eleven-year solar cycle. While a replay of the nineteenth century's geomagnetic hurricane is uncertain, more probable is the occurrence of a squall not as powerful as the Carrington Event but stronger than the solar wind that blacked out Quebec in 1989. These lesser incidents of space weather take place roughly every fifty years, give or take a decade or more.

On May 15, 1921, a glob of coronal plasma ten times more potent than its Canadian successor lit up Earth's magnetosphere. As *The New York Times* reported, "at 7:04 a.m., the entire signal and switching system of the New York Central Railroad below 125th Street was put out of operation, followed by a fire in the control tower at 57th Street and Park Avenue. Telegraph operator Hatch said that he was actually driven away from his telegraph instrument by a flame that enveloped his switchboard and ignited the entire building at a loss of $6,000. Over seas, in Sweden, a telephone station was 'burned out,' and the storm interfered with telephone, telegraph and cable traffic over most of Europe."[26]

These disruptions were relatively innocuous because industrialized society was far less dependent on electricity than it is now, and Earth's position relative to the incoming angle of the sun storm favored escape from most of its worst effects. Now that virtually every aspect of civilization runs on electricity, a repetition of 1921's geomagnetic gale colliding with our atmosphere at a more dangerous angle of attack would affect the modern world almost as severely as a Carrington Event, if only because of the grid's national and even international connectedness.

Nowhere throughout the 132 pages of the National Academy of Sciences' report will readers find so much as an allusion to the end of the Mayan calendar. Nor is it mentioned among any of the statements made by so many scientists in their serious discussions of the super sun storms that threaten to overturn human life. These scientists nonetheless concur that the next most favorable opportunity for a potentially disastrous encounter with the solar wind will arise when sunspot activity increases and proliferates throughout the second decade of our century. That scientific projections for a global calamity caused by the sun should coincide with ancient predictions of solar demons ravaging the world must at least give us pause.

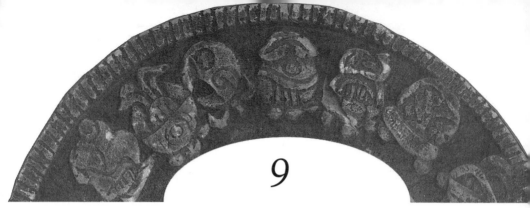

# 9

# Monsters from beneath the Sea

During July 2010, while British Petroleum executives were congratulating themselves on their containment of the previous April's catastrophic Deepwater Horizon oil spill off the coast of Louisiana, oceanographers were far from elated. They pointed out that the seabed in the general vicinity of the capped wellhead had risen as much as thirty feet since the disaster and continued to split with a growing number of lengthening fissures from which toxic gases were venting into the Gulf of Mexico. According to Terrance Aym, a science reporter for the Helium Internet site, "Methane levels in the water are now calculated as being almost one million times higher than normal."[1]

These conditions are particularly worrisome, because they match prerequisites for the eruption of a deadly megabubble as first described by an American paleobiologist in 1993. It was then that Douglas Erwin discovered that immense reservoirs of natural gas trapped mostly beneath the ocean floor were abruptly freed 251 million years ago to kill 96 percent of all land animals, marine creatures, and plant life on Earth. Physical science scholars have long known that this greatest of all extinction events closed the Permian Period but were unable to determine its cause.[2] Even a large meteorite or comet impact would not have resulted in such a thorough, almost universal extermination of all living matter at so many levels, extending even down into the sea. In comparison, the asteroid collision that wiped out the dinosaurs 65 million years ago destroyed about 58 percent of all life here.

Close examination of boundary rocks in Austria and Italy separating the Permian Period from the later Triassic Period revealed no trace of certain isotopes—iridium, platinum, ruthenium, rhodium, palladium, or osmium—associated with celestial impacts. Science reporters for the respected journal *Geology* concluded that physical evidence for a major meteor strike 251 million years ago could not be found.[3]

The first material evidence supporting Erwin's hypothesis was discovered a few months after he proposed it. On the other side of the world, geologist Richard Morante found traces of a massive release of carbon isotopes (chemical fingerprints left by a cataclysmic methane bubble) in ocean basins on margins along the periphery of the Australian continent.[4] The carbon isotopes were contemporaneous with the Permian Period die-off. Since the publication of Morante findings twenty-one years ago, Erwin's megabubble explanation for our planet's premiere extinction event has won growing recognition from other scientists. Among those most favorably impressed is Gregory Ryskin, a biochemical engineer at Northwestern University. His parallel research shows that at least one other mass death was caused by a catastrophic methane release. It took place during the Late Paleocene Thermal Maximum 55.8 million years ago, when one-third to one-half of all life on our planet was suddenly snuffed out.[5] Ryskin's investigation prompted his colleagues to wonder if similar megabubbles were responsible for other extinction events in Earth's checkered past.

A paleontologist at the University of California–Davis has done more than most to demonstrate how such a powerfully destructive phenomenon works and explore its special relevance to our time. Dan Dorritie discovered a new species of *Archaeocyatha,* a type of sponge that died out about 725 million years ago, now known to science as the *Polythalamia.* While researching possible mechanisms to explain the creature's disappearance, Dorritie learned about inconceivably immense stores of natural gas lying beneath the bottom of the ocean. Much of

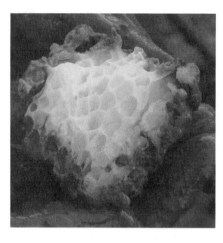

*Figure 9.1. A gas hydrate block embedded in sediment on the sea floor 3,800 feet beneath the surface of the Pacific Ocean off the coast of Oregon. Photograph by Wusel 007.*

this gas is in the form of methane bubbles prevented from rising to the surface by cages of ice known as methane clathrates, or gas hydrates.

As Erwin first suspected and other investigators have since determined, these hydrates were melted 251 million years ago by a range of volcanoes, the Siberian Traps, that erupted to heat the permafrost cover and set submarine landslides in motion around continental ridges. An estimated ten billion metric tons of methane—some ten times the amount of carbon dioxide in our atmosphere—were released. As a gas, methane rapidly oxidizes to disperse in open air. But when combined with water droplets, it moves across the face of Earth in low-lying clouds waiting to explode with a single lightning strike or encounter with a volcano, such as those of the Siberian Traps. Such an incandescent occurrence abruptly terminated most terrestrial life at the close of the Permian Period as well as 196 years later, in the Late Paleocene Thermal Maximum. No less lethal was the simultaneous poisoning of ocean waters down to their biological depths with methane and other toxic gases, including hydrogen sulfate, which is used today in state executions.

The megabubbles of methane released by melting hydrates were twenty miles across. When they burst, they produced high-pressure atmospheric waves devastating every living thing in all directions, followed by a tsunami towering three hundred feet tall to complete the initial phase of annihilation. Aym adds that "such occurrences can lead to the rupture of the methane bubble containment—it can then permit the methane to breach the subterranean depths and undergo an explosive decomposition as it catapults into the Gulf waters."[6]

Dorritie argues in his online book about methane-induced disasters that the modern world is in the process of initiating another mass extinction by overheating the planet.[7] For readers still unsure about scientific consensus concerning global warming, he lists several fundamental conclusions a majority of the world's twenty-five hundred professional climatologists have agreed upon as correct; namely, that temperatures are indeed climbing worldwide and will continue to rise, mostly because they are driven by the industrial burning of fossil fuels—oil, natural gas, and coal—to accommodate urban population expansion. This observation, the climatologists say, is underscored by nine of the ten warmest years recorded since systematic meteorological documentation was initiated by the United States Weather Bureau just before the start of the Civil War. Since 1880, when world temperatures were first annually documented, the years 1995, 1997, 1998, 2005, and 2010 were the hottest years on record. For two weeks, beginning on October 16, 2005, the most intense tropical cyclone ever documented in the Atlantic Ocean generated winds at speeds of 185 miles per hour. Hurricane Wilma killed more than sixty people and caused nearly thirty billion dollars in damage across Hispaniola, Jamaica, Cuba, the Cayman Islands, Nicaragua, Honduras, Belize, Cozumel, the Yucatán Peninsula, the Bahamas, Florida, Atlantic Canada, and Europe. September of 2014 averaged 60.3 degrees Fahrenheit, the hottest recorded late summer/early autumn, announced spokesmen for the National Oceanic and Atmospheric Administration. That same conclusion was separately determined by the National Aeronautics and Space Administration. Moreover, the first nine months of 2014 averaged a global temperature of 58.72 degrees, tying with 1998 for the hottest first nine months on record, according to NOAA's National Climatic Data Center in Asheville, North Carolina.

Climatologists also believe that global warming will exert increasing pressure on civilization in terms of freshwater scarcity and depleted agricultural productivity in the face of higher numbers of humans, with a subsequent negative effect on international economic life, to say nothing of an increasingly impaired natural environment and imperiled wildlife. Scientific consensus also holds that modern industry is putting greenhouse gas carbon dioxide into Earth's atmosphere at a much higher rate than has ever taken place in the whole history of the planet. As the oceans heat up, deep-sea hydrates will melt, freeing the megabubbles to rise to the surface, where they will burst 10,000 billion tons of methane. Given their projected rate of global warming and consequent climb in ocean temperatures, Dorritie and his colleagues conclude such a cataclysm must inevitably occur.

"Our own releases of carbon dioxide from the burning of fossil fuels well exceed, on average, those of the Siberian Traps," Dorritie writes. "What happened at the end of the Permian is long, long ago, but not far, far away. The catastrophic release of methane from the sea floor is not just something which was long ago. It could, unless we change our way of dealing with our planet, and change it fast, happen again tomorrow."[8]

He mentions that West Siberian peat bog—site of the volcanic eruptions that triggered the Permian extinction event—is already experiencing the melting of its permafrost, which caps one-quarter of our planet's methane hydrates. No less alarming, hydrates in the Bering Sea and Alaska's northern coastal region are likewise leaking methane. At mid-depths, southern ocean temperatures have increased 0.3 degrees Fahrenheit, while three miles beneath the surface of the North Pacific—at depths previously deemed too cold to be affected—seawater temperatures have risen 0.009 degrees Fahrenheit.

While these increases seem insignificant, they are spread uniformly over many thousands of square miles and, more impressively, increased in only fourteen years' time, between 1985 and 1999. The particularly cold depths of the North Atlantic were also considered impervious to heating increases of any kind, no matter how slight, until studies in 2000 revealed that levels as deep as nine thousand feet underwent a temperature surge of 0.06 degrees Fahrenheit.[9] In fact, industrial global warming has infused the world's oceans with enough energy to power California for the next two hundred thousand years!

Nor will this accumulation of hot energy rapidly dissipate. Water stores higher temperatures with great efficiency. As global warming continues to raise Earth temperatures, the oceans will necessarily heat up, until the hydrates that keep megabubbles of methane in check will melt, with consequences geologically documented in the Permian-Triassic boundary and at the close of the Late Paleocene Thermal Maximum. In 2008, David Archer, Bruce Buffett, and Victor Brovkin, geophysicists at the University of Chicago, determined that about 85 percent of the world's 3,000 billion metric tons of hydrate, accompanied by another 2,000 billion metric tons of methane bubbles, will be released when the ocean bottom warms by 5.4 degrees Fahrenheit. Even accelerated global warming would need at least another one hundred years or more to set this monster free.[10]

But the largest marine oil spill in the history of the petroleum industry may have pumped so much hot crude into the Gulf of Mexico that Archer and Buffet's critical 5.4 degree Fahrenheit trigger could be

*Figure 9.2. The last day of British Petroleum's Deepwater Horizon. Photo courtesy of U.S. Coast Guard.*

pulled much sooner than a one-hundred-year period based on previous projections.

Dorritie's manuscript, "Killer in Our Midst," was completed before BP's disastrous oil spill of 2010, which has accelerated his timetables, because, as Aym points out, the self-destructive Deepwater Horizon operation dumped 250 million gallons of oil as hot as 500 degrees Fahrenheit into the sea. Such a sudden, far-flung temperature spike threatens the hydrate ice cages with melting. Given the magnitude of the hot crude poured into the Gulf, geologists estimate a methane megabubble could be released at virtually any time. Given this unfortunate fact, the BP accident triggering a Permian Period–like extinction event thoroughly fulfills Mayan calendar prophecies for the future.

# *10*
# East-West Parallelisms

The sacred number five of Atlantis and the deluge that overwhelmed this Bronze Age civilization are crucial components of the Aztec Calendar Stone, but they are not the only outside influences apparently at work on the monumental almanac. Depicted at the Calendar Stone's center is the ferocious expression of the sun god Tonatiuh, which is the mirror image of the Lion pose, a facial exercise practiced by the followers of hatha yoga.

Derived from the Sanskrit *yuj* for "union" or "yoking," yoga is an ancient spiritual discipline of physical and mental procedures still used to focus on purification of the physical body as a prerequisite for purifying the mind. Goals range from improving bodily and emotional health to achieving liberation from all worldly suffering, particularly from the cause of all misery: the cycle of birth and death.

The yogic Lion pose calls for extending the tongue to its limits, tensing all facial muscles, widening the eyes, and stretching the fingers to resemble a lion's claws. This posture is identically displayed by the sun god on the Aztec Calendar Stone, including his talons. The hatha yoga exercise brings about the release of tension, an ending or completion, just as 4-Ollin marks the end of a tension-filled epoch, the Fifth Sun. The yogic Lion and Tonatiuh's face are, in fact, physically and symbolically indistinguishable from each other.

Although the oldest surviving references to yoga are found in the

Brāhmaṇas (commentaries on the proper performance of rituals), written circa 900 BCE, cylinder seals from the first Indus Valley civilization at Harappa depict figures in yoga postures going back nearly two thousand years earlier. Yoga was and still is the dominant spiritual discipline of Asia, particularly identified with ancient India generally and Buddhism specifically.

The appearance of hatha yoga's Lion face at the center of the Aztec Calendar Stone is not the Eagle Bowl's only curious connection with ancient India, however. According to Kenneth Caroli, the 5,150-year cycles of the Maya "certainly fit the traditional Hindu dates for Krishna and the juncture of Davpara with the Kali Yuga. If one accepts 2012 as the juncture of these two 'great years,' as it seems to be with respect to the winter solstice galactic alignment, the current 'great season' began around 10,959 BCE, very close to the sudden onset of the Younger Dryas stadial, the final cold phase of the last Ice Age."[1]

In Hinduism, the Kali Yuga signifies the end of the universe, the last of four *yugas*, or ages, just as the Maya knew four "suns," as showcased in their respective squares around Tonatiuh, the central figures of the Aztec Calendar Stone. The quartet of "suns" or epochs preceded a fifth or last period, the Fifth Sun. Both the Mayan and Hindu sets are "world ages" subject to cycles of creation, destruction, and renewal. The Aztec Calendar Stone's 4-Ocelotl, 4-Ehécatl, 4-Quihuitl, and 4-Atl parallel the Hindu Satya Yuga, Treta Yuga, Dwapara Yuga, and Kali Yuga. Beginning in 3112 BCE, the start of the Kali Yuga is a mere two years later than the start of the Mayan Fifth Sun in 3114 BCE. The Maya believed the demise of the Fifth Sun would be brought about by Macuilli-Tonatiuh, or the Clenched Fist of Tonatiuh, the god of destruction, portrayed on the Aztec Calendar Stone as the enraged face of a man with his tongue extended in the yogic Lion grimace.

So too, the Hindu Kalki Purana (a prophetic narrative) describes Kali, the demon of universal annihilation (not to be confused with the goddess Kali), who terminates the Kali Yuga in global upheaval, with a large lolling tongue. The violent end of both the Mesoamerican Fifth World, or Fifth Sun, and the Hindu Kali Yuga are presided over by the same god of destruction. As Caroli observes, "Clearly, the Maya thought in similar terms to the Hindus and early Buddhists, at least insofar as their scale went."[2]

Kali was the tenth avatar, or incarnation, of the beneficent deity Vishnu, which is similar to the Aztec Calendar Stone's Tezcatlipoca being the malevolent twin of Quetzalcoatl. In his guise as Kali, Vishnu declares in the Bhagavad Gita, "Whenever there is a withering of the law and an uprising of lawlessness on all sides, then I manifest myself. For the salvation of the righteous and the destruction of such as do evil, for the firm establishing of the Law, I come to birth, age after age."[3]

Recalculations arrived at by some modern Hindu scholars have shown that the vast spans of time separating the four yugas (1,728,000 years; 1,296,000 years; 864,000 years; and 432,000 years) are not to be taken literally. Instead, these otherwise unmanageable parameters, if understood in symbolic terms, indicate the present Kali Yuga will be catastrophically brought to a close soon after 2012.

The Hopi Indians of the American Southwest likewise tell of four "worlds," or ages, all ending in natural disasters instigated by the unbalanced behavior of humankind. They predict a Day of Purification, when "Saquasohuh Kachina dances in the plaza and removes his mask," according to Hopi Nation elder Dan Evehema.[4] In other words, modern civilization will be shattered as "the Blue Star appears in the sky."[5] In the Hopi language, *qatsina,* or literally, "life bringer," refers to anything in the natural world or cosmos, including natural phenomena, whether good or evil. "We are in the final stages now," said Chief Evehema, "so our prophecy says."[6]

Saquasohuh Kachina cannot be positively identified with any particular "Blue Star," although Sirius, the Dog Star, is sometimes suggested for its blue white color shift. If so, its relationship to the controversial winter solstice of 2012 seems unclear. At 8.6 light-years from Earth, we should not anticipate the appearance of Sirius in our skies anytime soon. The Hopi Blue Star is more likely a large meteor or asteroid that could approach the orbit of our planet.

In any case, their Saquasohuh Kachina prophecy was supposedly an ancient oral tradition shared with Presbyterian minister David Young by White Feather, a terminally ill elder of the Bear Clan, during the summer of 1958 and published five years later by the historical writer Frank Waters in *Book of the Hopi*. Dr. Allen C. Ross, a Santee Dakota educator and Lakota language scholar, relates that the same prophecy was uttered during the most important Hopi ceremony, the Wuwuchim, at least as long ago as early 1914. It may, in fact, predate even this early-twentieth-century instance by many years, perhaps generations.[7] It forecast in part:

> You will hear of a dwelling-place in the heavens, above the Earth, that shall fall with a great crash. It will appear as a blue star. Very soon after this, the ceremonies of my people will cease. These are the signs that great destruction is coming. The world shall rock to and fro. There will be many columns of smoke and fire such as White Feather has seen the white man make in the deserts not far from here. You will hear of the sea turning black, and many living things dying because of it. Turtle Island could turn over two or three times, and the oceans could join hands and meet the sky.[8]

Unlike the Maya, the Hopis are less definite regarding the arrival of these Earth-changing events, although at least some tribal elders have occasionally implied that an undisclosed section of the Wuwuchim ceremony did indeed correlate 2012's winter solstice—allegorically, it would appear—with the Blue Star. They are more willing to describe the last catastrophe that brought our present world into existence by destroying a former one. This former world, our ancestral homeland, was a large island in the Sunrise Sea, which one day rose up over the people, drowning most of them. Some were saved by the flood hero Kuskurza, who directed them to the back of a giant turtle. It carried them westward across the ocean, eventually coming to rest on the shores of a new land, which the survivors named after their means of rescue: Turtle Island.

Joining Kuskurza and his followers was a pair of antediluvian holy women, the Huruing Wuhti, today venerated as mother goddesses because they greatly increased the number of survivors. The Hopi version of the deluge states in part, "Down on the bottom of the seas lie all the proud virtue, and the flying *patuwvota*s [flying shields], and the worldly treasures corrupted with evil, and those people who found no time to sing praises to the Creator from the tops of their hills."[9]

The ancient Scandinavians were no less indefinite than the Hopi Indians regarding the exact moment when we might expect the next global cataclysm. But the Norse were not unlike Native American or Hindu cosmologists in their belief that the world had been destroyed several times over and would be again. Ragnarök, literally the Breaking of the Gods, was also referred to as *aldar rof,* the "destruction of the world," and in Germany as the Götterdämmerung, or Twilight of the Gods. In every case it was not a unique event but a global catastrophe that has occurred throughout the past and will continue to do so in the future. With each repetition the world is virtually destroyed, but a handful of survivors—sometimes no more than a single man and woman—escape to renew the cycle of life.

Ragnarök appears in the "Gylfaginning," or "Tricking of Gylfi," the first part of the *Prose Edda,* a collection of Norse myths, by the early-thirteenth-century Icelandic historian Snorri Sturluson. He describes the coming of a cosmic wolf, Fenrir, its eyes and nostrils spouting flames, reminiscent of the Aztec Tonatiuh. Fenrir's gaping mouth is so huge that it swallows first the sun, then the moon. Accompanied by a celestial snake, the wolf plunges out of heaven to attack Earth. The sky splits in two, allowing the sons of Muspell—the region of flames—to fall on the world. They set it on fire, led by their chief, Surtr, who wields an immense sword brighter than the sun.

"Already the stars were coming adrift from the sky and falling into the gaping void. They were like swallows, weary from too long a voyage, who drop and sink into the waves," relates "The Tale of the Mountain Dweller," a thirteenth-century Norse poem. The seas rise up, deluging the land. "Mountains will tumble, the Earth will move, men will be scoured by hot water and burned by fire," the tale continues. "What will remain after heaven and Earth and the whole world are burned?" Gylfi asks at the beginning of chapter 52. "All the gods will be dead, together with the *Einherjar* [mortal heroes], and the whole of mankind."[10]

Sturluson depicts the popular storm god, Thor, as a protector of Earth, furiously defending it from the cosmic serpent. He kills the monster but is himself slain in combat. Their last hope gone with Thor's death, people everywhere despair as they behold a gigantic dragon flying across the sky with millions of corpses in its mouth. Earth sinks into the sea; obscuring billows of steam rise, and flames shoot toward the heavens. The world has been destroyed, and virtually all life extinguished.

Ragnarök's astronomical character seems obvious, as does its Aztec-like fiery demise. The cosmic wolf, serpent in the sky, and flaming "sons of Muspell" are standard metaphors for destructive comets and meteor falls. Interestingly, both the Norse Ending of the Gods and Aztec 4-Ollin are global conflagrations caused by fire gods from above.

According to Norse legend, these calamitous events will be immediately preceded by Fimbulvetr, literally the Great Winter. The *Poetic Edda* poem "Voeluspá" reads, "Black become the sun's beams in the summers that follow, weathers all treacherous. A wind age, a wolf age—before the world goes headlong."[11] The first sign of Fimbulvetr will be three continuous winters without spring, summer, or autumn. In the resulting hardships, many wars of especially intense savagery will break out: "Brothers will kill brothers, sons their fathers."[12]

Some commentators conclude the concept of a Fimbulvetr occurred to the Norse because they inhabited areas of northern Europe that were undergoing dramatic climate change from warmer to colder conditions, starting around 1250 CE. This interpretation is challenged, however, by not only Norse, but Persian allusions to the Great Winter long before the Little Ice Age, a period of subnormal temperatures that beset the Western World for two hundred years, beginning around about 1350. With roots in eighth-century Iran, the *Bundahishn,* or "Primal Creation," associated with Zoroastrian cosmology, likewise forecasts three years of unrelieved wintery conditions just prior to the end of the world.

Fimbulvetr eerily presages the ice-age catastrophe associated with what is to come some time after 2012's winter solstice. While Norse cosmology did not set a precise future date for this Great Winter, its role in another version of the Ending of the Gods foreshadows climatologists' worst fears: "A long time ago, Creation was all ice. Then one day, the ice began to melt, and a mist rose to the sky. Out of the mist came Ymir, a frost-giant, from whom the Earth and the heavens were made after the gods slew him. That is how the world began. And that is how the world will end. Not by fire, but by ice. The seas will freeze, and the winters will never end."[13]

More specifically than Norse prognostication for a frigid Ragnarök, the ancient Chinese Book of Changes, like the Mayan calendar, indicates that the end of time would take place after the winter solstice of 2012. The I Ching is a system of symbols (*jīng*) believed to discern order or patterns from the apparent chaos of random occurrences as a means of determining the future. It is based on the constancy of change, the dynamic balance of opposites observed in nature, and the progressive evolution of events—one conditioning its successor—as part of an interrelating process. The I Ching text comprises oracular interpretations for sixty-four abstract line arrangements known as hexagrams. These are made up of six stacked horizontal lines forming sixty-four possible combinations. Traditionally, a hexagram was cast using yarrow stalks or coins.

Although the I Ching was preceded by the visionary experiences of Fú Xī in the early third millennium BCE, the sixty-four hexagrams upon which the system is based stem from another legendary emperor, Yǔ, whose reign began in 2194 BCE. This date illuminates our investigation because it indicates he ascended the throne just one year before the second global cataclysm, which occurred in 2193 BCE.

The virtually perfect coincidence of these two events suggests that the Chinese of Yǔ's time were recipients of an oracular tradition already developed elsewhere, from whence it was carried by refugee culture bearers expelled from their homeland, which was ravaged by natural catastrophe. The same familiar sequence of events was repeated on the other side of the world, when the natives of Yucatán received their prophetic almanac at the hands of flood survivors from the first worldwide disaster, which occurred 921 years before the second global cataclysm.

Despite apparent dissimilarity between China's I Ching and the Mayan time measurement, both were, in fact, calendars, as ethnobotanists and mathematicians Terence and Dennis McKenna found when they made a comparison of I Ching's hexagrams. They learned that the sixty-four six-line figures virtually matched the number of days in thirteen lunar months. In other words, one day multiplied by 64, multiplied by 6 equals the 384 days in thirteen lunar months.

Building upon this discovery, the brothers multiplied the 13 lunar months by 64 to arrive at 67 years, 104.25 days—the length of six minor sunspot cycles, each comprising 11.2 years. When multiplied by 64, the 67 years, 104.25 days, amounts to the +4,306 years that make up one pair of zodiacal ages. The +4,306 years multiplied by 6 equals 25,836 years, or a single precession of the equinoxes, one Baktun.

Indeed, this revelation of the Book of Changes as a solar-zodiacal almanac makes it seem far less traditionally Chinese than identifiably Mayan. Moreover, its essential reliance on six, one of the two Atlantean sacred numbers, connects the origins of the I Ching with the same sunken civilization from which Mesoamericans received *their* system for measuring time.

If, as the brothers found, the I Ching was a kind of celestial almanac, they presumed there must be an end date, like all premodern calendars. They set out to find it by composing a table of differences from one hexagram to the next. Over this table was superimposed a historical timescale indicating civilization's high and low points as peaks or troughs on a graph. Extraordinary periods of change in the past, referred to as "novelty," corresponded to differences among the hexagrams—so much so that the timescale lay upon them as a virtual template.

Tracing these parallels with all sixty-four hexagrams, the brothers observed that "novelty" attains its maximum potential for the first and only time when something unprecedented occurs. That singularity was indicated by their time-scale when overlaid on the I Ching, which terminated on December 22, 2012, the day after the controversial winter solstice. Applying this end date backward in time based on the thirteen lunar months, they discovered that 1.3 billion years from 2012 brought them back to the beginning of life on Earth.

Does their calculation mean that December 22, 2012, marked the beginning of the end of life on our planet? That date might signify "the dissolution of the cosmos in an actual cessation and unraveling of the natural laws, a literal apocalypse," according to the McKennas.[14] But they also theorized an alternate possibility, wherein 2012 could represent "the culmination of a human process, a process of tool-making, the dream of a union of spirit and matter"—in other words, the total transformation or replacement of our materialist civilization by something radically different.[15]

Dennis and Terence McKenna were not influenced by growing popular interest in the Mayan calendar's prophecy for 2012. Their work on the I Ching was completed by the early 1970s, at least fifteen years before they learned of the Mayan calendar's prediction, which was not generally well known, even to scholars, until the early 1990s. The publication of their findings in the original 1975 edition of *The Invisible Landscape* neither mentions nor references the Maya.

According to physicist Claude Swanson, the credibility of a prophecy increases when it is at least basically repeated by different sources unrelated to each other. As such, Chinese, Mesoamerican, Hopi, Hindu, Persian, and Norse prognostications share a generally similar conception that suggests the prophecy is at least fundamentally valid.

Resemblances particularly between the Mēxihcah 4-Ollin and Hindu Kali Yuga are so close in some important details that one appears to have been directly influenced by the other, despite India's location half a world away from Middle America. More probably, both the Olmec or Maya and their distant contemporaries of the subcontinent separately inherited the same calendrical tradition, as did the Chinese, from a common outside source—the long lost point of origin from which they and so many postdeluge peoples derived their cultural impetus: Atlantis.

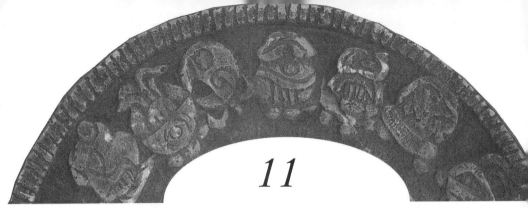

# 11

# The Incan Calendar

Although the Mayan calendar received attention for its focus on 2012, far less well known is the Incan calendar. While its Mesoamerican counterpart was far more complex, the two systems nonetheless share some fundamental similarities, suggesting both may have derived from a single contributor.*

Archaeologists believe little or no direct communication existed between the peoples of pre-Columbian Middle and South America, yet each calendar was divided into astrological and historical halves: the Mayan version for the prediction of coming developments; the Inca for the commemoration of past event horizons. Moreover, the Aztec Calendar Stone offers no chronologies for its various "ages."

Immediately after the Spanish Conquest, conquistadors and friars got to work dismembering the Inca Empire, plundering all its gold and purging its traditional belief system with monotheistic Christianity. Fortunately, at least the historical half of the Peruvian calendar was saved by a native convert to Catholicism, Felipe Guamán Poma de Ayala.

Born in Huamanga, in the central Andes Mountains, his father had been a provincial nobleman serving as emissary of the Inca Guascar to Francisco Pizarro when the conquering Spaniard was headquartering at Cajamarca. After receiving intense ecclesiastical indoctrination from

---

*This chapter first appeared as "The Remarkable Inca Calendar" in *Atlantis Rising* 12, no. 72 (November–December 2008). Republished here with permission.

local priests, de Ayala enthusiastically demonstrated his religious fervor by combating any perceived form of "idolatry." To assist him in doing God's work, he collected everything the natives told him about pre-Christian spirituality, all the better to extirpate it.

Between 1583 and 1613, de Ayala amassed an enormous collection of myths, folklore, and religious ideas in a twelve-hundred-page manuscript titled "Nueva corónica y buen gobierno," or "New Chronicle and Good Government." His chief intention was not to preserve the Indians' cultural legacy but to familiarize himself with it in his campaign against their faith. In so doing, however, de Ayala saved a great deal of the Inca's oral tradition, including their calendar, from otherwise certain oblivion.

Remarkably, the calendar not only reflects current Andean archaeology but also coincides with a global catastrophe that may have destroyed the motherland of civilization and dispersed its survivors throughout the world. The historical calendar comprises five ages, or "Suns," each roughly separated by one thousand years. The first belonged to the Wari Wiracocha Runa. Their name signifies "cross-breed"—referencing the camellid, offspring of a llama with an alpaca—because the Wari Wiracocha Runa were themselves the result of unions between native South Americans and the Viracochas. These were the followers of Sea Foam, the creator who traveled from his kingdom in the far west across the Pacific Ocean and made landfall in coastal Peru during the ancient past. Because the Viracochas were remembered as bearded, red-haired, fair-complected "giants," the Inca referred to all modern Europeans, who were somewhat similar in appearance as "Viracochas."

The Wari Wiraocha Runa were natives who knew only a rudimentary culture. According to de Ayala's native sources, they emerged as a people around 2800 BCE. This date matches the onset of an archaeological period known as the Preceramic Phase, when various Andean tribes began to coalesce into the fundamentals of organized society. De Ayala compared the Wari Wiraocha Runa to the pre-Flood people in Genesis because their era ended in a natural catastrophe reminiscent of the deluge from which Noah escaped with his family.

The Wari Wiraocha Runa were followed by the Wari Runa around

1800 BCE, when these more advanced Peruvians, likewise described as "Viracochas," introduced the benefits of agriculture. Two hundred years later, their era came to a sudden close when it, too, was terminated by a catastrophic deluge. Here, as well, de Ayala's chronology matches some important event horizons.

The year 1800 BCE sparked the Initial Period, a vital transition from a Preceramic primitivism to pottery manufacture and the rise of village life. The global flood cited by the Incan calendar circa 1600 BCE coincides with the eruption of Thera, a volcanic explosion that devastated the eastern Mediterranean in 1628 BCE. The black cloud above Thera, known today as Santorini, sixty miles north of Crete, filled with sixty thousand miles of ash, rising twenty-three miles into the sky.

It was the accumulation of seven cubic miles of rhyodacite magma ejected from a thirty-cubic-mile hole, and this colossal explosion left a crater nearly fifty square miles in area. Multi ton boulders were ejected into the stratosphere, and some have been found as far away from Thera as the Black Sea, seven hundred miles from the blast center. More than seventy miles to the east, more than a foot of ash fell on the islands of Kos, Rhodes, and Cyprus. Phaistos, Minoan Crete's second city, as though struck by the shockwave of a hydrogen bomb was carbonized in a flash.

This truly cataclysmic event was not limited to the Aegean Sea but instead part of a global disaster geophysicists, volcanologists, oceanographers, and scholars in related fields suspect may have been triggered by meteoric debris colliding with seismically sensitive areas of our planet. At the international convocation of professional researchers at Fitzwilliam College (discussed in chapter 4), they determined that the near miss of a comet in the early seventeenth century BCE set off a chain reaction of seismicity and volcanism expressed in monstrous tsunamis and unprecedented rainfall around the world.

While Thera erupted with the force of two hundred 500-megaton atomic bombs, New Zealand's Taupo Valley volcano simultaneously exploded, generating two-hundred-foot-high walls of water that traveled several hundred miles per hour as far as the Arctic Circle. Additional tsunamis were sent careening back toward the southwest by the contemporaneous eruption of the Akiachak volcano in Alaska. Islands standing in their way were overwhelmed and swept clean of every obstruction. Whole archipelagoes vanished or were utterly depopulated.

The Klamath Indians of south-central Oregon and northern California believe that Kmukamtch, a shining demon from the sky, endeavored to destroy Earth with his celestial flame, followed by a worldwide deluge. This reference to the comet associated with the Lemurian catastrophe is underscored by the appearance of the lost motherland's name in K*mu*kamtch.

To another California tribe, the Modoc, Kmukamtch means literally the "ancient old man from Mu," the creator of humankind. According to New Mexico's Ute Indians, "the Sun was shivered into a thousand fragments, which fell to Earth causing a general conflagration."[1] Their name for this heavenly explosion was Ta-wats, who ravaged the world "until at last, swollen with heat, the eyes of the god burst, and the tears gushed forth in a flood which spread over the Earth and extinguished the fire."[2]

It was this 1628 BCE catastrophe that may have been responsible for the final destruction of Lemuria, a high culture spread over island chains spanning the south-central Pacific Ocean. Also known as Mu, Kahiki, Hiva, Horai, Marae Renga, and many other names, it is memorialized in the oral traditions of numerous peoples throughout the Pacific realm, where the enigmatic ruins of Nan Madol, Kuai, Guam, Easter Island, and many other archaeological zones testify to its former existence.

The Lemurians were consistently portrayed as the possessors of an extraordinarily sophisticated civilization, who passed on its greatness to other peoples after calamitous events of the early seventeenth century BCE. Their story seems reflected in the Inca's historical calendar, which cites a contemporaneous flood that closed the age of the Wari Runa.

They were followed by the Purun Runa, or Wild Men, who applied the deluge survivors' advanced technology. Mining for precious metals—particularly gold and silver—was undertaken, and jewelry manufacture became an art. But these luxuries engendered greed that soon led to strife and even warfare. The Purun Runa's "Sun" is supposed to have dawned around 800 BCE, a critical moment in Andean archaeology, when the Initial Period transitioned into the Early Horizon.

This phase is most important for the founding of Chavín de Huantar. Located 155 miles north of Lima, the site is the first stone city of its kind in Peru, and it came to typify the entire epoch. De Ayala does not tell us how the age of the Purun Runa came to a close, suggesting perhaps that transition to the next epoch was peaceful.

In any case, the Auca Runa who followed in 200 CE instituted a decimal system; built mud-brick fortifications called *pucaras;* and worshipped *guaca bilcas,* translated by de Ayala as "supernaturals." They also invented the *ayllus.* These were social, religious, and ritual organizations that exerted political power through a combination of kinship and territorial ties. Once again, the Incan calendar accurately reflects a crucial archaeological transition. In this case, around 200 CE, during the Early Intermediate Period, the Moche civilizers began building cities along Peru's northern coast, while the Auca Runa seemed to fade from existence.

The Moche, like the Auca Runa, operated the first ayllus, erected pucaras, employed a decimal system as the basis of their construction projects and astronomical calculations, and, instead of confining their worship to variations of Viracocha, venerated a pantheon of "supernaturals." Although their day ended around 700 CE, the peoples who came after them—the Huari, Chimor, Llacuaz, Chachapoyas, and others— all at least fundamentally upheld and carried forward the cultural principles created by the Moche. Once again, de Ayala does not explain how or why the Auca Runa vanished, although the extensive warfare he implies through the construction of pucaras does typify those centuries leading up to the rise of the Inca.

The final "Sun" arose in 1200 CE, when the first Sapa Inca, or emperor, founded the Kingdom of Cuzco, the imperial capital. This last age did not end with the execution of Atahualpa, the last Sapa Inca, in August 1533. The Spanish Conquest only terminated an initial phase of an epoch that includes our own time. It is scheduled to climax in the next 192 years, around the turn of the twenty-third century. If the Inca made any prediction for the conclusion of the Fifth Sun, de Ayala did not include it in his "Nueva corónica y buen gobierno."

More certainly, the Incan calendar demonstrates that the Inca understood their history with at least a fundamental accuracy that went back some forty centuries before their own time. This record-keeping feat is made all the more remarkable when we realize that they kept no written documents; the only aids to memory they relied upon were devices such as *quipu,* knotted cords signifying numerical units.

No less impressive, each of their five Suns closely correspond to the major event horizons of Andean archaeology, including an early-seventeenth-century BCE global catastrophe that appears to have destroyed the Pacific Ocean motherland of civilization. It was, in fact, from a Lemurian kind of island kingdom that Viracocha and his followers were said to have escaped by sailing to Peru from the west.

The Incan calendar is testimony to the power of oral tradition, which is able to preserve the historic legacy of a people with surprisingly high levels of accuracy over the course of millennia. As such, it is proof that enduring myths are neither mere fables nor unreliable legends but, on the contrary, important truths enshrined in the national memory of a folk that may no longer exist.

# 12

# Doom Number

The early part of our century was bracketed by two specific dates—September 11, 2001, and December 21, 2012—respectively, the greatest single act of terrorism committed against the continental United States and the end of the Mayan calendar. If, as some observers suspect, something more than a coincidental relationship exists between these two events, its explanation must lie beyond the powers of ordinary human reason and in the world of numbers.*

The relationship between human destiny and numbers was recognized when the sixth-century BCE Greek philosopher Pythagoras observed that "all is number."[1] This dictum means that all existing things can be ultimately reduced to numerical relationships. He regarded numbers as the expression of those relationships and the universal spiritual force connecting every one of them as a network of energy laid over the whole breadth of creation.

In the *Epinomis,* Plato expanded upon the Pythagorean concept of numbers as keys to the synchronous interconnectedness of all phenomena: "All geometric constructions, all systems of numbers, all duly constituted melodic progressions, and the ordered scheme of all celestial revolutions disclose themselves through the revelation of a single bond of natural interconnection."[2]

---

*This chapter first appeared as "The Significance of the Number 11 in the 2012 Prophecey" in *Mysteries* 23 (2009). Republished here with permission.

The sacred character of numerical synchronicity was recognized by ancient Egyptian sages who regarded the universe as a composite whole, in which every part is related to every other part. To them, this universal entity represented a cosmic consciousness expressing its will in a hierarchy of levels. What humans perceived as "matter" was the materialization of that will, just as "mind" was awareness at a higher, and therefore invisible, level. The Pythagoreans sought to unlock the mysteries of cosmic consciousness through their study of numerical interrelationships, because they believed that numbers are the expression of function.

But only traumatic, widely recognized events—referred to by Terence McKenna as novelty—are potent enough to compel awareness of any relationship between destiny and numbers. The most recent example is the destruction of New York's World Trade Center in 2001. It took place on the eleventh day of the ninth month, or, as is commonly expressed, 9/11, the same digits used as a general emergency telephone number. Whether the attackers deliberately chose these numbers is unimportant; the point is that the parallel between the date of the event, its disastrous character, and the emergency number is significant.

Additionally, number 1 features prominently in the Twin Towers disaster. For example, $9/11 = 9 + 1 + 1 = 11$. September 11 is the 254th day of the year: $2 + 5 + 4 = 11$. After September 11, 111 days were left to the end of the year. The birthday of the Islamic prophet Muhammed is celebrated on the eleventh day of the ninth month.

The Twin Towers, standing side by side, resembled the number eleven. The combined windows in the Twin Towers numbered 21,800, or $2 + 1 + 8 = 11$. The first jetliner to collide with them was Flight 11. On board Flight 11 were 92 passengers: $9 + 2 = 11$. The other suicide aircraft, Flight 77, carried 65 passengers: $6 + 5 = 11$.

When President George W. Bush visited the ruins of the World Trade Center, he was photographed beside a fire fighter wearing a helmet emblazoned with the number 164: $1 + 6 + 4 = 11$.

At 1:11 on the morning of September 11, 2001, Geminorum-13, one of forty-eight stars in the constellation of Gemini, appeared inside the crescent moon. Gemini signifies the twins, while the crescent moon is the emblem of Islam.

Thirty years before the suicide attacks on the towers, numerologist Maria Valla wrote that people associated with the number eleven "can destroy anything that it touches, including self. You will conquer others, but in so doing, destroy yourself."[3] Among folk traditions around the world, the number eleven is traditionally associated with political instability and violence, lack of self-restraint, destructive transition, danger, and revolution.

These traits are generated by removing number one from the cosmic order, represented by the number twelve (the twelve houses of the zodiac, Christ's twelve apostles, the twelve hours of the day, the twelve months of the year, the human body's twelve pairs of ribs and thoracic vertebrae), and adding number one to the patriarchal number ten, which signifies political power or civilization (Plato's ten kings of Atlantis, the ten patriarchs of the Hindu god Manu, the original ten patriarchs in the biblical Genesis, the Babylonians' ten world rulers before the Flood).

In the Pythagorean system, eleven signified chaos because it was a cardinal number separating humanity or civilization—associated with ten—from the cosmic order embodied in the number twelve.

The troubling nature of eleven was introduced in the West after the Greek geometrician Pythagoras studied the mystical significance of numbers at the ancient Egyptian Mystery school of Heliopolis, meaning "City of the Sun." Could the early astronomers there have known about the sun's eleven-year sunspot cycle, and could that cycle be the basis for the number eleven's association with chaos?

As described in chapter 7, sunspots are cooler regions on the surface of the sun that seriously disrupt electronic communications and interfere with normal human thought processes. They discharge abnormally large concentrations of electronically charged particles, known as *photons*. These photons interface with radio, telephone, and television transmitters and receivers, as well as the neural network of our brains, overloading artificial and organic systems with power surges that push them beyond their limits.

During the early fourteenth century, the inexplicable disappearance of sunspots was coincidental with a relatively brief worldwide drought climatologists refer to as the Little Ice Age. They suspect that the eleven-year sunspot cycle is linked to the advance and retreat of glaciation over the past half-million years. Our sun also changes its magnetic polarity every eleven years, interfacing with Earth's own magnetic field to cause worldwide breakdowns in all forms of electronic communication.

But disruption is not confined to radio and television. From the mid-twentieth century, parapsychologists have traced a correlation between the solar flips and upsurges of emotional disturbances in human behavior. A study published in the December 1979 issue of *Psychology Today* reports that residents of U.S. day-care centers, nursing homes, and psychiatric wards all experienced an abnormally high frequency of anxiety attacks and erratic behavior during the apogee of the sun's eleven-year polar reversal. This May 1979 event also precisely defined an unusual upswing in violence and its precipitous decline experienced by prison populations across the United States and Mexico, according to the same *Psychology Today* article.[4]

Other mammals, even fish, appear to be affected. Writing for *Natural History* magazine, Dr. Dennis Duda describes a five-year study of whale vocalization undertaken by cetacean behaviorologists at the University of Oregon beginning in 1976. To their astonishment, they discovered that the leviathans sang original songs during a solar magnetic reversal; the unique sounds had not been made before nor have they been heard since.[5]

As recently as 2006, marine biologists from Chicago's Shedd Aquarium observed the disruption of lake trout spawning patterns correlated with the sun's polar flip. Researchers speculate that the bioelectric field of many creatures is directly influenced by the sun's eleven-year cycle.[6] If so, modern science and ancient mysticism begin to complement each other in the close of the Mayan calendar, whose inventors and operators, as explained in previous chapters, believed in a close relationship between solar cycles and human behavior.

As mentioned in chapter 5, the ecliptic of our star intersected with the galactic equator on the morning of 2012's winter solstice. The sun at that moment was one degree above the horizon at the equator (73 degrees west). Why did the Maya regard this cosmically unique event as the end of their calendar? The number eleven may provide an answer in our sun's eleven-year cycle associated with electrical disruptions on Earth.

The Mayan calendar officially terminated precisely on the morning of 2012's winter solstice at 11:11 UTC (Coordinated Universal Time). Millennia before the Christmas holiday, which usurped it, the winter solstice was humankind's greatest festival, the annual conquest of darkness, the original New Year's Day. Given the nature of the ancient holiday, the winter solstice of 2012—which was of greater importance in astronomical terms than other solstices—could signify the close of a dark, chaotic age and usher in the onset of human enlightenment.

The Maya were more explicit, however, if not entirely clear in explaining the termination of their calendar. It had begun with one catastrophe—the *Hun yecil*, the Great Flood—and would close with another they said would be known as the Rebellion of Earth.[7]

In both the magnitude and speed of deterioration, climate change continues to take natural scientists by surprise. Dr. George McKendry, director of the Massachusetts Institute for Earth Studies, stated in 2002 that just ten years remained for the implementation of major international improvements to head off "an irrevocable alteration in the life-support systems of our planet."[8] If decisive, preventive measures were not in place after that period, he maintained, not even the most radical solutions would be able to deter exponentially developing global instability. The increasing frequency and destructiveness of super storms—particularly hurricanes and tornados—together with unusually dry conditions, which contribute to major outbreaks of brush- and forest-fires, would typify our world in the twenty-first century.

Dr. McKendry may not have been aware that his deadline corresponded to the end of the Mayan calendar. Nevertheless, it is a dire prognostication underscored by the reappearance of the number eleven in our uncertain times.

# 13

# How Could They
# Have Possibly Known?

If the Maya were truly aware of some future catastrophe—a new ice age, perhaps—how could they have possibly learned of it? They possessed none of the deep-space telescopes, interplanetary satellites, or super computers that have enabled modern astronomers to make some of the discoveries with which the Maya and their predecessors were already familiar thousands of years ago.

Without these sophisticated technologies—relying entirely on their powers of observation with the naked eye over many generations—what abilities allowed them to see, from the perspective of at least 200 BCE, that the southern end of our galaxy's Dark Rift at midpoint in the Milky Way would form a perfect alignment with the winter solstice sun on the morning of December 21, 2012?

The Maya and their Olmec or Atlantean predecessors did not make such an incredible observation simply because they were wise. This calendrical achievement especially cannot be explained away by the mere fact of their obvious genius. Something as difficult to ascertain in deep prehistory as 2012's geo-solar-galactic alignment could have been determined only through simple observation with the assistance of modernlike technology or through psychic abilities. Each alternative seems unacceptable.

*Figure 13.1. Mexico City's National Museum of Anthropology illustration of an Atlantean Bacab supporting the sky atop Chichén Itzá's Pyramid of the Feathered Serpent, as the Mayan calendar cycles overhead toward its close in 2012*

To predict such an alignment so far into the future with pinpoint accuracy unaided by outside support of any kind seems impossible. It is understandable that the Maya could forecast, even by millions of years, the correct positions of Venus and other planets, stars, or constellations based on the regular cycles of these luminaries across the night sky. The 2012 event, however, was not cyclical in the same sense because such a galactic eclipse occurs every 26,000 years. Simple observations of precession would have required the passage of at least three such periods and uninterrupted preservation of their notation over the course of 78,000 years.

No society in human history has endured more than a fraction of that time. The world's oldest continuous civilization, the Chinese, has been punctuated over the course of its past four thousand years by anarchy, invasion, tyranny, natural catastrophes, book burnings, and other cultural revolutions that have all too often consigned its science and literature to oblivion. Human nature has repeatedly proved itself incapable of governing a society strong enough or resilient enough to endure seventy-eight or more millennia of unbroken stability.

If the Maya did not make their calculations for 2012 by naked-eye observation alone, could they have possessed supertechnologies that allowed them to see into the heavens, as we do now? Did they operate some third-century BCE forerunner of the Hubble Space Telescope? If Mayan astronomers had such an instrument at their disposal, no scrap of it has been found to date, nor has anything of the kind been so much as alluded to in their lengthy hieroglyphic texts or temple art.

Notwithstanding a lack of evidence, ancient-astronaut theorists believe extraterrestrial benefactors descended from outer space to tell the Maya all about the heavens and 2012. As material proof, they cite Palenque, where the Maya ceremonial center's Temple of Inscriptions contains a stone sarcophagus lid, the underside of which is adorned with a splendid bas-relief carving purportedly showing a seventh-century ruler—K'inich Janaab' Pakal, also known as Pacal II, the Great—at the controls of a spaceship.

In *Chariots of the Gods,* the famous Swiss author Erich von Däniken describes the scene: "In the center of that frame is a man sitting, bending forward. He has a mask on his nose, he uses his two hands to manipulate some controls, and the heel of his left foot is on a kind of pedal with different adjustments. The rear portion is separated from him; he is sitting on a complicated chair, and outside of this whole frame, you see a little flame like an exhaust."[1] Von Däniken's interpretation seems complemented by glyphs around the edges of the lid representing the sun, moon, Venus, and various constellations. On closer inspection, however, Pacal is clearly depicted descending into the jaws of Xibalba, the underworld—appropriately enough, because his body was entombed in this very sarcophagus. Moreover, the representation of a deity guarding the underworld appears to await the dead ruler's imminent arrival.

Equally as far-fetched as arguments of ancient astronauts sharing their celestial wisdom with Yucatán natives are prospects for psychic power the Maya perhaps employed to ascertain the significance of the winter solstice of 2012. Unacceptable as such a consideration might be to some serious investigators, it is, after all, the only conceivable method the Maya could have used to accurately forecast the rare astronomical events transpiring on the morning of a single day more than two thousand years beyond their time. The specific technique they probably employed to make such a long-distance observation was their equivalent to a practice known in the Western world since the late twentieth century as remote viewing.

Introduced by Stanford Research Institute laser physicist Harold Puthoff and parapsychologist Russel Targ in 1974, remote viewing refers to the acquisition of information about distant or unseen targets through extrasensory perception. Remote viewing is by no means the fantasy of spiritual hobbyists dabbling in the occult. As early as World War II, the U.S. government began funding paranormal researchers in the hope of turning them into psychic spies. These early programs lapsed after the cessation of hostilities but resumed with special interest after intelligence officers learned that similar programs were under way in the USSR and Red China.

In 1972, Puthoff was approached by representatives of the CIA's Directorate of Science and Technology, who put him in charge of a $50,000 project called Stargate following his successful remote viewing experiments. The results of his and Targ's investigations were published in *Nature* and in the proceedings of a symposium on consciousness sponsored by the American Association for the Advancement of Science. John McMahon, who headed the CIA's Office of Technical Service and later became the agency's deputy director, enthusiastically supported their work. With the Watergate scandal, however, the CIA was under pressure to quickly disassociate itself from anything unconventional, and in the late 1970s the agency turned over Project Stargate to the Air Force under the Foreign Technology Division.

Meanwhile, the U.S. Army's Intelligence and Security Command took up its own remote-viewing research under the command of General Edward Thompson, who acted as chief intelligence officer. He learned that contemporary investigations into the military application of paranormal abilities were receiving better funding and government support in the USSR and the People's Republic of China. At his urging, Project Stargate eventually moved from research into field operations with some notable successes. These included remote viewing a monster crane operating at a Soviet nuclear research facility; locating the crash in Africa of a Red Air Force bomber referred to by President Jimmy Carter in several speeches; and discovering a secret new class of Russian submarine, a feat carried out by three psychics. Thereafter, a special training program of military officers resulted in the formation of a military remote-viewing unit based at Fort Meade in Maryland.

By the early 1990s, the utility of remote viewing was firmly established when U.S. Army colonel William Johnson spent several months running another remote-viewing unit for locating military targets. Results were so positive that he insisted on the phenomenon's usefulness as an intelligence tool. With Republican control of House spending in late 1994, however, remote viewing was regarded as somehow irreligious, and the CIA terminated the project in 1995. That same year, an article in *Time* magazine reported that three full-time psychics were still working on a $500,000-per-year budget at Fort Meade, but they were due for termination.

Contrary to results over the previous twenty-five years, CIA spokespeople stated that remote viewing did not exist or could not be proved. Off the record, other government representatives confided that the phenomenon was authentic enough, but its viewers were unreliable, their performance varying in effectiveness from day to day. Soldiers required a reliable weapon, they explained, one they could depend on in any eventuality.

Some veterans of Project Stargate, however, are not convinced by the CIA's public pronouncements. They believe that advanced research into remote viewing continues in secret, together with its military application and use in espionage. Having learned everything they needed to know from civilians such as Harold Puthoff and Russel Targ, the government operatives summarily dispensed with them and now pursue their own classified remote-viewing agendas.

This very brief overview of extrasensory perception in the U.S. military illustrates that it is a real phenomenon that is only just being understood and put to use in modern times by world governments. The same practices appear to have been far better known to the Maya, whose entire culture was not only open to psychic abilities but took them for granted as part of the human condition and embraced them.

The Maya and other ancient peoples around the world often spoke about the flight of the shaman, a tribal seer who extended his or her consciousness to remote distances, in space and time, to bring back vital information to the people of the tribe. Skeptics refuse to acknowledge the possibility of these paranormal abilities, because their existence would undermine fundamental ideas about causality, time, the function of the human mind, and other principles currently held by the scientific community.

Nevertheless, the Mayan adepts were serious in the application of their psychic abilities, which they nurtured over the course of many centuries, as abundantly established by their surviving temple art. These powers may have enabled them to project their consciousness far into the future, where they beheld the event of December 21, 2012. They then returned and included it in the termination of their calendar. Given the ability of the Maya to project their consciousness, they may not have entirely disappeared with their civilization more than one thousand years ago but instead may walk invisibly among us as thoughtforms observing our time and beyond.

## PART TWO

# The Seer

*Edgar Cayce's*
*Spiritual Revelations of Atlantis*

# 14

# Plato and Cayce

If Jesus was asked what he thought of Mayan prophecies for our time, he might answer, as he is quoted as having said in the New Testament (Matthew 24:35–36), "Heaven and Earth will pass away, but my words shall not pass away. But of that day and hour no one knows, not even the angels of heaven, nor the Son, but the Father alone."

Undeterred by the apparent finality of this pronouncement, Pope Leo X assured his fellow Christians, "I will not see the end of the world, nor will you, my brethren. For its time is long in the future, five hundred years hence."[1]

According to the Pontiff, five centuries after he made his promise in 1514 the world would end, a mere two years following the Mayan calendar end date—that is, if he meant exactly five hundred years from the date on which he uttered his prediction. It would seem Leo X did not intend such precision but gave his flock to understand that the world would come to a close sometime around 2014. In any case, his prophetic statement very closely parallels the Maya's 4-Ahau 3-Kankin. Unlike them, however, the pope did not appear to base his prediction on any calendrical computations. As the highest priest in the Roman Catholic Church, he appears to have spoken out of a kind of religious ecstasy.

Another spiritual figure who allegedly foresaw distant happenings— both backward and forward in time—was Edgar Cayce, the twentieth-

*Figure 14.1. Edgar Cayce, the twentieth-century's Sleeping Prophet, stated that the consequences set in motion by the destruction of Atlantis are reverberating across the millennia into our time.*

century's Sleeping Prophet. While no one before Cayce's death in 1945 knew enough to ask him what he envisioned for the winter solstice of 2012 and beyond, he came closest to commenting on such an event when he said that similar "awareness during the era or the Age of Atlantis and Lemuria or Mu brought, what? Destruction to man, and his beginning of the needs of the journey up through that of selfishness."[2]

His trance-state utterance coincides with the moral underpinning for catastrophe stressed by Plato, the Mēxihcah, Hindu tradition, Hopi elders, and other sources linking the violation of natural law to the horror of physical consequences forecast by the Mayan calendar.

The mystical meaning of one of the Atlantean sacred numbers was additionally recognized by Cayce. He stated that five "represents man in his physical form, and the attributes to which he may become conscious from the elemental or spiritual to the physical consciousness, as the senses, as the sensing of the various forces that bring to man the activities in the sphere in which he finds himself."[3] His definition of this mystical number certainly reflects its significance from Plato's sunken kingdom to Mesoamerica.

During the Roaring Twenties the reincarnated memories of lost Atlantis began to surface for the first time in Cayce's "life readings." He would eventually leave behind 14,256 stenographic records documenting his clairvoyant comments for some eight thousand different clients over a forty-three-year period. Most of his readings produced during deep trances were concerned with diagnosing spiritual and physical health problems, with no references to vanished civilizations. His uncanny accuracy in personal analysis impressed not only thousands of sufferers who benefited from his curative insights but the medical establishment as well. As early as 1910, Cayce's psychic procedures were substantiated by Dr. Wesley Ketchum in a report to Boston's Clinical Research Society.

The success of the Sleeping Prophet's work was complemented by Cayce's natural piety and disinterest in material wealth. He never made a fortune from his gifts that so greatly helped others. Indeed, his achievement is an ongoing process of illumination, as people from around the world continue to study his collected remarks at the Association for Research and Enlightenment in Virginia Beach, Virginia.

Until his forty-seventh year, Cayce's life readings of the people who approached him for assistance never sparked any memories of past lives among the Atlanteans. During 1922, however, he began recalling life in a place with which he was totally unfamiliar. Hugh Lynn Cayce knew his father "did not read material on Atlantis, and that he, so far as we know, had absolutely no knowledge of the subject."[4] The evocative, often verifiable detail of his readings in which Atlantis was described is all the more astounding when we realize he knew nothing about the vanished culture during his waking hours. As his son wrote, "They are the most fantastic, the most bizarre, the most impossible information in the Edgar Cayce files. If his unconscious fabricated this material or wove it together from existing legends and writings, we believe that it is the most amazing example of a telepathic-clairvoyant scanning of existing legends and stories in print or of the minds of persons dealing with the Atlantis theory."[5]

Edgar Cayce's ignorance of the sunken civilization is not surprising.

His formal education was meager, and his points of reference were more conventionally religious than historical or academic. His grasp of the past was biblical, not scholastic. It seems clear, then, that the subject was outside the purview of both his personal background and essentially Christian view of the world. Yet his pronouncements are credible because they often contain information that made little or no sense at the time they were uttered but have since been confirmed by science. The objective reader cannot avoid the unmistakable impression that Cayce actually "saw" with his own inner eye a real place long since vanished.

Some important archaeological finds confirming Cayce's statements have come to light since he made them more than sixty years ago. In light of these fresh revelations, his life readings assume greater significance; they are made current as our own civilization enters a new epoch of hitherto undreamed of exploration in both inner and outer space. Within the Edgar Cayce life readings, the profusion of historic and geologic details and cultural correspondences—some of them unknown at the time he spoke of them—confirm that he did indeed "see" Atlantis. His clairvoyant utterances will be, therefore, all the more poignant and pertinent to a humankind in search of its origins. To realize where we came from is to know how we arrived at our present situation—and to understand where we may be headed.

Until the last decades of the twentieth century, most rational people would have deplored any attempt to combine serious research with the comments of a psychic. But times and perspectives have changed. Today psychics are often called upon by law enforcement agencies around the world, often unearthing valid clues and even solving crimes when conventional methods failed.

Closer to the subject of this investigation, California's Mobius Society is a group of remote viewers who work hand-in-glove with professional archaeologists to find traces of lost civilizations. Their track record is remarkable, with perhaps their most spectacular discovery being the underwater Ptolemaic harbor of Alexandria, lost since an earthquake caused it to collapse into the Mediterranean Sea nearly two thousand years ago. It seems only fitting, then, that with America's greatest psychic as our guide, we should seek the first and grandest of such lost worlds. Although pre-dated by Lemuria—more of a loosely affiliated union of religious communities spread across South Pacific archipelagos than a technologically progressive state—Atlantis was the earliest modern civilization, with all the economic, political, military, and social attributes that have fundamentally characterized all high cultures since.

Edgar Cayce often spoke of lost worlds during his deep sleeps. In fact, of the sixteen hundred people for whom he conducted life readings, about seven hundred described conditions in the vanished homeland of civilization. By comparing his recorded statements with what has been learned recently about Atlantis from archaeology and geology we may obtain an unusually clear, detailed, even credible glimpse of an otherwise dimly remembered age.

Throughout his adult life, Cayce's predictions were as numerous as they were accurate. He even correctly foresaw the date of his burial on January 5, 1945. More relevant to our discussion here, however, are his credentials as a genuine seer into the ancient past, which were revealed in two particularly outstanding readings, one of them concerning the Essenes. These were members of a small Jewish sect that began in the second century BCE. They lived a severe monastic existence focused on divine retribution for sin and proclaimed an impending last judgment that God would call down on an unrepentant humanity. When the Essenes' oft-mentioned end of the world failed to materialize after nearly three centuries, their cult vanished.

Cayce mentioned the Essenes during 1936, when he envisioned a woman client's incarnation near Jerusalem: "The entity was what would now, in some organizations, determine a sister superior or an officer of the Essenes. For the entity was associated with the school on the road above Emmaus near the road that goes down toward Jericho and towards the northernmost coast of Jerusalem."[6]

At the time of this life reading, scholarly opinion held that all Essene groups were exclusively male. Fifteen years later, however, the remains of Kirbet Qumran, the site of an Essene community that Cayce precisely described, were excavated just where he said they would be found. Graves in the area yielded skeletons of women as well as men, thus proving that the religious community was not exclusively male after all. Perhaps one of the skeletons unearthed by the archaeologist's spade was once inhabited by the same woman whose past life Cayce described.

His belief in the doctrine of reincarnation is evident here. A lifetime of similar readings assured him of the human soul's immortality, its survival after physical death, and its inevitable rebirth in a new body. Rather than seeing reincarnation as a pointless recycling of the spirit, Cayce regarded it as part of the great moral order of the cosmos in which each material manifestation of life on Earth was conditioned by a previous life—sometimes to gain knowledge through experience, to resolve ongoing problems, or simply to serve. In any case, each lifetime builds on an individual's sense of purpose and destiny.

The reincarnation theme appears again in this remarkable life reading: "For the entity was among those spoken of as a 'holy woman,' first the entity coming in contact with those activities at the death and raising of Lazarus and later with Mary, Elizabeth, Mary Magdalene, Martha; all of these were a part of the experience of the entity as Salome."[7]

The only Salome mentioned in the New Testament describes her as a witness to the Crucifixion, but not at the raising of Lazarus. In 1960, however, the Associated Press released information confirming the identity of Cayce's "entity" during a past life. Published in Long Island's *Newsday* of December 30, the Associated Press dispatch reports that Dr. Morton Smith, an associate professor of history at Columbia University, discovered a copy of a letter written by Saint Mark. Scholars at the Society of Biblical Literature and Exegesis established its authenticity and ascertained that the document originally belonged to Clement of Alexandria, one of the Christian Church's most important founders in the third century. The copy attributes the story of Lazarus to Saint Mark, an account previously found only in the Gospel according to Saint John. Saint Mark's version is virtually the same as that of John, save for a minor detail coinciding with Cayce's life reading: Clement of Alexandria's copy states that a woman witness to the miracle was called Salome.

These two verified examples underscore Cayce's glimpse of the world two thousand years ago, but his vision extended many centuries earlier, to a place far more remote in time. The earliest known person to describe it is also one of European civilization's leading intellectual figures. Together with Socrates and Aristotle, Plato is still generally regarded by classical scholars as among the most influential thinkers in the early history of the Western world. Declared the prominent twentieth-century metaphysician Alfred North Whitehead, "The safest general characterization of the European philosophical tradition is that it consists of a series of footnotes to Plato."[8] It is impossible to imagine a more credible source for Atlantis as fact.

Many historians believe Plato traveled to Egypt himself, perhaps to personally verify the account inscribed on a memorial column at the temple of the goddess Neith in the city of Sais, located near the southernmost end of the Nile Delta. The existence of this temple record was documented by two other influential thinkers: Proclus and Krantor.

The last major Greek philosopher, Proclus, wrote eight hundred years after Plato, but in his *In Platonis theologiam* (*Platonic Theology*) he cites the credibility of Atlantis by pointing out that the Egyptian column inscribed with the story was visited and identically translated more than half a century after Plato's death in 347 BCE.[9] The column was examined by yet another influential thinker, Krantor of Soluntum, who went to Sais as part of his research for Plato's first biography. Proclus writes that Krantor found the Atlantis story preserved exactly as described in the dialogues.

Unfortunately, the close inspection and documentation of the invaluable Egyptian column appears to have ended with Krantor. The enormous Temple of Neith was demolished down to its foundations on the orders of Christian authorities determined to purge every manifestation of paganism from Egypt. In the fifth book of *Historia Ecclesiastica*, written less than fifty years after their destruction in 391

CE, church historian Socrates Scholasticus tells how, "at the solicitation of Theophilus, Bishop of Alexandria, the Emperor issued an order at this time for the demolition of the heathen temples in that city; commanding also that it should be put in execution under the direction of Theophilus."[10]

First on the agenda was pulling down the Great Library of Alexandria and incinerating its million or so texts on medicine, botany, philosophy, astronomy, geometry, architecture, irrigation, agriculture, and virtually every aspect of classical civilization. "Thus this disturbance having been terminated," Scholasticus continues, "the governor of Alexandria and the commander-in-chief of the troops in Egypt assisted Theophilus in demolishing the heathen temples."[11] Among them was the Temple of Neith and all its original documents, including the history of Atlantis inscribed on the memorial pillar. With the wholesale obliteration of ancient source materials, it should hardly come as a surprise that Plato's two dialogues represent the only record of Atlantis still available to us. The wonder is that even the *Timaeus* and *Kritias* survived into modern times. Yet the account of the lost world in these dialogues is firmly supported by men of stellar credentials: Solon, Plato, Proclus, and Krantor.

Aristotle's only known comment about Atlantis—"he that created it also destroyed it"—is regarded by some skeptics to mean that Aristotle believed Atlantis was merely a fable concocted by Plato, who also invented its cataclysmic conclusion.[12] Aristotle's "he," however, might have just as likely referred to Poseidon, the sea god in Plato's account who laid the foundations of Atlantis and was responsible for later sinking it to the bottom of the ocean at the command of Zeus.

If Aristotle did regard Atlantis as fantasy, he was virtually alone among his scholarly contemporaries who affirmed the veracity of Plato's report. The Roman scientist Pliny the Elder applauded the geographer Statius Sebosus for his detailed description of Atlantis. Predating both Aristotle and Plato, Dionysus of Mitylene wrote "A Voyage to Atlantis" circa 550 BCE. Born around 50 BCE, Diodorus Siculus was a Greek geographer who described the Atlantean War. The first-century

Alexandrine theologian Philo Judaeus taught that Plato based his allegorical story of Atlantis on historical reality.

Ammianus Marcellinus, a fourth-century Roman historian, classified the destruction of Atlantis as a *chasmatiae,* a natural disaster in which seismic violence broke open great fissures in the Earth to swallow large tracts of territory during a single event. The famous Roman biologist Aelian reports in his third-century *The Nature of Animals* how "the inhabitants of the shores of the Ocean tell that in former times the kings of Atlantis, descendants of Poseidon, wore on their heads, as a mark of power, the fillet of the male sea-ram [perhaps frigate birds, whose habit of diving into the ocean may have inspired such a name], and that their wives, the queens, wore, as a sign of their power, fillets of the female sea-rams."[13]

Contrary to a general consensus of ancient Old World scholars affirming the veracity of Plato's account, modern skeptics, particularly archaeologists, are convinced Atlantis is only a legend. They fail to consider that, beyond his position as the seminal philosopher of Western civilization, Plato based his entire body of thought on the uncompromising pursuit of the truth. The *Timaeus* and *Kritias* cannot contain a fictional allegory for his notion of the ideal state, as some critics insist, because the Atlantis he described was far removed from his utopian conception, as presented in the *Republic.*

It seems likely, however, that Plato, had he completed the dialogue, would have used the rise and fall of Atlantis as a historical example illustrating the fatal consequences of civil degeneracy. In the *Kritias,* he did not inexplicably change from philosopher to historian. Instead, it appears more probable that he intended his citation of corrupted Atlantis to provide a factual basis for the dialogues.

Unlike Plato, who relied chiefly on a Greek translation of Egyptian temple records, Edgar Cayce's source of information was a kind of spiritual record he reviewed while experiencing an altered state of consciousness. Yet his descriptions of the doomed civilization seem to some researchers a mix of the credible and the fantastic. For example, his portrayal of the migration of Atlanteans to the Nile Valley following the destruction of their empire is entirely convincing. Many otherwise obscure names of people and places he associates with the Atlantis experience likewise seem to reflect real events. But when he said in the 1930s that the Nile River flowed across the Sahara Desert to the ocean in early Atlantean times, no scientist in the world would have even considered such an apparently outlandish possibility. Yet in 1994, nearly half a century after his death, a satellite survey of North Africa discovered traces of a former tributary of the Nile that in prehistory connected Egypt with the Atlantic Ocean at Morocco. Indeed, for someone of no formal education, Cayce grasped archaeology and geology in an extraordinary, even prophetic, way.

Perhaps most impressive of all, obscure, even fleeting references he made to Atlantis during the early 1920s were sometimes repeated only once, but within the exact same frame of reference, even after more than two decades. Cayce mentioned almost as an afterthought that old Jewish documents, unknown to the outside world during his lifetime but disclosed around the turn of the next century, would provide evidence for the former existence of Atlantis. In 2000, a Dutch science writer, Auguste Helaine, described an obscure Hebrew treatise on computational astronomy dated to 1378–1379 CE. It appears to be based on or even to paraphrase an earlier lost Islamic work about Atlantis, opening with a reference to the known inhabited regions of the Earth and the Atlantic Ocean: "Some say that they start at the beginning of the western ocean and beyond. For in the earliest times, there was an island in the middle of the ocean. Scholars were there, who isolated themselves in philosophy. In their day, that was the longitude of the inhabited world. Today, it has become sea, and it is ten degrees [about 300 miles] into the sea [i.e., west from Gibraltar]."[14]

Persuasive elements of Cayce's life readings such as these give even skeptics pause and encourage many investigators, regardless of their spiritual beliefs, to reconsider everything he had to say about Atlantis. But some are troubled by his unmanageable chronologies, which make out the lost capital to have been tens of thousands of years old, even going back to the early evolution of modern humans. No less disturbing is Cayce's repeated characterization of the Atlanteans as the inventors of a technology superior to twenty-first-century accomplishments. He describes them as the builders and operators of aircraft and submarines, who mastered all manner of electrical and chemical energies, including nuclear fission. Many serious researchers balk at Cayce's life readings when (to them) they begin to verge on science fiction but still feel that completely condemning his work for its apparent excesses would be throwing the whole Atlantean baby out with the fantasy bathwater.

Critical investigators striving to understand a credible Atlantis within the context of the documented past may accept his vision with a grain of salt, finding it especially useful for his commonly convincing insights, which personalize its participants and make the lost civilization come alive, as no one else has been able to achieve. They may not embrace all Cayce's statements without reservations, but they carefully examine each one, putting aside, not discarding, those that do not currently fit into the hugely complex Atlantean puzzle, while selecting those that, after close scrutiny, correspond to other pieces of information. To the surprise of honest skeptics, this careful comparative process more often validates Cayce's portrayal of Atlantis. Because he was correct in at least some important details, other Atlantologists believe he was telling the whole truth, however difficult it may be for us to grasp at the moment. He is the chief guide in all their research and is held in at least as high regard as Plato.

Regardless of the response Cayce continues to elicit, an important part of his legacy is the Association for Research and Enlightenment, operating in his former home at Virginia Beach. It maintains the largest library of its kind in the world, featuring not only all of his life readings but also many hundreds of books, papers, feature articles, and reference materials about the lost civilization.

Plato and Cayce do not disagree with each other about Atlantis. On the contrary, their discussions are complementary, at least in their general outlines. The American psychic fleshes out the story with real-life individuals, putting a human face on the Atlanteans presented in their broader cultural context by the Greek philosopher. Plato himself was not averse to extrarational means of ascertaining the truth, as he made clear in his post-Atlantis dialogue *Laws:* "The ultimate limits of the human mind are surpassed only by what the spirit may learn."[15]

Together, Plato and Cayce more fully present ancient civilization's greatest drama. While no important discrepancies contradict the two versions (separated by twenty-four centuries), they do feature some non-exclusionary differences. The most important are the Atlanto-Athenian War and ancient technology; the former plays a central role in Plato's report, but Cayce does not even allude to it, while the latter, which never appears in the dialogues, is a recurrent theme throughout the life readings. How can we reconcile these apparently major inconsistencies?

The answer may lie in the narratives themselves: both spoke of the same civilization, but at different periods in its very long life. By all accounts, Atlantean history spanned not centuries, but millennia. Cayce was concerned primarily with its early to middle years of internal religious strife, when its colonizers were traveling throughout much of the world. Plato's dialogues focus on its last period of overseas military involvement and final destruction. In other words, the two versions describe Atlantis in different epochs, separated by thousands of years. Plato and Cayce agree that, during the millennial interim, Atlantean civilization entered a decline from its former greatness, a degeneration that could have conceivably resulted in the loss of an earlier, higher technology, just as today we speak of lost arts from bygone cultures and eras.

That the story of Atlantis should have among its supporters the greatest philosopher and the greatest psychic in the Western world says much for its credibility, but had Plato's *Dialogues* failed to survive the collapse of classical civilization and the long dark ages that followed, Atlantis would be known today only in the enduring myths of various peoples affected by it and through Cayce's life readings. This is at the core of what the great Scottish Atlantologist of the early twentieth century, Lewis Spence, called "the problem of Lemuria."

No great thinker narrates the story of that earlier and parallel civilization, described in widely scattered folk traditions from Malaysia and

China to Polynesia and British Columbia, and beyond to California and South America. Punctuating this profuse if fragmented oral evidence are the sunken ruins recently discovered in Japanese waters and the remains found on dry land in Micronesia, on Easter Island, and in Peru. The Sleeping Prophet reconstructs them all and brings back to life a people predating Atlantis but who were perhaps even more similar to us, particularly comparable to the followers of New Age spirituality.

Edgar Cayce's provocative views of life in Atlantis and Lemuria, here updated in the light of new discoveries, are not merely valuable as history. They uncover an even more disturbing parallel between the catastrophic fate of a once richly powerful society and the modern world's similarly global and materialistic civilization.

America's preeminent visionary lifted the dark veil concealing our ancient Atlanto-Lemurian origins and identity. Perhaps if we look beneath the raised curtain, we may gaze into a mirror reflecting, to our surprise and even dismay, something of the image of our own times.

# 15

# Lost Motherland, Drowned Fatherland

No two peoples could have been more different from each other than those who dominated the Pacific and the Atlantic oceans. It is fitting that the Lemurians resided in the Pacific, in view of Lemuria's gentler society. The Atlanteans were politically extroverted and militaristic; the Lemurians, introverted and pacifistic. Even though the two seaborne civilizations were separated by thousands of miles, their inhabitants were far from unaware of each other. On the contrary, limited contacts had always taken place.

Cayce offers abundant examples of Atlanto-Lemurian relations, all of them cordial, some of them intimate, which more often occurred when Lemurians and Atlanteans happened to meet in overseas lands they both visited, especially Yucatán. He spoke of a time "when the people had come from Lemuria" to Atlantis "for the indwelling of the various activities."[1]

The Lemurians were uninhibited sexual activists whose family ties were loose and not clearly defined—shocking behavior to the devout Edgar Cayce, who shook his head at their perceived immorality. He condemned a "very much perverted activity by those from Mu."[2] Such freewheeling attitudes were part of the legacy passed down to their mixed descendants, the Polynesians, whose sexual behavior was likewise branded "licentious" by Christian missionaries. Freed from the necessity of working to survive because of the superabundance of food and the very hot climate in their homeland, where anything more than seminudity was less than practical, the Mu (as they are still remembered by the Hawaiians and Tibetans) developed a sensible, guiltless sexuality that was regarded merely as an aspect of physical life.

It was in the spiritual arts, however, that the Mu most excelled, even surpassing the skilled adepts of Atlantis, according to Cayce. The Atlanteans achieved "the highest or the greatest advancement in the earthly sojourning of individual entities or souls at that particular period—or the highest that had been save that which had been a part of the Lemurian Age."[3] The soul practitioners of first Mu and then Atlantis engaged in mass-meditation sessions involving hundreds, thousands, and occasionally *millions* of participants.

The psychic power generated from these single-minded assemblies went beyond anything experienced before or since. Levitation of otherwise immovable objects, psychokinesis, communal telepathy, remote viewing, metaphysical healing, the shifting of space and time, prophecy, interspecies communication, interdimensional travel—the whole gamut of known psychic phenomena and far more than presently guessed were supposedly developed by the Lemurians and later refined by the Atlanteans. Cayce told a client in 1935 that he once dwelled "in Atlantis during a higher state of civilization, teacher of psychological thought and study, especially that of transmission of thought through ether."[4]

Mass mental telepathy took place in "a great congress" shortly before the final destruction of Atlantis: "In the period when this became necessary, there was the consciousness raised in the minds of the groups, in various portions of the Earth, much in the manner as would be illustrated by an all-world broadcast in the present day of a menace in any one particular point, or in many particular points. And the gathering of those that heeded, as would be the scientific minds of the present day, in devising ways and means of doing away with that particular kind or class of menace."[5]

The Atlanteans were adepts at what would today be called "channeling," or, in the nineteenth century, "spiritualism," as they applied "the concentration of thought for the universal forces, through the guidance or direction of the saints (as would be termed today)."[6] They were masters too of astral projection: "Through the concentration of the group-mind of the Children [Followers] of the Law of One, they entered into a fourth-dimensional consciousness—or were absent from the body."[7] The Atlantean initiates had psychokinesis—the ability to influence physical objects by thought processes—literally down to a science, as Cayce revealed to a client who lived "in Atlantis before the second upheavals, a priestess in the temple through which mystics studied those tenets of the application of spiritual laws to material things."[8]

Common to his readings that describe these abilities are references to regular group activity: "concentration of thought for the use of the universal forces," "the consciousness raised in the minds of the groups," and so forth.[9] The implication here is that the coordinated mental exertion of perhaps thousands of persons, disciplined and working together at the same moment, concentrating all their psychological strength on the same object, generated unimaginatively powerful psychic energy. When focused into their "great, terrible crystal,"[10] the amplification of this energy must have been potent beyond measure—enough, perhaps, to destroy an entire civilization "in a single day and night," as Plato described it.

Cayce's readings suggest just such a psychic cause for the destruction of Atlantis: "In the Atlantean period those peoples gained much in understanding of mechanical laws and application of the night-side of life for destruction."[11] It was particularly because of these alleged paranormal powers that both Atlantis and Lemuria figure into our discussion of the Mayan calendar. While the rational science that went into the Mayan calendar's creation may have been carried to Mesoamerica by adepts from Atlantis, who may have themselves inherited these analytical skills from their Lemurian forebears, the kind of spontaneous prognostications made by Pope Leo X and Edgar Cayce appear to have had their ancient origins among the Lemurians alone, who became more reliant on a subtler intuition of the human subconscious.

Until the late twentieth century, professional archaeologists were virtually unanimous in their conviction that Mu, or Lemuria, was an unrealistic fantasy. Even scholars such as the well-known science fiction author L. Sprague de Camp, who conceded at least to the possibility of a factual Atlantis, perhaps thinking that the ancients had confused it with Minoan Crete or coastal Spain, were adamant that the existence of a Pacific Ocean counterpart was beyond all possibilities. The accidental find made by a diving instructor near Yonaguni, last in the southern chain of Japanese islands, during 1985, however, reopened scientific debate concerning Lemuria.

Kihachiro Aratake's discovery of a stone "citadel" seventy-five feet beneath the surface of the Pacific Ocean attracted the serious attention of certified researchers from around the world. With a few notable exceptions—among them, Boston University's Dr. Robert M. Schoch of Great Sphinx fame—most geologists agree with Professor Maasaki Kimura, commissioned by the University of the Ryukyus to survey the "monument," that the underwater anomaly is not only made by humans, but is at least three thousand years old. Others, such as Canberra's Australian National University Dr. Kurt Lembeck, believe the structure is much older, going back some twelve thousand years to allow for a seventy-five-foot rise in sea levels. Both investigators have dared to use the still controversial, formerly anathematized L-word to describe the sunken "citadel" as Lemurian.

The ruin is not an anomaly, however, because islands scattered throughout Polynesia, Micronesia, Macronesia, and Melanesia are replete with physical evidence in the form of arches, columns, statues, and pyramids—on land, as well as underwater—testifying to a high culture that long ago spanned the Pacific. This abundant, hard proof is richly supported and elucidated by the islanders' own oral accounts. They uniformly recall a huge, prosperous, and powerful kingdom that long ago dominated the ocean until it slipped beneath the waves and its survivors became culture bearers to foreign lands.

*Figure 15.1. Divers investigate a sloping wall at the base of Japan's sunken "monument" off the island of Yonaguni.*

A consistent theme threading these folk traditions stresses the spiritual disciplines mastered by this lost people. They are still often remembered as "sorcerers" adept in using unseen powers for healing, building monumental structures, remote viewing, or envisioning the future. On the Macronesian island of Pohnpei, native explanations for the offshore city of Nan Madol claim its 250 million tons of magnetized basalt were levitated through the air and stacked into place by a pair of brothers— Olisihpa and Olsohpa—magicians from their drowned homeland, Katau Peidi.

Lemuria was known by many different names wherever its representatives influenced the outside world. On Easter Island, it was remembered as Marae Renga. To the Japanese, it is Horai. Native Hawaiians refer to it as Kahiki. These appellations and all the rest were nothing more than various cultural inflections on the same motherland. More important, various oral traditions among outside cultures emphasized the extraordinary paranormal abilities exercised by the Mu.

Other than these persistent myths preserved over generations by folkish memory keepers, the ruins of Nan Madol or Yonaguni are mute witnesses to the special powers allegedly applied in Mu. Our only other possible source for information about them lies with the man who was himself part of that psychic otherworld known only too well to the lost Lemurians.

# 16

# Edgar Cayce's
# Dream of Lemuria

According to Edgar Cayce, "the Andean, or the Pacific coast of South America, occupied then [in predeluge times] the extreme eastern portion of Lemuria."[1] When he made this statement more than seventy years ago, oceanographers knew little of what lay beneath the Pacific. Only recently could they confirm that a subsurface archipelago was connected to the Peruvian coast as dry land until it sank sometime within the past ten thousand years.

With the collapse of the Soviet colossus and consequent end of the Cold War, hitherto secret U.S. Navy surveys of the world's sea floor were declassified and made available to the general public for the first time. California's renowned Scripps Institution of Oceanography at La Jolla used the military data to compile the most detailed and up-to-date series of maps, graphically revealing more than ever before what lay on the bottom of Earth's oceans.

The maps revealed several startling features. Among the most compelling of these was a sunken archipelago identified as the Nazca Ridge. This is a more or less contiguous group of former islands extending in a straight line for some 275 miles southwest from the Peruvian coast at the town of Nazca, south of the capital at Lima, and adjoining another group known as the Sala y Gómez Ridge. It bends almost due west for approximately another 350 miles in the direction of Easter Island. Both ridges were known before the new maps were released, but what the Scripps charts reveal is that they are part of a sunken archipelago that stood as dry land above the ocean in the recent geologic past. In fact, part of the Nazca Ridge is in shallow water, its topmost sections only one hundred feet or less beneath the surface.

Oceanographers now believe that, at least until the close of the last ice age some ten thousand years ago, a large archipelago of closely connected islands stood not far from the shores of Peru and extended into the Pacific more than seven hundred miles. With the discharge of melting ice at the close of the Quaternary Period's glacial phase, some twelve thousand years ago, the latest interval of geologic time, sea levels suddenly rose, deluging the entire archipelago. This appears to be precisely the sunken landmass Edgar Cayce said was part of Lemuria, nearly seventy years before it was identified by science. Although not a continent in a strict geological sense, Mu was indeed "continental" in its far-flung influences and vast cultural extent.

James Churchward, who first popularized the subject in his series of books about Mu in the 1920s, wrote that the aristocracy of Lemuria was white. Indeed, Polynesian legends still speak of white-skinned, fair-haired cultural heroes who fled to the Pacific islands after their homeland sank into the sea. The Chumash Indians of central and southern coastal California, whose name for today's Santa Cruz Island was historically Limu, display many anomalously Caucasian characteristics, such as full beards, not shared with other indigenous Americans. Moreover, these native tribes of white people told of their ancestral arrival from an island that sank into the sea. It also appears that a black population was in residence on Mu, descendants of which migrated westward into Micronesia, where they became today's Negritos. Other black Lemurians journeyed to the Americas, where they participated in Mexico's Olmec civilization and were memorialized by its ancient sculptors. These are the famous stone heads, eleven of which still survive, on display at La Venta Park Museum in Villahermosa, near Veracruz, in eastern Mexico.

Cayce tells us that Lemurians belonging to a brown-skinned lineage were the first of the great horde of strangers to reach Peru. These Lemurians formed the core ethnicity of native Peruvians (as well as of native Polynesians). Later, Peruvians also intermixed with people of Asia, India, and the Americas. Churchward, who published decades before the Cayce material was generally known, likewise stated that a brown-skinned ethnic group resided in the motherland.

Churchward wrote that Mu was subject to a white aristocracy, while Pacific island traditions imply that a theocracy prevailed in the sunken kingdom. In speaking of a client who brought Lemurian political ethics to South America, Cayce said, "The entity gave the peoples those principles of self-government that have gone to the best rule through many, many ages."[2] Later, Cayce addressed another past life in a similar vein: "The entity established much help and assistance to the peoples in that period, giving much understanding of division in a proper manner among the workers and the shirkers, among the well and the ill, the strong and the weak."[3]

Based on these utterances, the well-known writer of Native American subjects Vada F. Carlson concludes in her 1970 book, *The Great Migration,* that Mu was a democratic society not much different from our own. But equating modern democracy with Lemurian government, for whatever reasons, is a mistake.[4] Clearly, Cayce describes for Mu a religious oligarchy or theocracy, a system more reminiscent of Incan socialism. Idealizing the past, especially through the lens of one's own politically correct preferences, is to debase it and lose the truth. We cannot cast some admired, deeply ancient people in our own image without risking the most vulgar kind of self-flattery.

Cayce goes on to say that the Pacific civilization predated Atlantis, but both shared a fundamentally common fate: "Lemuria began its disappearance even before Atlantis, about . . . ten thousand seven hundred light years, or earth years ago."[5]

Cayce seems to be referring to a solar *calendar* ("light years, or earth years"), rather than the speed of light itself. The destruction of Mu begins to date, then, from around the year 8700 BCE. Let's take a closer look at this life reading. Cayce explains, "Lemuria *began* [author's italics] its disappearance" in 8700 BCE. It is entirely conceivable—and, in fact, far more likely, geologically—that the process of total submersion took millennia to complete. If we acknowledge this interpretation of Cayce's date, together with the archaeological evidence at Peru and Yonaguni, then Lemuria emerges as possibly the world's first civilization, antedating even Atlantis, with whom it was at least partially contemporaneous.

"According to Churchward," Carlson writes, "Mu was a continent in the Pacific. There were, he writes, four great cataclysms, the first taking place in the Miocene era, about eight hundred thousand years ago; the second and less violent episode about two hundred thousand years ago; and the greatest about eighty thousand years ago. A fourth and final event was the catastrophe of twelve thousand years ago that sent Mu and millions of her people to the depths in a 'vortex of fire and water.'"[6]

Carlson here confuses the Theosophists of Madame Blavatsky, Scott-Elliot, and their associates, whose version of Mu went back hundreds of thousands of years, with James Churchward, who while a colonel with the British army in India during the early 1870s learned from native sources about Mu. Indeed, his first book on the subject is titled *The Lost Civilization of Mu*. In it, he relates that the Motherland was destroyed around 10,000 BCE when some sixty-four million inhabitants perished in a natural catastrophe of tremendous violence. His prime sources were Hindu monastery inscriptions, the literal translation of which he used for the basis of his conclusions.

Comparisons of the archaeological record and oral tradition with Edgar Cayce's life readings do more than establish the Sleeping Prophet's credibility. They demonstrate that lost Lemuria was a real place, the motherland of humankind, as it was earlier characterized by James Churchward.

# 17

# He Saw Atlantis

In a five-thousand-year-old Sumerian account known as *The Epic of Gilgamesh,* the teller of the tale about escaping a great deluge, Utnapishtim, is described in the second half of the hero's story: "He was wise. He saw mysteries and knew secret things. He brought us a tale of the days before the Flood."[1]

The same might be said of Edgar Cayce, who told of three major periods of inundation that afflicted Atlantis. The single natural disaster described by Plato, which appears to have taken place in the late fourth millennium BCE, was a final destruction that came after the upheavals cited in Cayce's life readings. A combination of the Plato and Cayce material supports, therefore, the four global catastrophes defined by the Mēxihcah, Hindu, Persian, and other traditions. A typical life reading that mentions a time of upheaval took place in 1933, when Cayce told a client that he once dwelled "in the Atlantean land before the third destruction."[2]

Researchers since then have discerned three decisive geologic episodes in the history of an Atlantic island that originally was roughly the size of modern Spain. The first seismic unrest dropped much of its territory beneath sea level, followed several millennia later by renewed geologic violence, which sank the remaining dry land, save for the tops of its tallest mountains. These volcanic peaks became known in historic times as Madeira, the Azores, and the Canary Islands. Atlas was another volcanic peak, on which the city of Atlantis arose. The ultimate destruction of Atlantis took place when Mount Atlas detonated, hollowed itself out with ferocious eruptions, then collapsed into the sea.

Present interpretation of this evidence confirms the accuracy of Cayce's clairvoyant view of the Atlantean catastrophe. He said, "the destruction of this continent and the peoples was far beyond any of that as has been kept as an absolute record, that record in the rocks still remains."[3]

Cayce's account of major geologic upheavals in ancient times was verified by a 1958 doctoral dissertation presented to the Association for Research and Enlightenment titled "Earth Changes." After comparing fifty representative examples of Cayce's life readings dealing with planetary upheavals to modern knowledge of the Earth sciences, the dissertation concludes:

> Most of the readings on prehistorical subjects were given in the 1920s and 1930s, and were all on file before 1945. It is thus clear that the majority of the psychic statements antedate nearly all of the striking discoveries recently made by such youthful fields of scientific endeavor as deep-sea research, paleomagnetic research and research on the absolute age of geologic materials. Whereas the results of recent research sometimes modify or even overthrow important concepts of geology, they often have the opposite effect in relation to the psychic readings, in that they tend to render them more probable.[4]

Atlantologists have also had to catch up with Cayce's visionary grasp of the lost civilization's geologic past. His clairvoyant understanding of ancient Earth changes and their specific bearing on the fate of Atlantis explain the mass migration of its refugees across North Africa into Egypt. Skeptics long contended that such migrations through the vast expense of the Sahara Desert would not have been possible, but Cayce said, "What is now the Sahara was an inhabited land and very fertile."[5]

At the time of this utterance in 1932, geologists were certain that the Sahara Desert was at least several million years old and that living conditions there were no less hostile those many ages ago than they are at present, precluding any form of human habitation. Yet by 1955 the first extensive subsurface testing in the desert retrieved core samples proving the Sahara was indeed fertile enough to support herds of cattle as recently as 3000 BCE. Only in the centuries following did North Africa begin to lose its battle with the inexorable sands.

Almost simultaneous with these geologic revelations, archaeologists discovered the first evidence of a nomadic people who inhabited the Sahara and shared numerous points in common with the dynastic culture of Egypt. These civilized desert dwellers, or travelers, appear to have been the pharaonic Egyptians' own immediate ancestors, who migrated eastward into the Nile Valley from the seismic chaos of their Atlantean homeland, just as Cayce described.

No pyramids have yet been discovered in the Sahara, nor are any likely to be found there, because the wandering refugees from Atlantis probably recognized that the gradually desiccating conditions were increasingly unsuited to permanent habitation. During the late fourth millennium BCE, the desert was winning its struggle over the retreating fertile plains, with a consequent decline in the herds of bison and cattle that once roamed its grasses.

But the passing Atlanteans left their mark there too. Illustrations at Jabbaren and Aouanrhet in southeast Algeria, painted with the same red ochre the Egyptians used in their temple wall murals, show women wearing wreaths and headdresses identical to their Nile counterparts. The girls pictured with Egyptian facial features and blond hair at Tassili-n-Ajjer, a vast mountain range in Algeria that borders Libya and Niger, wear Egyptian robes, including Wadjet tiaras. (Wadjet was a cobra goddess, protector of the Lower Nile.) The figures are poised with worshipful gestures (their hands with raised palms in the Egyptian manner) before animal-headed deities commonly represented throughout the Nile Valley. The deities portrayed most often are the lion, falcon, and cow, which sports a lunar disk between her horns.

In the Egyptian religion, these beasts were Sekhmet, the goddess of fiery destruction, associated with the Atlantean disaster by twentieth-dynasty Egyptians; Heru (or Horus), the god of kingship, personifying the pharaoh's royal soul; and Mehurt (also known as Hathor and Mistress of the West), a goddess of the sky, joy, fertility, motherhood, and foreign lands. This trio composed a most ancient set in the Egyptian pantheon, all of them predynastic and said to have arrived "from the West." Interestingly, Mehurt means, literally, "the Great Flood."

The pastoralists, as archaeologists have come to refer to these Atlanteans in transit across the Sahara, practiced deformation of cattle horns, a curious custom shared only with the Egyptians, and employed animal breeding procedures used along the Upper Nile. Clearly, these refugees were the people Cayce envisioned when he spoke of the Sahara as fertile and inhabited by survivors migrating from the destruction of Atlantis into the Nile Valley.

Dynastic Egypt itself began quite suddenly with the arrival from the west of a technologically advanced people as told by the pioneering British archaeologist W. B. Emery. Known as the *Semsu-Hr* (Followers of Horus) and the *Mesentiu* (Harpooners), they came equipped with all the features of a full-blown civilization. Prior to their momentous arrival, the Nile Valley was sparsely populated by Neolithic tribes of indifferent farmers and artless potters who dwelled in mud-thatch huts and eked out a subsistence living on the riverbanks. Their lands were transformed virtually overnight by the creation of monumental architecture; complex, massive irrigation systems; a government hierarchy; divisions of labor; an institutionalized religion; visual arts of a high order; navigation; a written language; astronomy; geometry; surveying; a standardization of weights and measures—in short, all the elements of a culture that had already witnessed a long period of development elsewhere.

The advanced society that rapidly took root in the sands of Egypt was not merely some transplanted civilization, however. It was instead the outcome of native cultures blended with the genius of the arriving Followers of Horus and the Harpooners. This standard view of dynastic beginnings as a synthesis of foreign and domestic influences interacting during the late fourth millennium BCE is illustrated by a life reading Cayce made for a client who was "in Egypt at a time of coalition of natives, king, priest, Atlanteans, etc. Entity among natives in authority as counselor to various groups and historian of that to be preserved, native and Atlantean."[6]

The seafaring Semsu-Hr and Mesentiu are echoed in the life reading of a client who was "among those who came from Atlantis to Egypt in command of the fleets or ships, explored along waterways."[7] The beginnings of the Harpooners' civilizing efforts are clear when Cayce read for a man who was "among the Atlanteans who came into Egypt for preserving records and promises of Atlantean development."[8] The guiding leadership of the Followers of Horus and the Harpooners appears in a later reading: "Before that, the entity was in the Egyptian land among the Atlanteans who came in with those peoples in authority. For there the entity was one who personally cared for the records that were brought by the leaders of that people [the Atlanteans] for preservation in that portion of man's experience in the Earth."[9]

In his 1984 examination of Egypt's Great Pyramid, researcher William Fix stated that its internal chambers were places for rites of passage and initiation into the mystery religion of the human soul's rebirth after death. More than fifty years before, Edgar Cayce spoke of "the pyramid of initiation, where the opening of the records would come, that are as copies from the sunken Atlantis."[10] In 1941 he addressed another client as "the entity in the Atlantean and Egyptian lands—among those who came into the Egyptian experience for preserving the records of those activities—became a supervisor of the excavations—in studying the old records and in preparing and building the house of records for the Atlanteans, as well as a part of the house of initiate—or Great Pyramid."[11] Cayce told another client in 1942 that he once "aided the priest in the preparation of the manner of building the temple of records that lies just beyond that enigma that still is the mystery of mysteries to those who seek to know what were the manners of thought of the ancient sons who made man, beast."[12] Cayce's reference to "that enigma" and the man, made beast describe the Great Sphinx, an identification made all the more clear by its position "just beyond" the Great Pyramid, "the temple of records."

Even here, we find revealing details in Cayce's readings that point out the reality and accuracy of his statements. In a 1933 session with a client, he spoke of "the Sphinx, that was set later as the sentinel or guard."[13] Appropriately, the Egyptian word for the Sphinx was *Hu,* or "guardian." Of course, Egypt was not the only land settled by immigrants from Atlantis: "With the realization of the Children [Followers] of the Law of One that there was to be the final breaking up of the Poseidian-Atlantean lands, there were the emigrations with many leaders to the various lands."[14]

A life reading in 1934 told how his client "set sail for Egypt, but ended up in the Pyrenees in what are now Portuguese, French and Spanish lands."[15] The same period of eastern migration is described for another client who lived "in Atlantean land of Poseidian peoples when there was the breaking up of the land, among those who came first to the Pyrenees and then to Egypt, active in preserving records."[16] These migrations to the Pyrenees took place after the earliest geologic upheavals: "With this also came the first egress of peoples to the Pyrenees."[17]

The Pyrenees are mentioned in Cayce's life readings more often than any other area settled by the Atlanteans: "Evidences of this lost civilization are to be found in the Pyrenees"; "among Atlanteans who first came to Egypt, journeyed to what is now a portion of Portugal or the Pyrenees, where some Atlanteans had set up temple activity, aided in decorations of temple"; "in Atlantis at time of disputes when many sent to many lands, a mathematician, came to Pyrenees"; "came to Egypt from Pyrenees land, hence came with latter portion of those from the Atlantean land."[18]

Cayce sometimes identified Atlantis by an unusual name—Og. He could hardly have known in his waking state that Og had been used in different cultures to describe Atlantis, including the Scotch-Irish Tír na nÓg (Land of the Young), whose inhabitants caused a world-class flood; or Homer's Ogygia, an Atlantean isle visited by the hero Odysseus; or King Ogyges, the deluge survivor in Greek myth. There's even an Old

Testament reference to Og, who clung to the superstructure of Noah's Ark during the Flood.

The sheer number of Cayce's insights into the destiny and even precise location of the lost civilization have convinced many of its leading investigators that he was absolutely prophetic in 1941, when he said that it will "rise again" near the small Bahamian island of Bimini. It was there, in fact, that a 1,250-foot-long organized arrangement of square, pillowlike stone blocks arranged along the ocean floor just nineteen feet beneath the surface of the Atlantic and fifty-five miles due east from Miami, Florida, was accidentally found long after the Sleeping Prophet's death.

Attempts to dismiss the Bimini Road as nothing more than a natural formation of beach rock have been thoroughly undone by more than twenty years of on-site investigations led by underwater archaeologists William Donato (of Buena Vista, California) and Dr. Gregory Little (with the Association for Research and Enlightenment, Virginia Beach, Virginia).

They unquestionably established that the configuration was made by humans by, for example, revealing the stones' unnatural relationship to Bimini's shoreline; retrieving core samples from some stones demonstrating they are not native to the Bahamas; discovering Bronze Age anchor stones at the site; showing the artificial placement of one block upon another; and comparing the site's close resemblance to typical Bronze Age harbor works in the eastern Mediterranean Sea

These archaeological finds show that the Bimini Road was actually a walled breakwater or quay belonging to a docking facility of the kind built to accommodate ships in the ancient Old World, three thousand and more years ago. Stylistic comparisons with Bronze Age maritime engineering are supported by Bimini geology, which indicates that sea levels during the middle to late second millennium BCE were low enough for the site to have served as a harbor. These discoveries strongly suggest that during round-trip voyages from Europe to North America, Bimini was the last landfall for sailors in need of provisions, particularly fresh water, which is available in abundance on the limestone island.

In 1933, long before these disclosures came to light from the late 1980s to the early twenty-first century, Edgar Cayce spoke of "the sunken portion of Atlantis, or Poseidia, where a portion of the temples may yet be discovered under the slime of ages of sea-water . . . near what is known as Bimini, off the coast of Florida."[19] Eight years later, he told how "Poseidia will be among the first portion of Atlantis to rise again. Expect it in '68 and '69. Not so far away."[20]

A civilian pilot on a routine flight from Nassau happened to pass over the northern point of Bimini just as the sun's rays, instead of reflecting off the surface of the water as they usually do, momentarily penetrated the depths to reveal what appeared to him as a paved highway going across the bottom of the Atlantic Ocean. After landing in Miami Beach, he filed his report, inadvertently setting in motion the first of numerous diving expeditions to the Bimini Road. The year was 1968.

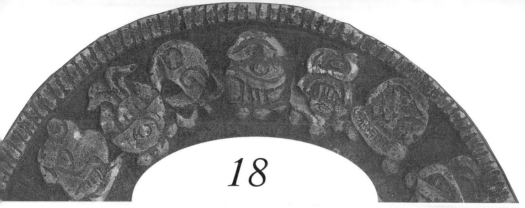

# *18*

# The Terrible,
# Mighty Crystal

Among Edgar Cayce's most controversial life readings are those describing a high technology developed and used by the people of Atlantis. Mainstream scholars are adamant that nothing resembling the modern physical sciences existed during preindustrial times, to say nothing of the ancient world. While praising the material greatness of the Atlanteans, Plato has nothing to say about any futuristic powers they may have possessed.

Cayce nonetheless tells of an electronic quartz crystal technology developed and mastered in Atlantis: "There were those destructive forces brought through the creating of the high influences of the radial activity from the rays of the Sun, that were turned upon the crystals into the pits that made for the connections with the internal influences of the earth."[1] And later, he mentions "the principles of the stone upon the spheres . . . these brought destructive forces."[2] "Both constructive and destructive forces were generated by the activity of the stone."[3]

"It was in the form of a six-sided figure," he explains, "in which the light appeared as the means of communication between infinity and finite; or the means whereby there were the communications with those forces from the outside [outer space?]. Later, this came to mean that from which the energies radiated, as of the center from which there were the radial activities guiding the various forms of transition or travel through those periods of activity of the Atlanteans."[4] Cayce goes on to say:

> The building above the stone was oval, or a dome, wherein there could be or was the rolling back, so that the activity of the stone was received from the sun's rays or from the stars; the concentrating of the energies that emanate from bodies that are on fire themselves— with the elements that are found in the earth's atmosphere.
>
> The concentration through the prisms or glass, as would be called in the present, was in such a manner that it acted upon the instruments with various modes of travel, through induction methods— [like radio-controlled drones] in the present day; the force from the stone acted upon . . . the crafts themselves.
>
> There was the preparation so that when the dome was rolled back there might be little or no hindrance in the application directly to the various crafts that were to be impelled through space, whether in the radius of the visioning of the one eye, as it might be called, or whether directed underwater or under other elements or through other elements. The preparation of this stone was in the hands only of the initiates at the time.[5]

Cayce speaks of "a crystal room" in Atlantis, where "the tenets and the truths or the lessons that were proclaimed by those that had descended to give the messages as from on High" were received by the initiates of a mystery cult. They "interpreted the messages that were received through the crystals."[6] Furthermore, he says, "The preparation of this stone was solely in the hands of the initiates at the time."[7]

Some of Cayce's clients were privy to these mysteries: "In Poseidia [Atlantis] the entity dwelt among those that had charge of the motive forces from the great crystals that so condensed the lights, the form of the activities—in conveniences of the body, as television and recording voice."[8] He describes another client as "active in recording messages and directing those forces. These were not only the rays from the sun, amplified by crystals, but were the combinations of these."[9]

None of this made scientific sense in the 1930s, nor could it have until the advent of the crystalline silicon chip nearly fifty years later. IBM's second-quarter stockholders report for 1989 echoes Cayce's life readings on the Atlantean crystals: "A crystal 'memory chip' has recently been invented by a German firm," informed Cayce's son, Edgar Evans, "that contains more than four million bits of information."[10]

Referred to also as the "firestones," the crystals of Atlantis were supposed to have had certain curative powers: "Through the same form of fire the bodies of individuals were regenerated; by burning—through application of rays from the stone—the influences that brought destructive forces to an animal organism. Hence, the body often rejuvenated itself."[11]

He speaks too of the "high influence of radial activity from the rays of the sun that were turned on the crystals." These produced "the super cosmic ray that will be found in the next twenty five years."[12] As he predicted, lasers were invented (reinvented?) around 1960. An article at the time in the *Physical Review* describes the basic principle of the laser in almost Atlantean terms: "The amplification is achieved by storing up energy in a small insulating crystal of special magnetic properties. The release of energy is triggered off by an incident signal, so that the crystal passes on more energy than it receives."[13]

The crystals of Atlantis themselves were beyond good and evil, according to Cayce: "About the firestone—the entity's activities then made such applications as dealt both with the constructive as well as the destructive forces in that period."[14] In the hands of well-meaning initiates, they were repositories for important information and survival tools for healing. But Cayce maintains that Atlantis in its final days was torn by internal discord. Struggle between two factions eventually focused on possession of the powerful crystals. Somehow, the Sons of Belial wrested them from their keepers, the "Followers" of the Law of One (as Cayce describes them), probably through seductive appeal to materialist weaknesses, and, as Plato writes, "human nature got the upper hand."[15]

Cayce, in fact, told a client he was "in Atlantean land during those periods when there was the destruction or separations of the land during the period of the first destruction—among those aided in the preparation of the explosives or those things that set in motion the fires of the inner portions of the Earth that were turned into destructive forces." Improperly used for purposes of exploitation and domination, it became "the terrible, mighty crystal; much of this brought destruction."[16] Shades of British Petroleum's Deepwater Horizon!

# 19

# North America's Atlanto-Lemurian Legacy

Oral traditions of the North American Indians are replete with memories describing the arrival of flood survivors from both Mu and Atlantis on the western and eastern shores, respectively, of Turtle Island. Tennessee's Cherokee believe Atali was an ancestral homeland in the Atlantic Ocean overwhelmed by a catastrophic deluge that ended a golden age of prosperity and power. In recounting Hokan-Siouan origins, mythographer Joseph Wherry tells how, "In the dim and distant past, the forebears of many California Indians lived on an island somewhere in the Western Ocean. This island was Elam, and they worshiped the powerful god named Mu."[1]

Cayce's trance-state insights throw an especially illuminating light on these abundant and enduring native accounts. He states:

> In the Atlantean lands, during those periods when there were the beginnings of the exodus, owing to the destructive forces that had been begun by the Sons of Belial, the entity was among the princes of the land that made for the separating of those influences wherein there might be established the journeying to other lands, with the keeping of the records, with the permanent establishments of activities that have become a part of that you call civilization in the present time.

Hence we find the entity making for the establishments in the Yucatan, in what became the Inca, in the North American land, and in what later became the land of the Mound Builders in Ohio; also the establishments of those activities in the upper portion of what is now the eastern portion of the land.[2]

Each of the cultures Cayce mentions—Mesoamerican, Andean, and North American Indian—were rich with accounts of light-skinned visitors from across the sea who arrived following a terrible flood and stayed to rebuild their civilization in cooperation with the native peoples. Likewise, Cayce tells of technologically endowed foreigners making various landfalls along both the Atlantic and Pacific shores of the Americas: "Hence these places partook of the earlier portions of that peoples called the Incal; though the Incals were themselves the successors of those of Og, in the Peruvian land, and Mu in the southern portions of what is now called California and Mexico and southern New Mexico in the United States."[3] Cayce's linking of Mu to southern California and New Mexico is especially pertinent because these states offer some of the best evidence for Lemurian influences in the Americas.

Cayce describes overseas influences in pre-Columbian America arriving from the Gobi Desert, among the most inhospitable places on Earth and utterly disassociated from civilization, ancient or modern. Yet he tells us that a great people once flourished there long ago, before the intolerable conditions for which it is now infamous overwhelmed the formerly fertile land: "There the entity was the priestess. And there may be seen some of those activities that are a part of the awareness to some in that land of Ohio, where there were those plans for such, in the mounds that were called the replica or representative of the Yucatan experience, as well as the Atlantean and the Gobi land. All of these are as open consciousness in the entity's activity."[4]

Natural upheavals did not alone trigger the mass movement of ancient peoples. According to Cayce, "Those in Yucatan, those in the adjoining lands as begun by Iltar, gradually lost in their activities, and came to be that people termed, in other portions of America, the Mound Builders."[5] He correctly recounts the movement of Mayan culture bearers from Yucatán to territories above the Rio Grande, where they were much later recognized as the Mound Builders. A growing number of archaeologists conclude that around 900 CE a large-scale, complex society did indeed leave the lowland regions of Middle America and finally settle in the Mississippi Valley. Here, they re-created their temple pyramids in soil, because stone was not as plentiful. They reinstituted astronomy, agriculture, social organization, and an organized priesthood.

America has always been a cultural melting pot, even in prehistory, as Cayce explains: "Before that we find the entity was in the land of the present nativity, during those periods when there were those peoples came that were known as the Lost Tribes, as well as from Atlantis, Yucatan, the Inca, and the land of On."[6]

A burgeoning richness of physical evidence supports diffusionist researchers, who believe the Americas were influenced by numerous peoples from various parts of the world millennia before Columbus. While Atlantean influences predominated in the early or formative periods of pre-Columbian civilizations, later epochs were touched by much smaller bands of Jews, who arrived in North and Middle America sporadically, as refugees from their numerous enemies. In the second century, after a failed rebellion against the Roman Empire led by Simeon Bar Kochba, "the Hebrews fled across the sea to a land unknown to them before."[7] These belong, in a general sense, to the same people Cayce loosely characterizes as the lost tribes. The Bat Creek Stone, discovered in Tennessee during the 1950s, is inscribed with markings similar to ancient Hebrew and is believed by some investigators to be a remnant of the Bar Kochba revolt. The leader in the inscription is referred to as "a star for the Jews."[8] The "On" Cayce mentions is a reference to Egyptians from a cult center known to the Greeks as Heliopolis, or City of the Sun. Cayce tells us here that survivors of Atlantis, Maya from Yucatán, travelers from South America, Lower Nile Egyptians, and even lost tribe Hebrews contributed to the mound-building culture of North America, which flourished along the Great Lakes, the Ohio River valley, and the Mississippi River valley and its tributaries from about 3400 BCE to the sixteenth century CE. These different influences, with their arrivals widely separated in time, explain the various phases through which that culture passed. Each one of North America's pre-Columbian periods parallels the melding of alien forces with local influences that Cayce states took place in North America: "They were portions of the entity's peoples that were a part of the experiences there of those peoples. For while confusions arose from the tenets of the Hebraic as well as the Atlantean, as well as the Inca, these became centralized or localized in the expressions of those peoples and those groups in that particular period of their activity. Yet the greater blessings that the entity in its activity rendered the people in that experience were in the building of individual homes."[9]

Cayce was particularly insightful in mentioning the corn growing activities of the later Mound Builders:

> The entity was in the land of the present sojourn [Pennsylvania] during the early activities of a peoples that had been banished from Atlantis. The entity was among those of the second generation of Atlanteans who struggled northward from Yucatan, settling in what is now a portion of Kentucky, Indiana, Ohio, being among those of the earlier period known as Mound Builders. Then the entity was among those who supplied to the peoples the fruits of the soil, learning how to crack corn, wheat and grain, that it might be prepared into foods through cooking—though much in those periods was taken raw.[10]

Cayce singles out the Iroquois as "the pure descendants of the Atlanteans."[11] Indeed, virtually every Indian tribe throughout the Americas has its own account of a great flood from which their forebears arrived in a new land. Yet prehistoric influences reached North American shores from a Pacific civilization as well. In 1934, Cayce informed a client that she once lived in that land now known as the American, during the periods when the Lemurian, or the lands of Mu and Zu, were being in their turmoils for destruction. And the entity was among those that—in what is now not far from that land in which the entity in this sojourn first saw the light, that must in the near future fade again into those joinings with the land of Mu—established a temple of worship for those that escaped from the turmoils of the shifting of the earth at that particular period.

The entity, in the name Oeueou, established near what is now Santa Barbara, the temple to the sun and the moon, for the satellite of the moon had not faded then, and there was enjoined as to the entity in the worship as the goddess to the moon and the sun.[12]

The "Zu" Cayce mentions was one of the closely associated islands in a string of Pacific archipelagoes that made up Lemuria. His association of the southern California islands with a Lemurian temple to the sun and moon is extraordinarily poignant, because the Santa Cruz area, as previously mentioned, was known as Limu to the Chumash Indians who dwelled in the region. They shared many aspects of their culture with the Mu, not least of all their worship of the heavenly bodies, particularly the sun and moon, as they were portrayed in surviving rock art and accurately described by Cayce.

In another reading, he tells of a past life

during those periods when the changes that had brought about the sinking of Mu or Lemuria, or those peoples in the periods who had changed to what is now a portion of the Rocky Mountain area: Arizona, New Mexico, portions of Nevada and Utah. The entity was then among the princesses of the land that established there the teachings of the Law of One, from the activities in the land which had brought destructive forces through the separations from those things that made for the love of the individual for the gratifying of selfish motives.

Then the entity established what may be called the home life in that land, as each home became then as the castle or place of worship—or activities that were separated, yet united in one as for purposes. The name then was Ouowu.[13]

This reading is especially significant, because the western states Cayce includes in connection with immigrants from Mu—Arizona, New Mexico, Nevada, and Utah—are those same areas where the most dramatic oral traditions about Lemuria are preserved among the Navajo, Paiute, and Shoshone Indians.

Here Cayce shows the continuing effect made on Native American spirituality, which is rooted in the Lemurian arrival:

Uzld was in the land of Og, now known as that of the American plateaus, or in the northern portion of New Mexico and such. The entity was among the peoples who first gave to those people the home and home's influence. The entity was in that land now known as the American during the periods when there were the sojournings of those from the Land of Mu, or Lemuria. The entity was then among the first of those that were born in what is now portions of Arizona and Utah, and among those who established the lands there for the building up or growing up of that civilization [the Anasazi?] in those experiences, and was in the name Uuluoou. The entity led many to a greater understanding of how there might be made the closer relationships with the material things and the spiritual thoughts of the people.[14]

Eventually, culture bearers from both Atlantis and Mu met in North America. An Atlantean named Amelelia who "acted as a priest-ess in the Temple of Light" was one of those, according to Cayce, "who oversaw the activities of the communications between the various lands, as from Om, Mu, the hierarchy land in that now known as the United States, in that particular portion of Arizona and Nevada, that are as a portion of the Brotherhood of those peoples from Mu."[15]

Underscoring Cayce, Carlson points out that "the Kootenay Indians of Washington and British Columbia have a legend stating that their forefathers came to America from 'The Land of the Sun.' 'Land of the Sun' and 'Empire of the Sun' were common names of Mu before its submergence."[16] The Pacific Northwest features a majority of native folk traditions describing ancestral arrivals from Mu. Cayce told a client he "was in that land known as Mu, or the vanished land of the Pacific, the Peaceful, and was among those that journeyed from Mu to what is now Oregon, and there may still be seen something of the worship as set up, in what was the development from that set up by the entity's associates, as the totem, or the family tree. Then the women ruled, rather than the men."[17]

Churchward appears to have correctly interpreted the destruction of Mu from recurring features on several totem poles raised by the Haida Indians of British Columbia. These tall, carved pillars of wood do not actually function as totems because the animals portrayed are often not worshipped. Instead, they are memorial or heraldic devices that preserve and relate in images the mythic-historical past of a particular household or tribe. Sometimes, an eagle attacking a whale is symbolically used as a kind of heraldry to designate the earliest beginnings of a family, whose current members can boast that their ancestors arrived along the Pacific Northwest coast after the flood that destroyed their tribal homeland.

Churchward and Cayce shared the opinion that at least some of these totem poles symbolically depict the demise of Mu (the whale) brought about by the judgment of the Great Spirit (the eagle). Oral histories support their common supposition about the totem poles. For example, the Haida still speak of the Steel-Headed Man, their founder, who arrived on the shores of Canada after a terrible flood that ensued when the whale, Namu, was killed by a sky god, the Thunderbird. Note the "mu" portion of the name Namu, a likely reference to the ancient land.

In the American Southwest, Cayce speaks of a postdeluge civilization still shrouded in mystery: "The entity was among the first that have become known as the cave or cliff dwellers, in that portion now known as Utah, Arizona, Colorado and New Mexico. In those environs and places did the entity make for its activities, in the name, then, Uramm."[18]

Cayce's cliff dwellers were the Anasazi, or the Ancient Enemies, as they were referred to by the Jicarilla Apaches, Navajo, Southern Paiute, and other Southwest tribes. Beginning about 1200 CE, the Anasazi built cities high up in the recessed areas of mountains or in remote valleys, such as Colorado's Mesa Verde. Although their immediate origins are obscure, their *kivas*—circular, ceremonial structures—embodied numerous features of the Omphalos religion practiced in Atlantis. Chief imagery of this Earth Mother mystery cult was the Navel of the World, represented by a natural cave or a subterranean temple signifying the sacred center of existence. In this sanctified precinct rituals for the eternal rebirth of the human soul were enacted. Perhaps like no other building of its kind to have survived from prehistory, the kiva typifies these esoteric principles first enumerated in Atlantis.

The Anasazi (or, at any rate, their shamans) might have had some Atlantean blood flowing through their veins and other links to the past that allowed them to preserve the old mysteries. Or they may have learned them from an even earlier people who had come into direct contact with adepts from Atlantis. In any case, more than a thousand years separate its final destruction from the moment the Anasazi began building their kivas and cliff dwellings.

Cayce sheds some light on another archaeological mystery far to the north:

> We find the entity there made use of the metal known as iron, or the combinations of iron and copper—which have long since been removed from use in the present, or copper so tempered by the use of same with a little of the iron, or in its formation in such a way and manner as to be hardened to the abilities for same to be used much in the way that many of those combinations have been found in the Egyptian, the Peruvian, and portions of the Chaldean lands—and more will be found in the Indo-China city yet to be uncovered.[19]

Plato describes the Atlanteans as great miners and metalsmiths whose national wealth largely depended on the world's highest grade of copper to produce extraordinary bronze. He refers to this superior copper as *orichalcum*. Little known to the general public is America's greatest archaeological enigma; namely, the excavation of at least half a billion pounds of copper ore in a stupendous mining enterprise that began in the Great Lakes region of the Upper Peninsula of Michigan about five thousand years ago. Although the identity of these prehistoric miners is unknown, Menomonee Indian tradition remembers them as the Marine Men—white-skinned, bearded foreigners who sailed out of the east.

Coincidental with the Michigan operations, the Old World Bronze Age began: high-grade copper, never in plentiful supply in Europe, was combined with zinc and tin to produce bronze. Both the American copper mining and the Old World Bronze Age came to a sudden halt in 1200 BCE—also the date for the final destruction of Atlantis, which lay between both continents.

In 1980, archaeologists stumbled upon what may be the world's oldest center for bronze making in northern Thailand. Perhaps Bang Chiang is the place Cayce meant when he said that ancient high-quality metalworking "will be found in the Indo-China city yet to be uncovered." And yet the process he describes of combining copper with iron refers to the lost art of "hardened copper," developed both in the Near East and in prehistoric Michigan. Perhaps another ancient city of the East will soon be found. In any case, if his description of the process is correct, it could unlock a metallurgical secret lost for centuries.

# 20

# Middle American Crucible

In one of his trance-state visions of the ancient past, Edgar Cayce tells a client, "Three thousand years before the Prince of Peace came, these peoples that were of the Lost Tribes, a portion came into this land, infusing their activities upon the peoples from Mu in the southernmost part of that called America, or the United States, and then moved on to the activities in Mexico, Yucatan, centralizing about the spots where the central of Mexico now stands, or Mexico City. Hence there arose through the ages a different civilization, a mixture again."[1]

Here Cayce explains that in about 3000 BCE, Semitic visitors from the Near East arrived in the southern United States—somewhere in the Gulf Coast region—before establishing themselves in what is now Mexico City. Since the middle of the past century, stone sculptures of men with distinctly Semitic countenances have been found associated with Mexico's earliest civilizations. Outstanding examples of fork-bearded people with aquiline noses are on display at La Venta Park Museum in Villahermosa, eastern Mexico, and at Monte Albán, a large archaeological site in the southern Mexican state of Oaxaca.

The earliest surviving documentation of Israel is found in the military records of Merenptah, the fourth ruler of the nineteenth-dynasty, who ruled Egypt from 1213–1203 BCE. It does not seem likely the Jews existed as a people much earlier than the thirteenth century BCE, so their arrival in America five thousand years ago is not credible.

Polychrome restoration of the Mēxihcah Cuauhtlixicalli, House of the Eagle, Eagle Bowl, or Vessel of Time—better, if improperly, known as the Aztec Calendar Stone.

A stone disk engraved with apparent numerical notation may be the earliest known example of the Mesoamerican calendar predicting the end of time on December 21, 2012. The object was discovered outside the important Olmec city of Izapa, where a Mayan inscription referring to that terminal date has been found recently nearby.

Replica of the original, 8-foot sun stone at the Coricancha, or Enclosure of Gold, at the Inca capital of Cuzco. Before its destruction by the Conquistadors, the disk was Peru's equivalent of the Aztec Calendar Stone.

A modern mural in the former Inca capital of Cuzco dramatizes Andean civilization dominated by Inti, the solar god of time. (Photograph by William Donato)

The Bahamas' Bimini Road, 55 miles east of Miami, Florida, is an Atlantean ruin, according to American psychic Edgar Cayce, who predicted its discovery 24 years before the structure was found. (Photograph by William Donato)

The culture of Lemuria was spread across island chains spanning the south-central Pacific Ocean until its people were overwhelmed by a natural catastrophe prior to the final destruction of Atlantis.

Southern Wisconsin's thirteenth-century Pyramid of the Sun at the prehistoric ceremonial center of Aztalan, the Aztecs' ancestral city, from whence they migrated into the Valley of Mexico. Appropriately, the Wisconsin pyramid was oriented by its builders to sunrise of the winter solstice.

The step pyramid at Chichén Itzá, Yucatán's ceremonial center, was dedicated to Kukulcan, the Mayas' Feathered Serpent, a flood hero who escaped the destruction of his homeland across the sea.

Visitors to Mexico's Villahermosa Archaeological Park encounter an Olmec Sky Watcher statue originally dedicated to astronomer-priests in charge of the sacred calendar. (Photograph by Claudete Nicholls)

Visitors at Chichén Itzá's Great Ball Court, below the Temple of the Bearded Man, where the non-Indian profile of Kukulcan, the Mayas' Feathered Serpent, appears inside as a bas-relief. (Photograph by Laura Beaudoin)

This jade mask depicts—as a basis for the Mesoamerican calendar—an Olmec priest in an altered state of consciousness, during which conventional understanding of time dissolves, enabling the human mind to glimpse several possible futures.

Model of an ancient Peruvian astronomer-priest of the kind who preserved a history of four global catastrophes associated with the rise of the Incas. (Photograph by William Donato)

Pachacamac, on the Pacific coast 25 miles southeast of the Peruvian capital at Lima, was pre-Columbian South America's leading oracle. Here, astronomer-priests preserved the secrets of their prophetic calendar. (Photograph by William Donato)

A low stone circle near the shores of Bolivia's Lake Titicaca was erected long before the rise of the Incas by astronomer-priests. From it, they made celestial calculations that went into the Andean calendar. The tower in the background is a chullpa, a mausoleum for the privileged dead. (Photograph by William Donato)

However, archaic Hebrew writing has been found on widely separated artifacts in Tennessee (the Bat Creek Stone), Ohio (the Newark Decalogue Stone), Michigan (the Soper-Savage Collection of inscribed tables), Illinois (Burrows Cave), and New Mexico (Hidden Mountain, Los Lunas). These sites tend to confirm Cayce's statements describing something like lost tribes of Israel in prehistoric North America.

The seafaring skills of the ancients combined with ocean currents acting as maritime highways rendered America a meeting ground of diverse peoples long before the Statue of Liberty was erected at Staten Island. Although the Atlanteans and Lemurians were the first of the civilized peoples to carry their influence to North America, they were followed by visitors from Bronze Age and classical Europe; medieval North Africa; and Asia, including the Near East and India—centuries and even millennia before Columbus.

For example, Carlson writes that "Siguenza y Gongora, a Mexican of the 17th Century, may have been correct when he made the statement that all Indians of the New World were descendants of Poseidon [ruler of Atlantis] and that Poseidon was a great-grandson of Noah."[2] One wonders what led Siguenza y Gongora to conclude that the natives of Mexico were descendants of Atlantis. It is conceivable that he heard Mēxihcah oral traditions of Aztlán, an island in the Atlantic Ocean.

Sometimes, the racial tensions of a bygone epoch echo through successive lifetimes. In speaking of a client who experienced an unaccountable sense of identification with ancient Mexico, Cayce characterizes the Aztecs as conquerors from the north, which is in accord with the archaeological record: "We find the entity in that period when changes took place in what is now known as Mexican country, in the subduing of the peoples as came down from the north [the Aztecs] by those coming up from the south [unknown, more powerful tribes]. The entity was then among those who were put in charge of the subdued people [the Aztecs], from which arose that people now known as Aztecs. [They, the red-skinned group, were] able to use in their gradual development all the forces as were manifest in their individual surroundings, passing through those periods of development."[3]

Aztalan, or the Place Near Water in the language of the local Ho Chunk Indians, was southern Wisconsin's foremost ceremonial center during the thirteenth century. Three palisaded walls interspersed at regular intervals with two-story watchtowers surrounded a trio of earthen pyramids oriented to the sun, moon, and planet Venus. The city of perhaps ten thousand residents led by astronomer-priests was also an important hub for commerce that supplied all of Mesoamerica with copper mined from the Upper Great Lakes region, beginning around 1100 CE and lasting until 1300 CE.

East of Aztalan lies Rock Lake, with its own pyramids—including a delta-shaped platform nine hundred feet long on each side—lying at depths of sixty, forty, and twenty feet beneath the surface. These stone structures are tombs flooded by a river that long ago spilled into the valley, thereby creating today's three-mile-long, figure-8-shaped lake. Aztalan originally straddled both sides the Crawfish River although an archaeological park open to the public since 1960 covers only one-half of the city on its western bank.

After some two hundred years of occupation, Aztalan was abruptly and entirely evacuated, its residents migrating en masse, according to Ho Chunk and Pottawatomie Indian oral traditions, disappearing forever toward the south.

Aztalan's unique history suggests Aztec origins, as they were described to Spanish conquerors in the early sixteenth century. The Aztecs claimed to have originated at Chicomoztoc, the Place of the Seven Caves or the Place of the Seven Wombs, a sacred lake in the far north, where seven related tribes formed a powerful coalition. It was from here that they left as a single group, eventually arriving in the Valley of Mexico, where they conquered and absorbed the high culture of the Mēxihcah.

Chicomoztoc was symbolized in temple art as a spiral, signifying an infant's spiral descent from the womb. Pottery shards at Aztalan were similarly decorated with the sacred spiral motif. Aztalan was abandoned shortly before the Aztecs entered the Valley of Mexico, lending credence to the possibility that the Aztecs inhabited Aztalan.

Cayce was correct in characterizing the arrival of the Aztecs as "the subduing of the peoples as came down from the north by those coming up from the south."[4] The newcomers were indeed suppressed by all other tribes in the Valley of Mexico until they clawed their way to political supremacy, becoming the dominant power in Middle America toward the end of the fourteenth century.

Long before their ascendancy, according to Cayce, religious influences from Atlantis had permanently dyed the cultural fabric of Mesoamerican civilization. For example, he identifies a female client of Atlantean background who "was then a princess in the Temple of the Sun, or the Temple of Light; though others have interpreted it as the Sun."[5] He implies that some worshippers venerated the sun as God incarnate, while initiates into the solar mysteries understood that the sun was only a metaphor for light or enlightenment of the universal consciousness that interpenetrates and orders the universe.

Cayce relates that these Atlantean temples functioned similarly on both sides of the ocean. He spoke of a woman client who "was in the Egyptian land when there were preparations of individuals for activities in other lands. The entity was among those who were prepared in the Temple Beautiful for those activities in what is now Yucatan."[6] This reading is revealing because it shows that people arrived in Yucatán not only as colonists from Atlantis or refugees following the destruction of Poseidia but also as Egyptians who traveled all the way to America for religious purposes.

Atlantean solar spirituality persisted among the Mexican people until the imposition of Christianity. Cayce tells a client that in a past life she was

in Yucatan land, during those periods of the early coming in of those from the western shores, or during the Spanish periods. There the entity was a priestess to the sun-god, who attempted to bring into the experience of her peoples the closer relationships to those peoples through the ability of the entity to depict in drawings, in the markings, upon even the face of nature, as well as upon the walls, the buildings of the peoples, that as would bring awe—and yet an inspirational awe—to so pattern their lives, their activities, as to be acceptable unto the higher influences that are ever creative in the experiences of individuals.[7]

Cayce here describes a woman who served as a priestess of the sun cult in Yucatán at the time of the Spanish Conquest, during the 1520s. He might just as well have been speaking about a practitioner thousands of years before.

Atlantean and Lemurian influences on the formative development of Mesoamerica often surfaced in the life readings of Cayce's clients:

With the leavings of the civilization in Atlantis [in Poseidia, more specifically], Iltar, with a group of followers that had been of the household of Atlan, the followers of the worshippers of the One—with some ten individuals—left this land of Poseidia and came westward, entering what would now be a portion of Yucatan. And there began, with the activities of the peoples there, the development of a civilization that arose much in the same manner as that which had been in the Atlantean land. Others had left the land later, others had left earlier.

There had been the upheavals also from the land of Mu, or Lemuria, and these had their part in the changing, or there was the injection of their tenets in the various portions of the land, which was much greater in extent until the final upheavals of Atlantis, or the islands that were later upheaved, when much of the contour of the land in Central America and Mexico was changed to that similar in outline to that which may be seen in the present.[8]

The late nineteenth-century archaeologist August Le Plongeon spent decades among the jungle ruins of Yucatán, where he discovered many important Mayan altars, one of which Cayce describes in an Atlantean context.

The stones that are circular, that were of the magnetized influence upon which the Spirit of the One spoke to those peoples as they gathered in their service, are of the earliest Atlantean activities in religious service, as would be called today.

The altars upon which there were the cleansings of the bodies [not human sacrifice, for this came much later, with the injection of the Mosaic, and those activities in that area] these were later the altars upon which individual activities—that would today be termed hate, malice, selfishness, self-indulgence—were cleansed from the body through the ceremony, through the rise of initiates from the sources of light, that came from the stones upon which the angels of light, during the periods, gave their expression to peoples.

The pyramids, the altars before the doors of the varied temples' activities, were injections from the people of Mu, and will be found to be separate portions, and that referred to in the scriptures as high places of family altars, family gods, that in many portions of the world became again the injection into the activities of groups in various portions, as gradually there were the turnings of the people to the satisfying and gratifying of self's desires, or as the Baal, or Baalilal activities again entered the peoples respecting their association with those truths of light that came through the gods to the peoples, to mankind, in the earth.[9]

The circular stone altars, which Cayce says belonged to the Atlantean religion, complement Plato's description of spiritually artistic and architectural designs throughout Atlantis, where concentricity dominated stylistic conventions. An altar precisely like the one Cayce describes was in fact discovered, not in Yucatán, but at a highly Atlantean site in western Italy, in a subterranean temple built 2,500 years ago by the Etruscans, near Lake Bolsena. Etruria is specifically cited in Plato's account as having been occupied by the Atlanteans, who brought the same kind of circular stone altars to Yucatán.

These artifacts belonged to a rich cultural legacy the Maya inherited from Atlantis, according to Cayce, after the island kingdom had been obliterated by a global cataclysm. His vision was paralleled by the words of an oracular jaguar priest in chapter 5 of the *Books of Chilam Balam,* a collection of calendrical, herbal, medical, astrological, cosmological, and historical texts: "The world was flooded and the sky fell upon the Earth. When the destruction and annihilation had been accomplished, the spirits of the Bacab began to re-organize the people of Maya."[10]

As described in chapter 4 here, Bacabs were pairs of long-bearded men supporting the sky with upraised hands. The Atlas-like Bacabs mentioned in the *Books of Chilam Balam* may represent the Atlanteans arriving in Middle America. Mexican archaeologists have associated the postdeluge appearance of the Bacabs in Guatemala with the foundation date of the Maya and the start of their calendar on August 10, 3114 BCE.

That Cayce envisioned all this decades before mainstream archaeologists made their discoveries lends potent credence to his prophetic statements.

# 21

# The Inca's Atlanto-Lemurian Heritage

According to Edgar Cayce, survivors of the Atlantean catastrophe fled not only to Mexico but beyond to South America.

> In the one life before this, we find the entity in the days of the peoples coming from the waters in the submerged areas of the southern portion as is now of Peru, when the earth was divided, and the people began to inhabit the Earth again. The entity was among those who succeeded in gaining the higher ground and then in the name of [which was changed afterward] Omrui, and changed to Mosases, for the entity became the ruler and the guide, or the patriarch of that age and gave much assistance to the few as were gathered about the entity.[1]

Cayce's description of immigrants from lost Atlantis seeking refuge in South America is also found in a native oral tradition recounted by the early-twentieth-century explorer Alexander Braghine: "The Paraguayan and Brazilian Guaranys possess a cycle of legends concerning their national hero, Tamanduare, who, with his family, was the only survivor spared by the catastrophe which destroyed 'The City of the Shining Roofs.'"[2]

The Inca themselves were proud to trace their lineage back to their own version of the Guaranys' Tamanduare: At-ach-u-chu, the tall, red-haired, bearded, fair-skinned culture bearer from a distant land in the east who arrived on the shores of Lake Titicaca after surviving some terrible deluge. He was remembered as the Teacher of All Things, who in South America established the arts of civilization, including agriculture, religion, astronomy, weights and measures, social organization, and government. At-ach-u-chu was the eldest of five brothers, who were known collectively as Wiracochas, or "white men."

At-ach-u-chu is better remembered by his title, Kon-tiki-Wiracocha, or White Man of the Sea Foam—in other words, a foreigner who arrived by ship, *sea foam* being a poetic description of its bow wave. All features of this supremely important figure in Andean tradition, beginning with the *At* in the beginning of his name, clearly define him as the leader of survivors from the final destruction of Atlantis, who reestablished themselves by creating a hybrid civilization, a mix of local cultures with Atlantean technology, in Peru and Bolivia.

At-ach-u-chu, who resembles similarly fair-faced culture bearers appearing after a great natural disaster in the Atlantic Ocean, is an Andean version of the Aztecs' Quetzalcoatl and the Maya's Kukulcan. These related founding heroes from over the sea apparently represent the effect native peoples experienced from the large-scale arrival of Atlantis refugees.

The South American At-ach-u-chu appears to derive from Atcha, known to the ancient Egyptians as a far-off, splendid, but vanished city echoing lost Atlantis. At-ach-u-chu could mean "the Man from Atcha." In any case, Cayce seems to have had At-ach-u-chu in mind when he told a client he "was in the Atlantean land when there were those periods of the last upheavals, or the disappearance of the isles of Poseidia. The entity was among those groups into what later became known as the Inca. For the entity was then in the line of the house of Inca, and was the mother of an Inca in the Peruvian land, as called in the present."[3]

The combination of Atlantis and South America turn up in other readings as well. Cayce says of another female client that she "was in the Inca land when there had been the journeyings of the Atlantean peoples for setting up what later came to be known as the Incal activities. There the entity was a companion of the one that had acted in the capacity of a leader in setting up the customs, rituals and activities in that land following the destruction of Atlantis."[4] A year before his death, Cayce told a client that he "was among those that went from the Atlantean land to what is the Peruvian or Inca land."[5]

The South American continent, however, is also washed by the Pacific Ocean, which brought its own human influences to bear on the development of Andean civilization. Cayce states: "In this experience the entity was a priestess in those interpretations of what later became known as the Incals, the Lost Tribes, the people from the Atlantean land, and the people . . . from the Lemurian land."[6] We should find Cayce neither confusing nor vague when describing simultaneous influences in Peru from Atlantis and Lemuria. South America lay between these oceanic powers, which were, after all, contemporaneous, so detecting both Atlantean and Lemurian themes in Andean civilization is not contradictory or even surprising.

As Cayce says of another client, "The entity was among those that were to become the emissaries or the sojourners in what is now the Incal land, or the Peruvian land. Later from that sojourn the entity came to what is now the Central American land, aiding in the establishing not only of the tenets but the manners and the forms of worship during those sojourns. The entity was among the princesses of the land, not only of the Atlantean, but of the Ohlm and Og lands, and later Muri [Mu]."[7]

This is a particularly interesting reading because Cayce, apparently oblivious to his own words, seems to be tracing the movements of "the entity" from Atlantis into Peru and beyond to Lemuria. It is a credible sequence of events that complements everything known about these three ancient, interrelated civilizations. It also demonstrates the supposition, held by many investigators, that Atlanteans and Lemurians were not unknown to one another. For example, Churchward repeats a Lemurian tradition that the figure deified in Egypt as Osiris was actually a mortal Atlantean who journeyed to Mu, where he learned the esoteric principles associated with his name.[8]

Cayce says that a man who came to him "was among those that

were the leaders of the Ohums [an earlier people, any one of the several cultures that preceded the Incas] where there was the breaking up of the deeps, and the land disappeared and reappeared."[9] Here Cayce implies a rise and fall of sea level, precisely the fluctuation that did indeed take place over thousands of years following the last ice age, when Cayce says Mu was lost and the underwater structures at Okinawa were covered.

Among the wonderful surprises found throughout the life readings are numerous details that are small but conspicuous for their accuracy. These little gems go far to establish that Cayce was indeed in contact with some alternative source of information beyond other human beings. A case in point is his reference to the Inca, who built "walls across the mountains."[10] Although their construction achievements were generally appreciated in Cayce's lifetime, no one knew of any walls they may have built in the Andes until more than twenty years after his death. During the late 1960s, the first reports of what newspapers immediately dubbed "the Great Wall of Peru" were published. Winding its way through jungle and around some of the highest peaks in South America, the stone structure has been dated by archaeologists to Incan builders in the mid-fifteenth century. Its full extent is still unknown, but investigators believe it may be at least several miles long. The portions that have been discovered are essentially intact.

The Inca also excelled in the production of textiles to a degree far greater than any other pre-Columbian people, a skill reflected in a Cayce life reading: "In the one before this we find [the entity] in the Peruvian country, now known, in the days of the first Incal, as known. [The entity was] then the one who gave the first of the draperies to the temples of that period, and the entity lost in that period of experience through self-aggrandizement of position held. The urge as is seen is the love of fine linen and as any work raised as figures on cloth, and the entity sees beauty in any raised figures in such, and often wonders why."[11]

As Cayce suggests, there was also a dark side to the intermingling of native Peruvians with the Atlantean newcomers.

Then, with these destructive forces, we find the first turning of the altar fires into that of sacrifice of those that were taken in the various ways, and human sacrifice began. With this also came the first egress of peoples to that of Pyrenees first, of which later we find that peoples who enter into the black or mixed peoples, in what later became the Egyptian dynasty.

We also find that entering into the Og, or those peoples that later became the beginning of the Inca, or Ohlum, that built the walls across the mountains in this period, through those same usages of that as had been taken on by those peoples; and with the same, those that made for that in the other land, became first those of the mound dwellers, or peoples in that land. In the one [life], then, before this we find [the entity] in that land known as the Peruvian, and when there was the end of the Ohums and their rule over the land. The entity [was] then among those of the first people who brought in the sun worship to that land.[12]

Cayce continues: "The entity was among those that came from the Atlantean lands and gave the peoples much of the impulse of the added forces in a practical building up of the material things of life, as pertaining to court hangings, ritualistic forces, even to that of the offering of human sacrifice, for the entity was the first high priestess to the sun of that land, making the first human sacrifice in that period."[13]

Cayce's description of the Atlanteans as worshippers of a sun god is also found in the writings of a sixth-century BCE Greek mythologist. Hesiod writes that a previous civilization he referred to as an *oikumene* (from which our word *ecumenical* derives) established itself worldwide. It flourished in an age of gold, but the "gold" Hesiod mentions was the gold of the sun, which was adored as a god. Like all religions, this solar cult had its esoteric and exoteric aspects. While the uneducated masses believed the star around which our planet revolves was quite literally God himself, initiates into the solar mysteries understood that the sun was a metaphor for spiritual principles of enlightenment.

Yet the suggestion of human sacrifice adds an unsettling factor, as

Cayce relates: "The one life before this we find in that land now known as the Peruvian, and the entity was then among those who—as a high priestess—led a people into a northern land now known as Yucatan, and the entity was the priestess in the temple as builded there. . . . In this experience the entity was rather the sun worshipper and the taker of blood."[14]

There is no evidence, either in the Cayce readings or from more conventional sources, for human sacrifice in Atlantis itself. The practice was doubtless common enough among Native Americans long before the Atlanteans arrived. While it reached monstrous proportions under the Aztecs, who degenerated into cannibalism, human sacrifice was far less prevalent among the Andean civilizations, especially under the Inca. They appear to have employed it on relatively rare occasions.

William H. Prescott (1796–1859), the first American scientific historian, told of an infrequent ceremony in which the most beautiful girl and boy were chosen from among all the children of the community, dressed in the finest clothes and precious ornaments, and paraded in public on raised thrones with great pomp and honor. Afterward, they were given a powerful narcotic, then ritually killed while deep in sleep, usually by a single blow to the head. In recent years the preserved remains of Inca and possibly pre-Inca children or young adults have been found on the cold, dry mountaintops of the Andes, where they were deliberately exposed to death surrounded by rich offerings. The motives behind these human sacrifices and those occurring in Mesoamerica are entirely different. The Inca offered to God the most precious things they knew—their loveliest children.

Conversely, the Aztec aristocrats employed the spectacle of ritualized human sacrifice to overawe the Indian masses, to terrorize them into submission and obedience. The cosmic consequences of such imbalanced behavior, Cayce maintains—and the Maya would have concurred—were the precipitous downfall of pre-Columbian civilization and the virtual extermination of its peoples.

# 22

# Edgar Cayce's
# Atlanteans and Lemurians

Historians and archaeologists can tell us much about Atlantis and Lemuria—the appearance of their temples and palaces, their wars, their colonies, and their final destruction—but what about the people, the individuals, great and small, who were part of this tremendous drama? They seem utterly lost to even the best scholars bent on resuscitating the vanished civilization.

Only Edgar Cayce restores them in the life readings of those who came to him for help with spiritual, personal, and emotional problems. He was able to show many of his clients that the roots of their difficulties lay in the deeply ancient past, among energies reverberating down through subsequent incarnations from Atlantean times. As such, his readings are all in the nature of therapy, not history.

In tracing these unsuspected influences from a former time, so long ago, Cayce often describes his clients in their lives as men and women of Atlantis and Lemuria. He thereby sheds an absolutely unique light on the inhabitants—frequently the movers and shakers of society—who shared a great and terrible destiny. Nowhere else in all the twenty thousand books and magazine articles written about these lost worlds may we learn so much about the individual human beings who lived and died there, or fled their homeland's violent demise to become survivors in foreign lands, contributing thereafter not only to their own subsequent incarnations but also to the development of all humankind. In these personalized life readings, Edgar Cayce appears to fulfill the words of Roman emperor Claudius, in 54 CE: "The men and women who laid the foundations of this world are gone, but their voices echo in the words of our great interpreters of the past."[1]

The following names Cayce recalls are heavily weighted toward Atlantis because he describes or mentions far fewer Lemurians than Atlanteans, perhaps due to the more serious karmic consequences he says were generated by the latter people, which, more than historical concerns, interested him. Originally the inhabitants of Atlantis, as both Cayce and Plato concur, were a virtuous people who developed several spiritual disciplines and whose principles influenced the development of religions throughout the world, down to the present time.

The Atlanteans, however, eventually succumbed to the lure of self-indulgence, and they largely turned away from the gods. A reaction against this decline arose in the monotheist Followers of the Law of One, who were opposed by the aggressively materialist Sons of Belial. In the midst of their confrontation, Atlantis suffered the sudden catastrophe that utterly destroyed the land. Individual decisions and actions produced by this drama resulted in effects reverberating down the millennia through numerous lifetimes.

The Lemurians had fewer soul complexities to work out. They did not undergo the internal stress of religious turmoil, and the loss of their homeland was less traumatic. Their society did not decline and degenerate because it was not progressive. Atlantis was an advancing technological state cut in the style of modern Western civilization and was therefore caught in the inescapable cycle of growth, strength, prosperity, stagnation, decline, degeneration, and extinction. The Lemurians were not bound by this cycle. They cared far less for material wealth or indefinite progress. Their chief focus as a religious society (similar to today's Tibetans) was spiritual enrichment. The gentler demise of their islands seemed less a cataclysmic judgment than a catalyst for the dispersement of their piety to other parts of Earth.

As such, the Lemurians incurred less karmic debt, resulting in fewer confused souls for Cayce to heal.

The selected life readings that follow illuminate characters who played their roles in the separate but parallel dramas of the deep past. Cayce also refers to myths and traditions of peoples affected by the Atlanteans and Lemurians, which sheds light on the origin of concepts and the blending of cultures in the ancient past. Furthermore, the life stories presented here illuminate how the forgotten men and women of those lost places of long ago contribute to the destiny of those living in the modern world.

# A

**Aahuen**    An Atlantean religious scientist, Aahuen was "persuaded" by political leaders to assist in the misuse of spiritual energies for material purposes. The experiment was unsuccessful, culminating in the obliteration of Atlantis.

**Aa-rr-ll-uu**    An inhabitant of Poseidia, the western outpost of Atlantean civilization in the Caribbean, Aa-rr-ll-uu lived at a time of intense foreign migrations and worked as an esoteric chemist (alchemist) who was not above abusing his powers at the expense of his clients. His name is very similar to a term used for a great ancestral island described in a Babylonian account of the Great Flood.

In Babylonian tradition (circa 2100 BCE), Arallu was a great mountainous island in the Distant West (the Atlantic Ocean), a kind of paradise, where freshwater springs and a year-round temperate climate were enjoyed by the spiritually enlightened inhabitants. Arallu was the Babylonian version of Atlantis.

Aalu is ancient Egyptian for the Isle of Flame, descriptive of a large volcanic island in the sea of the Distant West, which physically matches Plato's Atlantis virtually detail for detail: mountainous, with canals and luxuriant crops, a palatial city surrounded by great walls decorated with precious metals, and so forth. Aalu's earliest known reference appears in *The Destruction of Mankind,* a New Kingdom history (1299 BCE) discovered in the tomb of Pharaoh Seti I at Abydos, site of the Osireion, a subterranean monument to the Great Flood, which destroyed a former age of greatness. On the other side of the world from Egypt, the Apache Indians of the American Southwest claim their ancestors arrived after the Great Flood destroyed their homeland in the ocean of the *east,* still remembered as the Isle of Flame.

The Hurrians occupied Anatolia (now known as Turkey) from the early third millennium BCE. Many of their religious and mythic concepts were absorbed by their Hittite conquerors, beginning after 2000 BCE. Among these traditions we find the story of Alalu, the first king of heaven, a giant god who made his home on a mountainous island in the sea of the setting sun. His son, Kumarbi, is synonymous with the Greek Kronos, a mythic personification of the Atlantic Ocean through Roman times.

**Ahajah**  An important culture bearer from Atlantis, Ahajah landed in the Atlantean kingdom of Elasippos (modern Portugal) and traveled through Gadeiros (Spain), eventually settling in the Pyrenees Mountains. A virtuous diplomat, Ahajah did much to establish early civilization and the high-minded tenets of religion on the Iberian Peninsula through friendly collaboration with the native people. His legacy is associated with accounts of the Holy Grail, allegedly headquartered at Castle Monsalvat in the Pyrenees.

**Ahasus**  A princess who lived at a time of social unrest and geologic upheaval in Atlantis, Ahasus used her talent as a skilled practitioner in the Followers of the Law of One mystery cult to pacify conditions through music. She and her fellow initiates believed the power of harmonics could bring an accord between humans and their environment. Her efforts were successful, and she presided over a period of spiritual and material greatness. Her philosophy of music was undoubtedly carried by Atlanteans to Greece, where these same precise principles were expounded by later philosophers, particularly Plato and Aristotle.

**Aian**  An administrator at the Temple of the Sun, the most important solar powerhouse in Atlantis, Aian saved many lives through his personal and brave initiative during the final destruction. He escaped with them and other survivors to Egypt, where he was an early worker in the Temple of Sacrifice and the Temple of Beauty.

**Ajax-ol**   A statesman-historian, Ajax-ol escaped the destruction of Atlantis and settled in Egypt, where he achieved even greater authority and helped direct the wholesale intermarriage of Atlantean refugees with native Egyptians. He also supervised the placement of specially selected documents from lost Atlantis into a house of records, which he commissioned and built near the Great Pyramid, which he likewise contributed to in a lesser way.

**Ajxor**   An Atlantean admiral, Ajxor successfully navigated his fleet from the catastrophe to the open sea, eastward across the Mediterranean, and finally to Lower Egypt. In his charge were some of the leading historians and political leaders of Atlantis, who became important culture bearers in the new land. Ajxor helped to develop Egyptian riverways for commerce, even exploring undiscovered reaches of the Nile, where he opened trade relations with new peoples, such as the Nubians. (See *Istulo,* on p. 212)

**Alpth**   An extraordinary linguist, Alpth was a translator who accompanied the leading Atlantean political leaders in Egypt during their culture-bearing mission through the Nile Valley. In time, he changed his name to its Egyptian equivalent, Ob-thet.

**Alta**   An Atlantean masculine name, Alta means "new life" and is associated partially with the eastern littorals of Florida. In 1993 the Atlantis Organization (of Buena Park, California) launched Project Alta, a sonar investigation in the vicinity of the underwater Bimini Road, believed by some researchers to be a remnant of Atlantean civilization.

**Amaicaca**   Amaicaca is remembered by the Carib Indians of Venezuela as a deluge hero who escaped in "a big canoe,"[2] which settled at the top of Mount Tamancu after the floodwaters receded. Amaicaca resembles Edgar Cayce's Amaki (see below) and the Colombian Amuraca. Scholars now believe it was from the native word *Amaicaca* or *Amuraca,* not the first name of an Italian mapmaker (Amerigo Vespucchi) from which the newly discovered continent of America actually derived its name.

**Amaiur** The legendary first king of the Basque, Amaiur parallels the biblical Tubalcain, a grandson of Noah, the flood hero in Genesis. His name means "Monarch of Maya," a kingdom referred to as the Green Isle, sunken in the Atlantic Ocean. In Greek myth, Maya was one of the seven Pleiades, daughters of the goddess Pleione and the Titan Atlas, and therefore an Atlantis, or daughter of Atlas. See his resemblance to the Carib Amaicaca, above.

**Amaki** A city in Poseidia, the Atlantean kingdom of the Caribbean, Amaki was a center for fire worship, a cult that spread into North America at least as far as southern Wisconsin, where the remains of several pyramidal sites still survive.

**Ambeno** One life reading describes the materially advanced state of Atlantean society in its last days, when its people were obsessed with the gimmickry and luxury afforded by technology. Ambeno was a princess who lived near "the great crystals that so condensed the lights [of the sun, moon, and stars] . . . as to guide not only the ship upon the bosom of the sea but in the air and in many of those now known in the transmission of the voice, as in the recording of those activities . . . for television, as it is termed in the present."[3] As a supporter of the Followers of the Law of One, Ambeno believed in class collaboration and rejected the "self-indulgences" of her time.

**Am-ee-lee** A high-ranking librarian, Am-ee-lee lived in Atlantis during a period of serious civil disorder between the Followers of the Law of One and the Sons of Belial. Afraid the conflict would escalate to undermine civilization, Am-ee-lee organized and dispatched several missions to transfer vital religious, scientific, and historic records for safekeeping to other parts of the world, especially Egypt. He migrated to a retreat in the Pyrenees Mountains but died frustrated because he never knew whether his emissaries reached the Nile Valley with their precious documents.

**Amia-ieou-lieb** A most important person (or would have been) and the last prince of the royal house, the successor to the throne, Amia-ieou-lieb was killed in the catastrophe that destroyed Atlantis.

**Amiee** A queen of Poseidia, the Caribbean outpost of Atlantis, Amiee was infamous throughout the empire for her iron-heeled rule, which resulted in predictable civil unrest.

**Amielee** Today's equivalent of a labor organizer, Amielee was also a skilled agriculturist. Perhaps because of his success as a mediator among the working classes, Amielee was ordered to the Atlantean kingdom of Azaes (Yucatán), where his work in instituting the garden-bed production of local crops survived him by many centuries in the farming policies of the Maya. In later life he achieved a position of high authority, which he used with benevolence in establishing the Followers of the Law of One religious principles. These likewise carried over, at least partially, into subsequent Middle American belief systems.

**Aneecl** Ruler of the Gate of Gold, a city in Poseidia, the Caribbean kingdom of Atlantis, Aneecl worked in applying the "nightside" of natural forces, which led to excesses of materialism, with subsequent cataclysmic results.

**Aoun** The first man to cross the Atlantic Ocean (from Atlantis to Yucatán) in an aircraft. Thanks to the new technology of human-operated flight, Aoun traveled far beyond Mexico to Mongolia and Southeast Asia.

**Apex-el** Sailing with his colleagues from the destruction of Atlantis, the scholar Apex-el made for Egypt but was blown far off course to land on the French coast. There they tried "to create a temple activity for the followers of the Law of One."[4] Though unsuccessful, they left "marks" (inscriptions?), which survived at least until 1934, in the chalk cliffs of Calais. After prolonged travels in France and Iberia, Apex-el and his followers finally arrived at the Nile Delta, where they found a new home among the large colony of surviving Atlanteans.

He subsequently played a seminal role in the rebirth of civilization by establishing a library in Lower Egypt that, over the course of centuries, grew to become the Great Library of Alexandria. Many documents pertaining to Atlantis were stored among its more than one million volumes, until they and the rest of this vast body of knowledge were lost when the library was burned by a Christian mob in the fifth century. Had this catastrophe been avoided, we would have far more than the fragmentary accounts of Plato and Edgar Cayce to tell us about the civilization of Atlantis.

**Apsa-Elarz**   An Atlantean born in Egypt, Apsa-Elarz collected folk music of the various peoples who had settled along the Nile and served as a choral director in the Temple of Sacrifice and the Temple of Beauty, where the power of sound (applied acoustics) was employed for physical healing and spiritual advancement.

**Aptheno**   While a young man in Atlantis, Aptheno abandoned himself to the excessive self-indulgence and crass materialism of its final days. Although he survived the destruction, Aptheno utterly despaired for the loss of all his worldly goods. Only sometime after his arrival in Egypt with his fellow survivors did he begin to gradually undergo a process of personal enlightenment. His transformation came about through service in one of the early hospitals, where he eventually went into medical research and studied the use of sound in healing.

**Arsth**   A keeper of records in the Atlantean colony of Azaes (Yucatán), Arsth administered documents that survived at least until 1944 and "may eventually be found again."[5]

**Asa-masa-me**   No longer a young woman but still an active priestess in the Followers of the Law of One religion, Asa-masa-me escaped the destruction of Atlantis and sailed in company with many other survivors to the Nile Delta. She arrived in ill health but recuperated enough to participate in the preservation of essential documents for the reconstruction of Atlantean civilization in Egypt. Her task was mainly the translation of original Atlantean documents into Egyptian records.

"These may be found," Cayce says, "especially when the house or tomb of records is opened, in a few years from now."[6]

**Asme**  An Atlantean geneticist, Asme worked with her colleagues to conduct experiments on human physical perfection, including outward beauty and an accelerated internal capacity of the body to heal itself.

**Asphar**  Among the technicians who preserved the scientific knowledge of metallurgy from the destruction of Atlantis by resettling in the Nile Valley, Asphar used electroplating when working with precious metals and assisted in the electrical combination of copper, zinc, and tin for the production of bronze, so important in the ancient world. He also serviced a scalpel that generated coagulating energies for bloodless surgery in medical operations.

The electroplating techniques employed by Asphar found possible validation in the Baghdad Battery, recovered from an Iraqi archaeological dig and subsequently dated to Persia in the second century BCE. Using citrus juice as an acid, it generated enough power to electroplate a statuette. Thirty years after Cayce described the Atlanteans' "electrical knife," just such a surgical tool was invented (reinvented?) by medical researchers in the United States.

**Atso, or Gyatso**  Tibetan for *ocean, Atso,* or *Gyatso,* is associated with the most important spiritual position in Bon Buddhism, the Dalai Lama. The Mongolian word for *ocean* is "dalai," a derivative of the Sanskrit word *atl,* for "upholder," and is found throughout every Indo-European language for "sea" or "valley in the water" (as that created by high waves): the Sumerian *thallath,* the Greek *thallasa,* the German *Tal,* the English *dale,* and so forth. The term *dalai,* according to Tenzin Gyatso, the fourteenth Dalai Lama of Tibet, stems from the Tibetan word for *ocean* that forms his name. Although "Dalai Lama" has sometimes been translated as "Ocean of Compassion or Wisdom," it really means "Wise Man (Guru) of (or from) the Ocean," a title that appears to have originated with the pre-Buddhist Bon religion, which was partially absorbed by the creed introduced from India in the eighth century.

Atlantologists have speculated since the late 1800s that the history and religious tenets of Atlantis are still preserved in some of Tibet's secret libraries or even encoded in the very ritual fabric of Tibetan religion itself, although these suspicions have never been verified by documented evidence. Other investigators discern traces of the Lemurian mystery cults in Bon Buddhism, particularly the central importance placed on the doctrine of reincarnation. Tibetan sand mandalas designed to portray the celestial city, with its concentric layout of alternating rings of land and water, are powerfully reminiscent of Plato's sunken capital, even to the sacred numbers and elephants. These considerations seem underscored by Atlantean influences in the high-holy terminology of Tibetan just discussed: *gyatso, dalai,* and so forth.

Edgar Cayce speaks of an unnamed person from the land now known as Tibet who visited Atlantis at a time when Atlantean teachings were being disseminated. Perhaps this refers to the early spread of spiritual concepts to Tibet from Atlantis and accounts for the Tibetan Wise Man from the Ocean. In other life readings, Cayce mentions a correlation between Atlantean thought and Mongolian theology.

**Ax-Tell** His name is mentioned more often than any other in the Cayce Atlantis readings. Ax-Tell's importance stems primarily from the large personal following he won in Atlantis and took with him into Egypt. He also preserved "those records of the Atlanteans as to the abilities for the use of the unseen forces."[7]

**Ax-tent-na** Traveling from Atlantis to the Lower Nile Valley, Ax-tent-na "was the first to set the records that are yet to be discovered or yet to be had of those activities in the Atlantean land . . . from the chambers of the way between the Sphinx and the pyramid of record" (i.e., the Great Pyramid at Giza).[8]

**Ax-Tos** Not all the Atlanteans described by Cayce were great or powerful. Ax-Tos was a humble physician who administered to working-class patients during the imperial period of Atlantis, when the empire was aggressively spreading its control and influence over much of the world. He was also a priest of the Followers of the Law of One (healers were invariably spiritual practitioners as well), who argued against the materialist Sons of Belial then in control of society.

**Ax-Tutem**   A great leader among Atlantean energy technicians, Ax-Tutem furthered the peaceful application of natural forces for private residences and public buildings, including heating and motive power. Although Cayce compares them to electricity, the precise nature of those forces is not disclosed.

# B

**Boob**   As the early Atlanteans began to broaden their civilization to other lands, according to Cayce they were confronted by masses of powerful and dangerous animals that threatened their expansion. Interestingly, the Aztecs had a similar tradition, known as Ocelatihu, wherein human beings took up counsel for a kind of war with these beasts for world domination. Cayce describes Boob as one of the council members, second in authority, who helped organize the successful defense of humankind against the rampaging animals.

**Bus-Lu**   The regent of Sus, an Atlantean city, Bus-Lu was obsessed with the "misapplication of the truths" found in science, which reduced him to becoming a narrow-minded technocrat.[9]

# C

**Caphala**   She was a companion to the leader of refugees from Atlantis during the city's early geologic troubles. Caphala arrived as a youngster in Peru and was so taken with the country's mountainous scenery, native ceremonial life, and abundance of gold that these impressions, according to Cayce, continued to resurface in subsequent lives, including in her twentieth-century incarnation.

**Checho**   Even after the Sons of Belial succeeded in destroying Atlantis, they tried to reassert themselves throughout Egypt, the new

Atlantean homeland. Among them was a refugee priestess, Checho, who attempted to regain her former power by causing disturbances in the Nile Valley, but she failed because the Followers of the Law of One now exercised supreme power through the Temple of Sacrifice, the religious and temporal administrative authority in Egypt.

**Chi-Eloir** "Among the first of the off-spring of the Atlanteans in the Egyptian land," Chi-Eloir grew up at a time when survivors from the Atlantis catastrophe were still arriving in the Nile Valley.[10] She was a dancer in the Temple Beautiful (or Temple of Beauty), but her performances would bear no resemblance to anything known in the West today, because all the arts, including dance, were strictly regulated by laws laid down according to the leading principle that all aesthetic expression was sacred.

Consequently, Chi-Eloir's dances in the Temple Beautiful were regarded as spiritual experiences. About the only modern comparison may be found in the whirling dervishes of Sufism, wherein the dancers, dedicating their revolving steps to Allah, enter altered states of consciousness in order to approach the divine. This originally Atlantean concept survived at least into classical Greek times, when the sacred or Apollonian dance was clearly distinguished from mundane or profane dances in the spirit of Dionysus.

# D

**Diu** One of the many simple peasants on the island of Atlantis, Diu was noted for his brotherly love, which was expressed in storing food for less fortunate individuals. Interestingly, the name appears related to later developments in Greek and Latin (both influenced by Atlantean speech) for the words Deus and Deo, or God. In a separate life reading, made thirteen years later, Cayce speaks of another Atlantean, a recorder of messages, named Deui. Ignatius Donnelly, the nineteenth-century founder of modern Atlantology, concludes that "the words we use every day were heard, in their primitive form, in their [the Atlanteans'] cities, courts and temples."[11]

**Duo-She-Dui** This name is interesting chiefly because it represents one of the few instances in which Cayce provides a direct translation from the original Atlantean into English. Duo-She-Dui means "the Duo Teaching" or "the Dual Life as One," and refers to the activities of a refugee in Egypt's Temple Beautiful, where he trained ministers from various lands in the tenets of both native and Atlantean theologies. As such, Duo-She-Dui appears to be more a title than a given name. It also demonstrates how at least some Atlantean words have survived into modern English: our word *dual* comes from the Atlantean word *duo*. The melding of spiritual ideas appears to have been a convention invented by the Atlanteans to integrate their modes of thought with the native beliefs still current in the Nile Valley. The eventual result was dynastic civilization, a harmonious synthesis of the two cultures.

This was Cayce's vision of pharaonic origins, and it is in perfect accord with both Egyptian myth and modern archaeology; the former recounts that seafaring foreigners (the Mesentiu, or Harpooners) arrived from the west to create the first dynasties; the latter claims evidence for the appearance of a sophisticated society that transformed the Nile Valley from a Late Stone Age conglomeration of loosely related agriculturists into a full-fledged civilization virtually overnight.[12]

# E

**Ececo** An early chemist, Ececo was one of the investigators who helped develop the civilian use of explosives, a knowledge that would be lost with the destruction of Atlantis.

Donnelly concludes that explosives were invented in Atlantis: "Having traced the knowledge of gunpowder back to the most remote times, we are not surprised to find in the legends of Greek mythology events described which are only explicable in supposing that the Atlanteans possessed the secret of this powerful explosive."[13]

**Eesmes** Among the first generation of Atlanteans born in Egypt, her abilities as a writer (or, more probably, a scribe) served Eesmes well as a group organizer. The name has an authentic ancient ring and may be a variation of Esses (better known as Isis) or, more appropriately, Sheshat, the Egyptian Mistress of the House of Books, the divine inventor of writing and heavenly record keeper.[14]

**Elam**  He was a worker who assisted in the operations of "the crystal, the mighty, the terrible crystal."[15] In Elam's reading, we get a glimpse of Atlantean crystalline technology, which was superior to ours in at least a few respects. Cayce does, in fact, say that the Atlanteans "reached even a higher state of application of material things (hence called civilization) than even in the present day."[16] Elam and his colleagues were busy "photographing from a distance"; they possessed "the ability for reading inscriptions through walls, even at a distance," and were capable of "overcoming of (termed today) the forces of nature or gravity itself [levitation?]."[17]

Elam is also the biblical name given to an important civilization in southwestern Iran, approximately equivalent in area to modern Khuzistan. Almost as old as Sumer, Elam was the first known civilization in Mesopotamia's Fertile Crescent (beginning about 3500 BCE) and was a major, although distinct, Mesopotamian state that flourished as late as the Persian Empire. It formed a satrapy (or province) under King Darius I after more than two thousand years of existence. Given its profoundly ancient origins, Elam may have derived its name from an Atlantean culture bearer or a refugee family from Atlantis.

Elam's Lemurian provenance is made clear in the Native American oral traditions of California's Washo Indians. Their flood story tells of a terrible natural catastrophe that engulfed a huge and magnificent kingdom, whose leaders escaped over the sea to North America. Before its inundation, the ancestral island, known as Elam, was home to a primarily agricultural people, who called their chief deity Mu.

**Elchi**  An Atlantean navigator, Elchi has an intriguing parallel with the very ancient town of Elche in southeastern Spain, on the Rio Vinalopo. It was here that a polychrome stone statue known as La Dama de Elche (The Lady of Elche) was found in 1897 during a nearby archaeological dig. Stylistically, the statue resembles nothing else of its kind but has suggested Atlantean provenance to many researchers, including the leading archaeologist in Spain during the 1920s, Elena Maria Whishaw.[18] Her conclusion is underscored by the statue's place of discovery in Alicante province, described by the Greek philosopher Plato twenty-four centuries ago as the location for a kingdom of Atlantis in Spain (Gadeiros, from which the modern Spanish city of Cadiz derives its name).

The name of the town appears to have remained phonetically unchanged over time, going back to the Arab Elix and the Roman Ilici, itself a derivation of a Phoenician word taken directly from the Atlantean language.

**Elem**  A prince in the royal house of Atlantis and a son of the Most High, Elem panicked "when the destructive forces came" and tried to save himself, rather than help others, as his duty demanded.[19]

**Elie**  "Worshiped by the peoples of a portion of the land," Elie was a famous if egotistical musician in the temple at Poseidia, where "sounds of all natures were produced upon the instruments of the day."[20]

The post-Atlantean, pre-Roman Etruscans were known to mount full-fledged orchestral performances, which appear to have been part of their legacy from Atlantis, where elaborate, large-scale musical ensembles, like those suggested in this reading, were often heard.

**Ellisy**  This beautiful, manipulative priestess was forced against her will to leave Atlantis because of serious religious upheavals taking place in her homeland prior to its geologic destruction. Arriving in Yucatán, Ellisy moved on to Peru, charming her way to wealth as she went, leaving a swath of discontent behind her in the process.

**Ellm**  This man, Ellm, "was among those in the temple worship of the period" who "were afterwards worshiped by the people."[21] Here we learn that after their deaths, mortal human beings, if they had been particularly virtuous, were sometimes elevated to revered deities in Atlantis, perhaps equivalent to today's postmortem status of sainthood bestowed by the Catholic Church on its most devout followers.

**Elmeur**   The son of the Atlantean ruler Ajax, Elmeur lived during a very early period in the history of Atlantis, when the Followers of the Law of One cult was just coming into being. His name appears to be a phonetic variant of Evenor, described by Plato as the first king of Atlantis.

**Emesersea**   A high priestess for the Followers of the Law of One, Emesersea intuited the final, most violent destruction of the Atlantean lands, but, loving her homeland deeply, she was reluctant to leave it just because of a frightening premonition. "It was with foreboding, and with doubts and fears, that the entity almost by force was carried first into the Pyrenees land—or Spain and Portugal."[22] Emesersea finally settled in the Nile Valley, where her instinctive ability served in the early rebuilding of civilization.

**Exina**   The wife of Axel, an Atlantean ruler, Exina accompanied her husband to Egypt. There she personally engaged in melding the tenets of the Followers of the Law of One with native beliefs in the Near East, particularly Assyria.

Exina appears to have been memorialized and even deified in this part of the world as the very early Mesopotamian grain goddess Exinu.

# H

In Iroquois myth, At-o-tar-ho was a female monster whose head was covered with writhing snakes instead of hairs, similar to Medusa. The "At" in At-o-tar-ho implies an Atlantean connection.

**Hy-Poc-Rax-El**   Emery notes the sudden emergence of medical technology in the Nile Valley at the outset of dynastic civilization, during the late fourth millennium BCE, while Cayce mentions the migration of a medical practitioner, Hy-Poc-Rax-El, from his Atlantean homeland to Egypt, where he was "very close to the one who headed the department of hospitalization (as would today be called), or the department of healing arts, or the application of the influences of nature into man himself."[24]

Cayce describes early Atlantean medical practices as surprisingly modern and holistic: "The study was then, as it should be now—that man is a part of that which was made—all that was made, and took upon himself a manifested part of same—through the mental expression that became crystallized in material forces. Hence, in the natural forces about man, added with the mental and the spiritual, there is that which will bring the connecting of man's relationship to his material environment."[25]

# I

**Iel**   An Atlantean immigrant in Egypt, Iel taught "the art of weaving and making of linens and the finer arts of not only the decorations of the body, but the weaving of materials and styles [representing] various stations in life."[26] In other words, a person's rank or status was indicated by the cut of his or her clothes.

The loom was an innovation, together with every aspect of pharaonic society, that appeared suddenly and fully developed in the Nile Delta around 3100 BCE.

**Ilax**   After immigrating from Atlantis, Ilax became "the princess of fire" in rituals for the Followers of the Law of One cult.[27] She was the mistress of shamanistic ecstasies, wherein her altered states of consciousness were meant to establish communication with the spirit world. Her renowned transformations contributed to the mystery cults later instituted by Isis, Ra, and Hermes. After achieving substantial influence and prestige, however, Ilax mistakenly sided with the wrong faction in a native rebellion and lost all her political power. She subsequently devoted herself to the performance of menial tasks in active service to the Followers of the Law of One.

**Iltar**   With just ten followers, Iltar, a member of the household of Atlan and an adherent to the Followers of the Law of One cult, left Atlantis to settle on the shores of Yucatán. Several temples were built there, but they were destroyed during the almost worldwide geologic upheavals that destroyed his forsaken Atlantean homeland. He survived these natural turmoils to build many new sacred structures, which profoundly influenced the development of Mesoamerican architecture. Cayce predicts that "the temple of Iltar will then rise again."[28]

Cayce also indicates in this reading that "those in Yucatan, those in the adjoining lands as begun by Iltar, gradually lost in their activities; and came to be that people termed, in other portions of America, the mound builders."[29]

**Ishod**   An Atlantean metalsmith and forger of weapons, including chariots, Ishod also worked in more decorative silver and gold.

In Plato's description of Atlantis, he characterizes its chief industry as metallurgy and its craftspeople as busy in the production of military bronzes, as well as the manufacture of luxury items in more precious metals, with which they even bedecked the walls of their public and sacred buildings.

**Ishuma**   During the second series of major geologic upheavals that afflicted Atlantis, Ishuma was a low-ranking, albeit ambitious, priestess in the Temple of Light, which belonged to the Followers of the Law of One cult. Advancement through the religious hierarchy was obstructed by her superiors, particularly the elders, who sought, unsuccessfully, her dismissal. They were scandalized by Ishuma giving birth to "seventeen sons by seven different men."[30]

Not even powerful cult leaders were able to force her removal from the prestigious Temple of Light, some indication, perhaps, of the moral freedom that prevailed in Atlantean society, at least during its middle period. The elders of the Followers of the Law of One cult, on the other hand, Cayce identifies as less open-minded.

**Istulo**   An Atlantean immigrant in Egypt, where she was a "healing assistant,"[31] or nurse, specializing in the care of children, Istulo somehow fell afoul of her superiors to the extent that she was forced to leave

Egypt. She resettled in Abyssinia and there tried to continue her practice among the native young people but was so intoxicated by the local culture that she gradually replaced her scientific medical practices with "the rhythm of incantations" and native beliefs.[32]

Her reading is additionally interesting because it shows that Atlantean influence reached even as far as East Africa. A remnant of this influence appears to have survived as late as the fifth century BCE, when Nubia (modern Sudan, incorporating much of present East Africa) was ruled by an Atlanersa. The title means "prince or royal descendant (ersa) of Atlan."

# M

**Mayr**  An Atlantean priestess, Mayr resettled in Egypt, where she became an emissary to lands as far away as the Indian and Pacific oceans.

**Meg**  "Before the second of the upheavals," Meg, a priestess, "interpreted the messages that were received through the crystals and the fires that were to the eternal fires of nature [natural energies]."[33] In Meg's time, there were "new developments in air, in water travel . . . these were the beginning of the developments at that period for the escape."[34] Although the first examples of this evacuation technology were becoming available, "when the destructions came, the entity chose rather to stay with the groups than to flee to other lands."[35]

In ancient British myth, Meg was a giantess able to throw huge boulders over great distances. Her memory still survives in the Royal Navy, where battleship guns are referred to as Mons Megs, from "Long Meg." It is not inconceivable that Cayce's Meg and the Atlantean cataclysm were transmuted over time into the British Meg, which seems to describe an erupting volcano ejecting its lava bombs.

**Mu-Elden**  A woman survivor from the destruction of Atlantis, Mu-Elden immigrated to the Nile Valley, where she assisted in the Temple of Sacrifice and the Temple Beautiful. Her name indicates Lemurian origins.

**Mufuti**   Cayce enigmatically describes Mufuti as "an Atlantean and a Lemurian in purpose."[36]

**Muglo**   This female spiritual advisor in Atlantis with a decidedly Lemurian name, Muglo, indicates the Pacific effect on the Atlantic civilization.

# O

**Ogriae**   A princess at a time when Atlantis was reaching the zenith of its greatness, Ogriae "kept away from those of the opposite sex, for the love was given in one of low estate and could not bring self to the conditions necessary for the consummation of the desires in each other's inner self."[37] Doubtless, those "conditions" would have entailed Ogriae's renunciation of her high place in the royal family.

Her name exemplifies a common theme of the Atlantis phenomenon in which certain words or sounds survive among some of the cultures influenced by the lost civilization. For instance, names composed of or deriving from "Og" are associated in ancient Irish and biblical contexts with a world-class deluge, such as the former's Tír na nÓg, a kingdom beneath the sea, and the latter's Old Testament Og, who in Genesis was a giant hitching a ride on Noah's Ark. After a terrible flood destroyed their homeland, Ogllo (alternate spelling, Ocllo), together with her husband, Manco Capac, arrived in South America on the shores of Lake Titicaca, Bolivia, to found Andean civilization, according to the Inca's story of creation.

In Greek myth, Ogyges, the first king of Greece, was the son of Poseidon (the sea god) and reigned during a great flood. Homer wrote of Ogygia, a mid-Atlantic island where Calypso was the high priestess of a magic cult that turned men into servile beasts, not unlike the genetically engineered "things" Cayce says made up the unfortunate laboring classes of Atlantis. He describes a genetically engineered subclass deliberately modified by the Atlanteans to serve as human beasts of manual labor.

In Cayce's life readings, Og is one of the three principle islands belonging to Atlantis at the time of its final destruction.

# P

**Pfstxie**    She was the priestess of a sun-worshipping cult is what is now the Ohio Valley, where hundreds of ancient earth mounds may still be found. Cayce says these mounds "were called the replica or representative of the Yucatan experiences, as well as the Atlantean . . . All of these are as one consciousness in the entity's activity."[38]

Archaeologists agree with Cayce that the prehistoric Mound Builders probably worshipped in a cult of the sun god, judging from important solar alignments, particularly orientations to the solstices, originally built into many of the structures. Diffusionist scholars point to abundant evidence that connects the Mississippian Period of pyramidal mound building throughout the Midwest and much of the South with close parallels in Yucatán.

An earlier phase of mound building, known as the Adena, spread from the Atlantic seaboard to Wisconsin after the final destruction of Atlantis, about three thousand years ago. Although most of North America's prehistoric mounds were not tombs, all of them were sacred. Surviving Native American tradition depicts some of the earthworks as "schools" for students of shamanism. Most mounds appear to have been raised in communal efforts under the direction of these holy men and women (like Pfstxie) as concentrations of telluric, or Earth, energies. In other words, the architects of these formations built them to focus spiritual power.

Cayce suggests these structures were Atlantean in the sense that the mounds ritually duplicated Mount Atlas, the holy mountain from which the city Atlantis, meaning "daughter of Atlas," derived its name. Plato informs us that Atlas was not a god but a semidivine being, a Titan, the son of a god, Poseidon, by a mortal woman, Kleito.

Pfstxie was a native priestess who perpetuated the Ohio Valley's sun-worshipping cult brought to North America before her time and memorialized in the earthworks of the Midwest.

# R

**Rariru**   Instrumental in blending newly arrived Atlanteans with prehistoric Peruvian society, Rariru instituted "the worship of the sun and the solar forces"[39] and took charge of every detail of the new "ritualistic forces," even those "pertaining to court hangings."[40] Rariru "was the first high priestess to the sun in the land, making the first human sacrifice in that period."[41]

Rariru adopted the name in the early stages of her priestly career, or she may have been simply born into the sun cult, given the solar significance of her name. Ra, of course, was the supreme Egyptian sun god, but he never demanded human sacrifices. On the other side of the world, on Easter Island, the word Ra was used in many mythic contexts with regard to the deified sun. In Rariru's Peru, the Inti-Rai-mi was the Inca's most important ceremony (still performed today) on behalf of their sun god, who likewise received no human sacrifices.

**Rhea**   In describing this high priestess for the Followers of the Law of One, Cayce provides some indication of the high levels of spiritual enlightenment reached by the Atlanteans, especially in regard to progress they made in elevating the group mind. Rhea and her colleagues achieved "the concentration of thought for the use of the universal forces, through the guidance or direction of the saints (as would be termed today)."[42]

There are few terms in the present that accurately describe their state of consciousness, save that through the concentration of the group mind of the Followers of the Law of One, they entered into a higher, fourth-dimensional consciousness—or were absent from the body. This was a state of mind or soul wherein behavior equaled identity and thought equaled action. It was a level achieved in a "light" or "astral" body, separate from but connected to the physical body.

"Thus they were able to have that experience of crystallizing through the Light the speech from what might well be termed the saint realm, to impart understanding and knowledge to the group gathered."[43] Rhea became proficient as "the interpreter to the groups of the messages attained or gained from the periodical meetings with those from the universal realm, for instruction, for direction, for understanding in those periods of activity."[44]

It appears that progress in psychic development among the Atlanteans went beyond almost anything known since. In this respect, the difference between their time and ours is crucial, because modern Western society generally dismisses paranormal phenomena as useless superstition, invalid, or nonscientific. In Atlantis, however, psychic research was universally acknowledged as not only authentic science but also the highest scientific endeavor. Consequently, modern Western humans are spiritually vacuous and provincial materialists, while the Atlanteans were getting in touch with the higher forces of Creation.

The ancient Greeks revered Rhea as the Great Mother Goddess, the Mother of the Gods, and the daughter of Gaia and Uranus—Mother Earth and Father Sky. In this parentage we see Cayce's Rhea, whose psychic work involved connecting the mundane Earth with the spiritual heaven.

The husband of the goddess Rhea was Cronos, associated with the Atlantic Ocean. His fellow Titan, Atlas, assumed leadership of the war against the gods after Cronos resigned this position. All this places Rhea in the Atlantic realm at a time defined by Plato as the war between Athens and Atlantis—the same conflict reflected in Greek myth.

Who, then, was the Rhea described by Cayce? Did she derive her name from a goddess worshipped first in Atlantis whose cult spread to Greece? Or perhaps the high priestess achieved such renown that she was remembered and eventually deified by the Greeks as one of their most important goddesses.

# S

**Saail** He was a defrocked priest, punished because he used splendid temples belonging to the Followers of the Law of One church as rendezvous sites for "sin." Turning to the Sons of Belial, Saail participated in active rebellion against his former faith.

What makes his reading of particular interest is Cayce's mention of "the mysteries of the black arts" practiced by Sons of Belial cultists.[45]

We thus learn that the Followers of the Law of One were opposed not simply by another spiritual doctrine, but by a sophisticated, perhaps destructive, movement with its own set of mysteries.

**Sailuen**  Traumatized by the overwhelming geologic cataclysm she experienced in the destruction of Atlantis, Sailuen's spirit would be troubled by inexplicable, inborn fears of earthquakes—the intuitively felt recollections of her Atlantean sojourn—throughout successive incarnations.

Before the advent of these troubles, she tried to "prevent the activities of the peoples towards self-engorgement, or the taking on of self in the manner of worshiping self's abilities, rather than applying self as a channel or the motive through which universal forces might act."[46]

Here, Cayce acts as a psychiatrist, explaining for his client the root of her deep-seated but unreasonable fear of seismic and social upheavals. In view of his statement that numerous Atlantean souls are reincarnating in our time, one wonders how many people today are suffering from the same inexplicable (to them) anxieties?

His description of Atlanteans just prior to their destruction as wallowing in the "engorgement" of vulgar materialism could just as well apply to modern Americans more interested in "worshiping self's abilities"[47] than becoming "the channel or the motive through which universal forces might act."[48] This last and wonderfully succinct characterization of the self's true function is at the core of all genuine spiritual attempts and the central goal of meditation striven for by practitioners of Tibetan Buddhism.

**Segferd**  He lived in Atlantis during its technological heyday as the equivalent of a modern electrical engineer. In this reading, Cayce provides insight into the applied science and research known to the Atlanteans. Like us, they were able to transmit sounds, electricity, and "color" (movie projection, television?), but they were also interested in the transmission of thoughts.[49]

He describes the Atlanteans as "well advanced in those things that are still being sought today—the very means and manners of turning the forces of nature into that channel as a servant for the mind of man."[50]

**Segund**    "Before the breaking up of the Atlantean land," Segund was "very close to those in authority" as "the keeper of the portals, as well as the messages that were received from the visitation of those from the outer spheres." Who or exactly what these visitors might have been is not made clear.[51]

Immediately prior to the worst outbreaks of seismic violence, Segund used his position as a "messenger . . . or the means through which transmissions of activities were set up,"[52] to organize evacuations to nearby Og (one of the Atlantean islands; it too would later be destroyed), Yucatán, the Pyrenees, Greece, and Egypt, and as far away as India, Southeast Asia, and Mongolia. The vast extent of these mass migrations provides some measure of the Atlantean population, which must have been enormous.

**She-Aba**    Born in Egypt of Atlantean parents, She-Aba designed "the various characters of robes, the dress of the peoples of the various positions in the court, as well as in the fields of service," in the Temple of Sacrifice and the Temple of Beauty.[53]

**Shu-Su-Mu-Lu-r**    Born of mixed Atlanto-Egyptian parentage, Shu-Su-Mu-Lu-r appears to have been a propagandist "for the presenting of ways and manners in which the race might be changed."[54]

With their homeland utterly destroyed, many (most?) Atlanteans resettled in the Nile Valley, where they sought to create a new society by interbreeding with the native people. Shu-Su-Mu-Lu-r was one of the first members of this hybrid offspring. She must have been a positive example, because she was chosen to represent it and promote the ongoing process of interbreeding. Judging from the results (i.e., pharaonic civilization), the blended outcome was successful, perhaps in some measure because the indigenous people of the Nile were probably related (at least distantly) to the Atlanteans, with whom Egypt had been in contact for centuries prior to their mass migrations.

Shu-Su-Mu-Lu-r's part Atlantean heritage was reflected in her name, Shu being the Egyptian Atlas.

**Shu-Tu** After becoming a priestess for the Followers of the Law of One, Shu-Tu was forced to leave Atlantis during the terrible geologic upheavals, which eventually sank her homeland beneath the sea.

Arriving in Yucatán, she learned that survivors from a somewhat similar but earlier catastrophe settled in what is now southern California and New Mexico. These were refugees from the Pacific Ocean civilization of Mu, long familiar to the Atlanteans. Although temperamentally poles apart, the two peoples engaged in amiable spiritual dialogue, and visitors from Atlantis (mostly diplomats, scientists, and theologians) were not unknown in the Pacific.

The Lemurians were not as outgoing or aggressive and were less frequently seen outside their spheres of influence, a notable exception being the queen of Mu's journey to Egypt for the Great Pyramid's consecration. These spheres expanded to include Asia and the Americas after the destruction.

Shu-Tu embarked on a long journey to find these lost Lemurians. Her quest was successful, and she learned a great deal about the spiritual ideas that originated in Mu. They were then beginning to influence religious thought in India, Southeast Asia, and East Asia, where they would survive to varying degrees in Buddhism, particularly in Tibet, and in Shinto, the indigenous religion of Japan. She was fascinated by these new (to her) concepts, which, however different from what she knew from the Followers of the Law of One, were still complementary to her Atlantean beliefs, and even in some instances expanded upon them. Shu-Tu began "correlating the tenets" of the two belief systems.[55]

This synthesis of Atlantean and Lemurian, together with local spirituality, survives in the largely secret lodge traditions of the Hopis, Navajo, and other tribal peoples of the American Southwest.

**Sonl** A living example of the familiar axiom that "absolute power corrupts absolutely," Sonl "ruled with an unlimited power" over the sacred Atlantean city of Peos, much "to his soul's undoing."[56]

His tyranny nonetheless provides us with a glimpse of the authoritarian political system that governed Atlantis. In the hands of enlightened leaders, the immense power of the Atlanteans was used to good effect, raising civilization to heights of material and spiritual greatness never seen before or since. But when that power was surrendered to the abuses of a Sonl, the noble society declined into self-destruction. That is the supreme lesson of Atlantis for our time and civilization.

**Su-Er-To**    A princess high in Atlantean aristocracy, Su-Er-To was also a gifted priestess for the Followers of the Law of One. She fled for her life from the cataclysm that obliterated Atlantis, suddenly reduced to a mere refugee dependent upon the hospitality of foreigners. Emotionally disoriented, she had great difficulty adjusting to a new life in the Nile Valley, where her former greatness now counted for little.

But she had not lost "the ability to aid by the very high vibrations of the body itself,"[57] and Su-Er-To eventually regained her former self-confidence through healing others with the laying-on of her hands, a natural power that continued through numerous incarnations and also was present in Edgar Cayce's twentieth-century client.[58]

**Sululon**    An aggressive leader of the Sons of Belial, Sululon indulged in a torrid affair with a female follower of the despised Followers of the Law of One. They were lovers at a time when strife between the two cults was approaching its peak, and Sululon was forced to flee Atlantis under the accusation of traitor.

He landed on the shores of Yucatán, the first Atlantean to arrive there, and was welcomed as a god. Together with a few friends who accompanied him, they organized the willing populace into work crews for the creation of the first stone temples and palaces in America.

Sululon and his companions established law and order; temporarily put an end to human sacrifice; and instituted agriculture and irrigation, astronomy, literature, the arts, metallurgy, medical care, and all the other advantages of the distant home left behind forever.

Restless by nature, he decided to leave after a few years. The native people wept to see him and a few of his original companions go. (Some remained behind as chief administrators and married local women.) He tried to comfort them by saying that he would return someday; if not, then surely one of his descendants would come back to reclaim the kingdom he was leaving in their hands.

Sululon journeyed south into Bolivia and Peru, where the same series of events was repeated. Again, he grew unsettled after a few years and left his sorrowing new people with a promise to return. This time he traveled north, far beyond Yucatán, into what is now the state of Virginia. There his journey would come to an end. His wanderlust got the better of him, and he vanished into American myth as the Feathered Serpent.

**Su-Son**   One of the most peculiar individuals in the life readings, Su-Son was regularly mistaken for the most powerful prince in Atlantis. The two men were physically identical, although utterly unrelated, a situation that inevitably led to numerous misunderstandings with serious political ramifications—"until the union of their purpose and activity made for the preventing of turmoils arising from the experience of Su-Son."[59]

# T

**Tek-Ia-Eln**   He was in Egypt "when there were the coalitions made with the Atlanteans, as well as the natives, and those of other lands."[60] Tek-Ia-Eln matched work assignments and careers with those men temperamentally suited to them—"the stonecutters, the farmers, the herdsmen, the miners. All of these were trained for the service to the peoples as a unit, not as individuals."[61] This last statement is a credible, hence revealing, look at a part of ancient Egyptian society as it was being forged by the combination of cultures.

**Tujar**   A kind of servant or combination nursemaid and teacher, Tujar lived and worked in the household of an Incan prince at a time when Atlantean influences were transforming Peru. She applied herself "to the edifying of the young" by excelling in basket weaving, painting, book making, and rug designing, while dutifully attending to the weak and disabled.[62] In her twentieth-century incarnation, her talents lived on as a painter of pastoral scenes. Cayce reveals that "ever to the entity there must be either the mountain or the sea in the viewing of same," a tendency that echoes Tujar's soul memories of ancient days.[63]

# Z

**Zurumu**   An Atlantean priestess with a Lemurian name, Zurumu worked in Yucatán's Temple of the Sun.

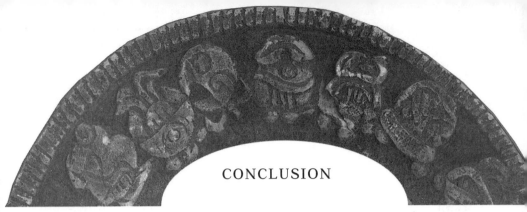

# Fireballs and Poisoned Bees

In the early morning of February 15, 2013, a shooting star streaked across the clear skies over Siberia. The fireball seemed to suddenly swell with brilliance and then explode in a momentary flash that was brighter than the rising sun. Staccato thunderclaps rode hard on the heels of rapidly spreading compression waves, the largest infrasounds ever recorded by a United Nations' monitoring system. These waves were so powerful that they reverberated around our planet several times, taking more than twenty-four hours to dissipate. The shock waves damaged 7,200 buildings in six cities, such as Chelyabinsk, where nearly 1,500 people were injured by shards of flying glass. In the same city, a zinc factory's 2,000-square-foot roof collapsed.

Heavier than France's Eiffel Tower, the 18,000-ton culprit was a 4.5-billion-year-old meteor falling at 41,750 miles per hour, approximately fifty times the speed of sound. When air friction caused it to superheat, the resultant explosion equaled 500 kilotons of TNT. Most of this energy was absorbed in the upper atmosphere, where detonation occurred at an altitude of 14.5 miles above Earth. Had the fireball's trajectory differed only slightly, however, a 2,000-foot-high air burst thirty times more potent than the atomic bomb that destroyed Hiroshima at the end of World War II would have vaporized Chelyabinsk's 1,130,000 inhabitants.

They would have made up only a fraction of the total victims. The city at that time was used as a depot for collecting the former Soviet military's vast stores of bacteriological and chemical arms gathered from all over Russia for decommissioning. The meteor exploded perhaps two seconds before it could ignite these true weapons of mass destruction, with inconceivably lethal consequences for the whole world.

Apparently, civilization escaped the Mayan calendar's catastrophic prophecy, just fifty-five days after its termination the previous December, by a paper-thin margin. The Maya themselves might have smiled on Siberia's near miss as a hopeful message from the cosmos, confirming that our species, generally at least, has begun to incline, however so modestly, toward enlightenment and consequently avoided 4-Ollin's Rebellion of Earth. Was the Chelyabinsk fireball supposed to have been the agent of that global disaster? If so, did its premature explosion signify that humanity did not deserve extinction after all? You will note that a meteoric event did not figure into my list of potential candidates for cataclysmic change. Astronomers do not anticipate similar threats from outer space anytime soon. But then, the Siberian event took them by complete surprise.

*Fox News* reports that scientists at NASA have "so far detected only about ten percent of the near-Earth objects that are wider than eighty-seven miles across."[1] The Chelyabinsk meteor had a diameter of just sixty-five feet. NASA observers estimate "that there may be hundreds of thousands of such objects within one-third the distance from Earth to the sun that remain unknown."[2]

To be sure, we live in a cosmic shooting gallery, where major collisions have radically altered the history of our planet and will undoubtedly do so again, sooner or later. How any of them may relate to the Mayan prophecy or similar prognostications is unknown. But at least 2013's close call conformed with their belief that nothing is foreordained; that alternative futures lie before us in a field of potentiality; and that our collective behavior can, in effect, decide which one we will experience. The same might be said of yet another global catastrophe not included in my list of end-times scenarios.

Just after America's first atomic bomb was detonated near Alamagordo, New Mexico, in 1945, a newspaper reporter wondered if nuclear weapons might lead to the final destruction of civilization. "No," Albert Einstein replied, and suggested something less obvious. "If the bee disappears from the surface of the Earth," he said, "man would have no more than four years to live. No more bees, no more pollination . . . no more men!"[3]

His pronouncement was remarkably prescient, because it was uttered sixty years before the advent of colony collapse disorder, the sudden and drastic mortality of honeybees around the world. The phenomenon first appeared in late 2006 to early 2007, when their rate of attrition abruptly skyrocketed, with a total loss in the United States alone of 45 percent. Such die-offs had occurred in the past, but never before of such scope, and the hives always rebounded soon after. But during the early twenty-first century, their radical decline persisted and worsened over subsequent years. In Scotland, apiculturist Andrew Scarlett lost 80 percent of his 1,200 hives during 2009. Three years later, the Swiss reported that about half of their country's bee population had not survived the winter. Ireland's losses were greater than 50 percent. Overall, German honey production fell more than 40 percent, but in usually high-yield regions, such as Baden-Württemberg, two-thirds of all bee colonies were wiped out.

A number of theoretical causes were suggested, but none took hold until 2012, when several peer-reviewed, independent studies were able to determine that pesticides were primarily to blame. William Stockwin reports in the *Examiner:*

> Neonicitinoids [*sic*] are systemic poisons that mimic the effects of nicotine, and differ from other insecticides, because they also enter the pollen and nectar of the plant, not just the leaves. When foraging bees take up the poison-laced pollen and nectar from plants treated with neonicitinoids, such as *Imidacloprid* or *Clothianidin,* the effect on their central nervous system makes them disoriented and unable to find their way back to the hive. Those that do get

back to the hive deliver the poisoned pollen and nectar, killing the rest of the colony. . . . Since *Imidacloprid* was registered for use in the U.S. in 1994 by Bayer Crop Science, neonicitinoids have become the most widely used group of pesticides in the U.S.[4]

During early 2013 the European Food Safety Authority announced that neonicotinoids posed an unacceptably high risk to bees and told how the industry-sponsored science upon which regulatory agencies' claims of safety have relied was "criminally flawed."[5] In April 2013 the European Union passed legislation banning the use of several insecticides for two years. These measures have been condemned by apiculturists everywhere, however, as too little, too late, because of the environmental persistence of pesticides in irrigation channels and soil after decades of intensive application. The clean-up measures necessary to effectively remove them would be costly in the extreme and virtually impossible to thoroughly complete. Meanwhile, hive attrition rates continue to soar internationally.

If these rates do not radically decline before midcentury, Einstein's prophecy is in danger of coming to pass, because bees pollinate approximately one-third of all crop species in the United States alone. Such a deleterious effect on food production would stress an already frazzled international economy beyond the breaking point, bringing to the industrial world widespread famine, which, without the murdered bees, could only get worse and would never be solved. Conditions in Africa and India, where starvation is already endemic, would cause many millions of deaths and unprecedented social dislocation among the living.

In all these lethal event horizons, humans play a crucial role. Our greenhouse gases are heating the polar regions, thereby depressing the Northern Hemisphere's jet stream and speeding up nature's timetable for the next ice age. Our civilization, because we engineered it to depend entirely on electricity, is a sitting duck for the next Carrington Event. Propelled by insatiable greed, our drilling for yet more oil is jeopardizing the sea bottom's ice cages with rising temperatures that could unleash enough methane to kill all life on Earth short of 4 percent, as happened during the Permian Period extinction event. Had Chelyabinsk been struck, the effects of 2013's meteor would not have been limited to a single Siberian city. Instead, vast supplies of bacteriological and chemical nerve agents, ejected into the atmosphere, would ride air currents around the world. The bees, which make possible one-third of the food we eat, are being killed off by pesticides made by humans.

Any one of these possibilities not only fits a global upheaval associated with termination of the Mayan calendar, but eerily parallels a former civilization. The people of Atlantis were alleged to have created a long-lived, culturally rich, economically powerful, and virtuous society. But over time, in Plato's words, they "became too diluted too often, and with too much of the mortal mixture, human nature got the upper hand. Then, they being unable to bear their fortune, became unseemly, and to him who had an eye to see they began to appear base, and had lost the fairest of their precious gifts. But to those who had no eye to see true happiness, they still appeared glorious and blessed at the time when they were filled with unrighteous avarice and power."[6] To some investigators, such as the renowned French Freemason scholar Serge Hutin, these words refer to the Atlanteans' racial purity ("the fairest of their precious gifts"), which became less important to them than the pursuit of material gain: "Plato tells of the growing decadence that afflicted the Atlantean people. He attributes it to increased cross-breeding. In a sense, the great Greek philosopher was clearly a racist: he regarded the increase in cross-breeding as a calamity."[7]

To other researches, such as Desmond Lee, a British translator of the dialogues, Plato meant to say that the Atlanteans, being originally descended from Poseidon, diluted their godly inheritance by intermarrying with ordinary mortals. But this interpretation lacks conviction, because the Atlanteans never interbred with other deities following Kleito's encounter with Poseidon.[8]

In any case, Cayce's life readings take up where Plato left off: "With the continued disregard of those who were keeping the pure race and the pure peoples, Man brought in destructive forces combined with those natural resources of the gases, of the electrical forces made in

Nature, caused volcanic eruptions [like the Siberian Traps] in the slow cooling of the Earth."[9] If these words bring to mind British Petroleum's 2010 oil disaster, they seem more evocative when Cayce tells how "that portion now near what would be termed the Sargasso Sea [the Gulf of Mexico] first went into the depths" with Atlantean drills.[10] "These, not intentionally, were tuned too high, and brought the second period of destructive forces to the peoples of the land."[11]

Cayce says that "the terrible crystals," which concentrated limitless energy from the hidden wellsprings of nature, had been taken over by the materialistic Sons of Belial to dig into the Earth for the extraction of wealth in the form of precious minerals. But they penetrated too deeply and set off subterranean forces that resulted in catastrophic consequences. Remarkably, several Native American tribes, such as the Menominee of the Upper Great Lakes region, recount in their oral traditions how a world flood was precipitated by greedy foreigners, the white-skinned Marine Men, who dug into Earth Mother for underground riches, especially copper.[12]

The Tuaoi stone, the great crystal at the center of Atlantis, according to Cayce, was used in "the application of spiritual power in the physical world."[13] In this pursuit, the Tuaoi was abused. Early twenty-first-century events appear to mirror the self-destruction of Atlantis. There, according to Cayce, two rival factions struggled for control of their people's destiny: the Followers of the Law of One and the Sons of Belial. The former does not appear to have been merely some monotheistic cult but seems to refer instead to the One Law, or the predominance of natural law, with emphasis on healing and psychospiritual values.

The Sons of Belial, however, were only interested in using natural resources for their own material gain. The origin of contention between the two groups was, as Plato explains, rooted in racial problems. Cayce agrees: "And there crept those pollutions, or polluting themselves with those mixtures that brought contempt, hatred, bloodshed and desires of self without respect to others' freedom, others' wishes—and there began then, in the later portion of this period, dissentings and divisions among the peoples of the lands."[14]

Cayce informs a different client that he once lived "in Atlantean land during those periods when there was the divisions between those of the Law of One and the Sons of Belial, or the offspring of what was the pure race and those who had projected themselves into creatures that became 'the sons of men,' as the terminology would be, rather than the creatures of God."[15] Three days later, he describes a different client as having dwelled "in Atlantean land when there were the greater questioning between the Sons of the Law of One and the Sons of Belial, or between those that were purified by keeping the pure strain."[16]

One of Cayce's last life readings about Atlantis includes "a priest of the Law of One pitted self against many of those things that were presented by a people that were being drawn gradually into self-indulgence. This was during the time when there was the breaking up of the Atlantean land. When there was then waging of the eternal Laws of One with those that worshiped Belial—and those that worshiped the satisfying of physical desire—those that worshiped ease and pleasure in the material world."[17]

This spiritual-materialist struggle preceded natural catastrophe, as Cayce describes for a client who lived "in Atlantean land when there were those activities that caused the first upheavals and the use of those influences that brought destruction to the land—among those of the Law of One, but was persuaded by and with leaders of the land to apply spiritual laws for material gain—thus brought or aided in bringing what eventually became the destruction of the material lands."[18]

Plato reports that the island of Atlantis was swallowed up by the ocean after a day and night of exceptionally violent seismic activity, followed by an extraordinary degree of magmatic debris that pervaded the seas outside the Strait of Gibraltar for literally centuries thereafter. But its final destruction may not be entirely understood in purely geologic terms. With fascinating consistency, the cataclysm is linked to the spiritual decline of the Atlanteans, from Plato and Cayce to the folk traditions of Wisconsin's Ho Chunk Indians and the Basque in Spain. Formerly known as the Winnebago, the Ho Chunk preserve generational accounts of an ancestral people who sinned against their original goodness by fighting among themselves until they were punished by the gods with a terrible flood. Basque racial memory of "the Green Isle," Atlaintika, lost in a cataclysmic storm brought about by the immorality of its inhabitants, is a version of Plato's Atlantis.

The precise relationship between social decay and physical annihilation is defined in none of these accounts, although they do provide a model for what might have occurred. Despite an apparently natural disaster that obliterated the oceanic civilization, Plato argues that the Atlanteans brought about their own demise. Their sins against the very foundation of not only society but life itself so offended the natural order of the universe that the keepers of that divine order, the gods, condemned them to oblivion. Cayce, who was unfamiliar with the dialogues, seconds the *Kritias* in his telling of a corrupt people punished with the annihilation of their fabulous island. Plato's theme of an Atlantean judgment was repeated in faraway cultures he never dreamed existed, from the Hopi Indians of the American Southwest to African tribes of the Ivory Coast.

This world memory, indelibly stamped in the consciousness of dozens of peoples often separated by thousands of miles and as many years, substantiates the verity of lost Atlantis. On another level, the resemblance of that fallen land to the present condition of world civilization is more than uncanny. Perhaps the ultimate significance and power of Atlantis to affect our time will be revealed when modern humans realize that we have allowed our society to slip almost as far.

Cayce wonders if comparisons between the modern world and Atlantis are being drawn by an influx of Atlantean souls into our time: "Be it true that there is the fact of reincarnation, and that souls once occupied such an environ [Atlantis] are entering the Earth's sphere and inhabiting individuals in the present, is it any wonder that—if they made such alteration in the affairs of Earth in their day, as to bring destruction upon themselves—if they are entering now, they might make many changes in the affairs of peoples and individuals in the present?"[19]

The apparent collapse of long-established religious and political institutions, along with the rapid deterioration of the global economy, with its attendant corporate corruption and larceny on an unprecedented scale, suggest to some that the spirit of Atlantis is reemerging in our time, as Cayce says it would. Perhaps the Followers of the Law of One have returned as the idealists who today work for the protection of our natural environment, while the despoilers of our planet's rain forests or the industrial exploiters are the reincarnated souls of the Sons of Belial.

According to Hugh Lynn Cayce, his father believed that "many individual souls [or entities] who had one or more incarnations in Atlantis are reincarnating in the Earth in this century [the twentieth century], particularly in America. Along with technological abilities, they bring tendencies for being extremists. Often they exhibit individual and group karma associated with selfishness and exploitation where others are concerned. Many of them lived during one of the periods of destruction or geological change in Atlantean history."[20]

As Edgar Cayce himself says, "Even today, either through the direct influence of being reincarnated in the Earth, or through mental effect on individuals' thoughts, they may influence individuals, groups and nations in the present."[21] The Atlanteans failed the crisis they themselves brought about and were utterly destroyed. Now, as the world again approaches a question of "to be or not to be," as Hamlet wondered, their spirits are returning to work out once more the eternal dilemma of survival.

Certainly, the most compelling parallel afforded by Cayce's life readings is the destruction of Atlantis itself. Because the Atlanteans were insatiable for unlimited material prosperity, all the previous values that made them great and powerful were discarded, even despised. They broadened their uncontrolled exploitation of the natural environment until Earth, pushed too far for too long, turned on them with overwhelming fury, annihilating them and all their works. In a single day and night, their wealth, technology, and self-indulgent power were reduced to ashes floating on the sea.

The deities associated with Atlantis—such as Poseidon, Atlas, Thaut, Kukulcan, and Viracocha—metaphorically represent the forces of history and nature to poetically complement Cayce's life readings. Thanks in large measure to Cayce and Plato, it seems more than significant that the Atlanteans' fate has come down to us at this critical moment for our planet. They made their indelible imprint on America's pre-Columbian civilizations, which rose to their own heights of cultural greatness as pyramid builders and astronomers, but fearing the loss of control over an expanding population, they increasingly resorted to physical coercion of the bloodiest kind. When a regime has sunk so low on the scale of human decency as to require mass murder as part of state policy, it has relinquished any right to exist and dooms itself to eventual extinction.

The Aztecs, however, were neither the first nor the last example of this practice in America. History—ancient and modern—is tragically replete with government leaders for whom power became an end in itself and security became inseparable from terror. The cosmic balance between ethical behavior and its physical consequences was the focal point of the Maya's cosmological understanding of humanity's relationship to life, and this was expressed in their calendar. It later evolved into the Cuauhtlixicalli, the Aztec Calendar Stone. This was the ominous Vessel of Time that accurately ticked off the final moments before the great city over which it stood was razed to the ground. Now, the same Mesoamerican calendrics point to a time beyond the morning of December 21, 2012, to a coming period that is not clearly defined.

The Maya would have explained that the events symbolized by that date will be a reflection of humankind's harmonious interdependence with nature or, conversely, our many generations of self-indulgence. In other words, our civilization will be either rewarded with continued existence, perhaps even the advent of a new golden age, or punished with all the demons of the Underworld "when Bolon Yokte descends."

To be sure, positive energies are at work in the world, striving to correct the destructive imbalance created by past centuries of unlimited gratification, uncontrolled acquisition, and suicidal exploitation of those very forces that brought us into being and sustain our existence. Compassion for sentient beings everywhere; love of all things natural;

spontaneous generosity; and building, thinking, and living in harmony with higher human nature have not yet been entirely eradicated by unmitigated decadence, arrogant intolerance, egotistical cynicism, or tyranny masquerading as democracy. Whether our nobler instincts sufficiently tip the scales in favor of all humankind was either suggested in the affirmative by 2013's near miss over Siberia or is yet to be revealed by the shape of things to come. However remarkable may have been the Maya's accurate prediction of astronomical alignment on the winter solstice morning of 2012, it had no power in itself but was only an interesting juxtaposition, one visible only from our terrestrial perspective.

It was, in short, a solely visual phenomenon. Moreover, the distances separating Earth and the sun from other celestial bodies in our galaxy are far too great for gravitational forces to have acted upon us in any way. If, in hindsight, some geophysical change is to ever be associated with December 21, 2012, it may be found in the precessional wobble that alters our planet's angular relationship with the sun, the cause of ice ages. Perhaps some unknown factor associated with the heavenly alignment would bring this about, or perhaps it was only an omen of our future, merely a signpost along the way with no direct effect on our final destination.

Before his death at ninety years of age in 2002, the renowned Australian geologist S. Warren Carey observed, "Our present interglacial has probably nearly run its course. While the world worries about a nuclear winter, we may suddenly find the seas lowering by one hundred meters or more, as the next glacial stage advances over Europe, Asia, and North America."[22]

According to John Imbrie, the paleoceanographer at Brown University who received numerous scientific awards for verifying Milanković's theory of Earth rotation as the cause of glaciation, "during the past two million years, no interglacial lasted more than twelve thousand years. Most lasted only ten thousand. Statistically speaking then, the present interglacial is already on its last legs, tottering along at the advanced age of ten thousand years."[23]

Columbia University professor James D. Hays, quoted in chapter 6, believes that "previous interglacial mild intervals comparable in warmth to the present one lasted only about ten thousand years. If it is truly similar to earlier ones—and if Man's activities do not alter natural trends—it should be nearly over."[24]

Curiously, long before 2012's galactic alignment predicted by the Mayan calendar was generally known, scientists were already concerned about the unknown repercussions of just such an event. As long ago as 1970, Craig B. Hatfield and Mark J. Camp broached the subject of "mass extinctions correlated with periodic galactic events" in the *Geological Society of America Bulletin*.[25] Fourteen years later, astronomers Richard D. Schwartz and Philip B. James described "periodic mass-extinctions and the Sun's oscillation about the galactic plane" for readers of the journal *Nature*.[26] Furthermore, a "possible relation between periodic glaciation and the flexure of the galaxy" was suggested by astronomer George E. Williams in 1975.[27]

While a new ice age is inevitable at some point, its current onset seems at least suggested by climate change. More closely imminent is the arrival of a solar hurricane, because such an event could coincide with heightened sunspot activity, which is responsible for coronal masses of plasma hurled at our planet. Their collision with Earth's magnetosphere might short out modern civilization's electronically run infrastructure. Resulting social dislocation may push the Western world toward extinction, thereby fulfilling the darkest hints of the Mayan prophecy.

A cataclysm of that global magnitude, if not too severe, might be, in fact, the catalyst for the positive change some researchers interpret as the true end of the Atlanto-Mesoamerican calendar. Drastic reduction of world population could restore the lost balance between ourselves and our environment, removing in one stroke the fundamental cause of civilization's self-destructive traits. While downsizing us from 6,763,557,000 individuals to a few million survivors or less seems like the worst holocaust of all time, nature regards such die-offs as nothing more than necessary readjustments.[28] Genetic studies show, for example, that the eruption of Indonesia's Mount Toba seventy-five thousand years ago virtually exterminated humankind.

"At one point," reports *National Geographic*, "our species may have been down to as few as two thousand individuals" from an estimated worldwide population of two *million*.[29] Yet, it was this near-extinction event resulting in our genetic hardihood, adaptability, and resilient immune system that made us everything we are today, enabling us to survive and evolve over time. Perhaps another cataclysmic restructuring for the greater good of our species is in the offing. Such a blow would also perform what we ourselves seem unable to do; namely, purge our political, economic, social, educational, cultural, and religious systems that have resulted in the world's present condition. Then, like our premodern ancestors, we would be forced to either adapt or die. That decisive challenge could galvanize our innate genius for building an altogether different way of life for the continuous fulfillment of our higher destiny.

For now, our species hesitates on the brink of something impending and momentous we sense but cannot yet clearly identify. At worst, we are collectively experiencing an instinctive anxiety attack in response to one of several lethal threats moving invisibly, if irrepressibly, toward us from the future. Indeed, we are not exempt from the same kind of natural process that has erased so many other obsolete creatures before our relatively recent appearance. The real tragedy lies not in our passing away, however well deserved, but in our squandered potential for becoming something better. On that slim excuse we have reason to hope that our descendants, as survivors, may yet live to achieve it.

One thing at least is certain: The present age and all its works cannot long endure; they must vanish, one way or another. The triumph of universal mediocrity and mendacity will end. And whatever is to come—final annihilation or unprecedented greatness—cannot be avoided. The prophecy of the Mayan calendar will be fulfilled.

# Glossary

**Atlas**   The first king of Atlantis, from whom the city, island, and surrounding Atlantic Ocean derived their names.

**Azaes**   One of Plato's Atlantean kings. He gave his name to a Mayan people, the Itza, in coastal Yucatán, where Chichén Itzá, with its depiction of Atlas-like figures, was built.

**Aztlán**   A "white island" in the Atlantic Ocean, homeland of Mēxihcah ancestors, who brought with them the first sacred calendar to Middle America.

**Bolon Yokte**   The Mayan god of the underworld, who will close out the Fifth Sun.

**Bronze Age**   The preclassical millennia from 3100 BCE to 1200 BCE, characterized by a transition from copper to superior bronze metallurgy.

**Chalchiuhtlicue**   The Mēxihcah Lady of the Turquoise Skirt, a mythic figure personifying the final destruction of Atlantis and the cataclysmic deluge that terminated 4-Atl, or 4-Water, the Fourth Sun.

**Cuauhtlixicalli**   The Eagle Bowl or Vessel of Time, the original Mēxihcah name for the Aztec Calendar Stone.

**Fimbulvetr**   In Norse sagas, the Great Winter, three consecutive years of unbroken winter conditions preceding the end of the world.

**Followers [Children] of the Law of One**   According to Edgar Cayce, a monotheistic cult that failed to achieve control of Atlantis before the island was destroyed.

**Hun yecil**   Described in the Maya's *Popol Vuh*, or *Book of Counsel*, as the Drowning of the Trees, a deluge that ravaged the world just before Kukulcan arrived on the shores of Yucatán.

**I Ching**   The ancient Chinese *Book of Changes*, a system of symbols believed to discern, as a means of divination, order or patterns from the apparent chaos of random occurrences.

**Kleito**   Described in Plato's *Kritias* as the Atlantean woman who bore Poseidon five pairs of male twins, progenitors of the royal houses of Atlantis.

**Kukulcan**   The Mayan Feathered Serpent, the bearded founding father of Mesoamerican civilization.

**Macuilli-Tonatiuh**   Clenched Fist, the destructive aspect of the sun depicted at the center of the Aztec Calendar Stone. He presided over the close of an age in 2012, but some predict his awesome fury will yet come to pass.

**Magdalenians**   Upper Paleolithic Europeans contemporary with Plato's Atlanteans.

**Mictlán**   The Mēxihcah realm of the dead.

**Nahui-Ollin**   The Mēxihcah 4-Ollin, or 4-Movement, the Mayan calendar's final age or sun, which concluded on the winter solstice sunrise of 2012.

**Ragnarök**   The Ending of the Gods in Norse cosmology, a recurring cycle of global destruction.

**remote viewing**   The acquisition of information about distant or unseen targets through extrasensory perception.

**Saquasohuh Katchina**   The Hopi Blue Star, said to appear as a messenger of worldwide chaos and calamity.

**Semsu-Hr and the Mesentiu**   Respectively, the Followers of Horus and the Harpooners, described by ancient Egyptians as the progenitors of dynastic civilization who arrived at the Nile Delta after their homeland, Sekhet Aaru, was overwhelmed by the sea.

**Sons of Belial**   A materialistic cult Edgar Cayce stated was in charge of Atlantis at the time of its destruction.

**taurobolium**   Bull sacrifice as practiced by the kings of Atlantis in the Temple of Poseidon.

**Tenochtitlán**   The Aztec capital, a city originally built by the Mēxihcah.

**Tezcatlipocha**   Smoking Mirror, the virtuous Feathered Serpent's evil twin, synonymous with the darkness and annihilation time cyclically visits upon the world.

**Tortuguero**   Place of the Turtles, located in Mexico near the border with Guatemala, where the earliest and so far only known written Mayan reference to the end of their calendar has been found.

**Tuaoi**   Described by Edgar Cayce as "the terrible, mighty crystal" that the Atlanteans abused, leading to their self-destruction.

**Yonaguni**   A small island at the end of a Japanese chain known as the Ryukyus, where a sunken "citadel" associated with Lemuria was discovered in 1985.

**yugas**   Hindu epochs or eras within a cycle of four ages.

# Notes

## INTRODUCTION.
## REWINDING THE MAYAN CALENDAR

1. Friedrich Nietzsche, *The Birth of Tragedy* (Cambridge: Cambridge University Press, 1999), 121.

2. David Hatcher Childress, *Lost Cities of North & Central America* (Kempton, Ill.: Adventures Unlimited, 1992).

3. Lars Franzen and Thomas B. Larsson, "Landscape Analysis and Stratigraphical and Geochemical Investigations of Playa and Alluvial Fan Sediments in Tunisia and Raised Bog Deposits in Sweden—A Possible Correlation between Extreme Climate Events and Cosmic Activity during the Late Holocene," in *Natural Catastrophes during Bronze Age Civilizations: Archaeological, Geological, Astronomical and Cultural Perspectives,* ed. Trevor Palmer and Mark E. Bailey (Oxford, UK: Archaeo Press, 1998), 592.

4. Allen J. Christenson, trans., *Popol Vuh: The Sacred Book of the Maya* (Norman: University of Oklahoma, 2003), 53.

5. Ibid.

6. Robert M. Schoch, *Forgotten Civilization: The Role of Solar Outbursts in Our Past and Future* (Rochester, Vt.: Bear and Co., 2012).

7. Jennifer O'Mahony, "Solar Storm Could Leave Britain without Power 'for Months,'" *Telegraph,* June 7, 2013, www.telegraph.co.uk/.../Solar-storm-could-leave-Britain-without-power-for-months.html.

8. L. Bolduc "GIC Observations and Studies in the Hydro-Québec Power System," *J. Atmos. Sol. Terr. Phys.* 64, no. 16 (2002): 1793–1802.

9. Paul Bedard, "Massive Solar Flare Narrowly Misses Earth, EMP Disaster Barely Avoided," *The Washington Examiner,* July 31, 2013,

http://m.washingtonexaminer.com/massive-solar-flare-narrowly-misses-earth-emp-disaster-barely-avoided/article/2533727.

## CHAPTER 1. HISTORICAL ATLANTIS

1. Ramses Seleem, *The Illustrated Egyptian Book of the Dead: A New Translation with Commentary* (New York: Sterling, 2001), 424.
2. Robert Kohlmann, trans., *The Edfu Texts* (Dallas: University of Texas Press, 1968).
3. Philipp August Böckh, *Commentary on Plato,* trans. Robert Pearson (London: London University Press, 1928), 45.
4. Plato, *The Timaeus and the Kritias,* trans. Desmond Lee (London: Penguin Books, 1977), 121.
5. Ibid., 24.
6. Kenneth Caroli, private e-mail correspondence with the author, February 20, 2009.
7. Plato, *The Timaeus and the Kritias,* 132.
8. Ibid., 130.
9. Ibid., 128.
10. Caroli, private e-mail correspondence with the author, February 20, 2009.
11. Desmond Lee in Plato, *The Timaeus and the Kritias,* 129.
12. Caroli, private e-mail correspondence with the author, February 20, 2009.

## CHAPTER 2. SPIRITUAL ATLANTIS

1. Plato, *The Timaeus and the Kritias,* trans. Desmond Lee (London: Penguin Books, 1977), 130.
2. Ian Kerner, *She Comes First* (San Francisco: Collins Living, HarperCollins, 2004).
3. "Wells, Joseph Warren," *Atlantipedia,* atlantipedia.ie/samples/wells-joseph-warren.

## CHAPTER 3. SACRED NUMBERS

1. Plato, *The Timaeus and the Kritias,* trans. Desmond Lee (London: Penguin Books, 1977), 133.
2. Carl Olson, *The Theology and Philosophy of Eliade: A Search for the Centre* (New York: St. Martin's, 1992), 56.

## CHAPTER 4. THE CALENDAR STONE

1. Daniel G. Brinton, *The Books of Chilan Balam* (Philadelphia: Stern, 1882), 102.
2. Carpenter, Louis. "Teobert Maler: Early Photographer of the Maya," *Art and Archaeology Magazine* 22, no. 18 (March 1981): 17.
3. Brinton, *The Books of Chilan Balami,* 59.
4. Ibid.
5. Allen J. Christenson, trans., *Popol Vuh: The Sacred Book of the Maya* (Norman: University of Oklahoma, 2003), 77.
6. Bernal Diaz del Castillo, *The True History of the Conquest of New Spain,* trans. Alfred P. Maudslay (London: Hakluyt Society, 1910), 98.
7. Zelia Nuttall, *The Fundamental Principles of Old and New World Civilizations,* vol. 2 (Cambridge, Mass.: Peabody Museum of American Archaeology and Ethnology, 1901), 72.
8. del Castillo, *The True History of the Conquest of New Spain,* 38.

## CHAPTER 5. FOUR GLOBAL CATASTROPHES OF THE ATLANTO-MAYAN CALENDAR

1. Marc Davis, Piet Hut, and Richard A. Muller, "Extinction of Species by Periodic Comet Showers," *Nature* 308 (1984): 33 (www.nature.com/nature/journal/v308/n5961/abs/308715a0.html).
2. Ibid.
3. Kenneth Caroli, private e-mail correspondence with the author, February 20, 2009.
4. Plato, *The Timaeus and the Kritias,* trans. Desmond Lee (London: Penguin Books, 1977), 130.
5. Plato, *The Timaeus and the Kritias,* 131
6. Max Heindel, *The Message of the Stars* (New York: Cosimo Classics, 2006).
7. Robert Ballington, *Encyclopedia of World Myth,* vol. 7 (London: Prior Publishers, Ltd., 1889), 631.
8. Jorge Luis Borges, *Atlas of the Mountain* (New York: Pranger, 1980), 45.
9. C. A. Burland, *The Gods of Mexico* (London: Eyre and Spottiswoode, 1970), 88.
10. Graeme R. Kearsley, *Mayan Genesis: South Asian Myths, Migrations and Iconography in Mesoamerica* (London: Yelsraek, 2001), 174.
11. Allen J. Christenson, trans., *Popol Vuh: The Sacred Book of the Maya* (Norman: University of Oklahoma, 2003).

12. C. A. Burland and Werner Foreman, *Feathered Serpent and Smoking Mirror* (New York: G. P. Putnam and Sons, 1975), 104.

13. Michael D. Coe, *Mexico* (New York: Praeger, 1966), 44.

14. Ballington, *Encyclopedia of World Myth*, 372.

15. Victor von Hagen, *The Ancient Sun Kingdoms of the Americas* (Cleveland: World Publishing Company, 1957), 138.

16. Franzen and Larsson, *Natural Catastrophes during Bronze Age Civilizations*, 593.

17. Alexander Besant, "European Genetic History Mystery Uncovered Using Ancient DNA," *Global Post*, April 24, 2013, www.globalpost.com/dispatch/news/science/130424/european-genetic-history-mystery-uncovered-using-ancient-dna.

18. Ibid.

19. Ibid.

20. Ibid.

21. Anton Mifsud, *Malta: Echoes of Plato's Island* (Valleta: Prehistoric Society of Malta, 2000).

22. Thomas Abel Brimage Spratt, *On the Geology of Malta and Gozo* (Philadelphia.: Nabu Press, 2010).

23. Franzen and Larsson, *Natural Catastrophes during Bronze Age Civilizations*, 592.

24. John Noble Wilford, "Collapse of Earliest Known Empire Is Linked to Long, Harsh Drought," *New York Times*, August 24, 1993, www.nytimes.com/1993/08/24/science/collapse-of-earliest-known-empire-is-linked-to-long-harsh-drought.html?pagewanted=all&src=pm.

25. "Greenland Ice Sheet Project 2," Institute for the Study of Earth, Oceans and Space, University of New Hampshire, www.gisp2.sr.unh.edu.

26. Karen Wright, "Empires in the Dust," *Discover*, March 1, 1998, http://discovermagazine.com/1998/mar/empiresinthedust1420.

27. Franzen and Larsson, *Natural Catastrophes during Bronze Age Civilizations*, 592.

28. Baille cited in Franzen and Larsson, *Natural Catastrophes during Bronze Age Civilizations*, 479.

29. Ibid.

30. Denis Murphy, *The Annals of Clonmacnoise* (New York: Cornell University Library, 1896), 217.

31. Richard William Howard-Vyse, *Operations Carried on at the Pyramids of Gizeh in 1837,* vol. 2 (1839; repr., New York: Eca Associates, 1988), 26.

32. Ibid.

33. Kenneth Caroli, private e-mail correspondence with the author, October 29, 2002.

34. Ibid.

35. Masse cited in Franzen and Larsson, *Natural Catastrophes during Bronze Age Civilizations,* 437.

36. Elizabeth Kolbert, "The Climate of Man—II: The Curse of Akkad," *Annals of Science,* May 2, 2005, http://faculty.washington.edu/lynnhank/The_Curse_of_Akkad.html.

37. Caroli, private e-mail correspondence with the author, October 29, 2002.

38. Han Yu, *The Veritable Record of the T'ang Emperor Shun-tsung,* trans. Bernard S. Solomon (Cambridge, Mass.: Harvard University Press, 1950), 110.

39. Plato, *The Laws,* trans. R. G. Bury (Cambridge, Mass.: Harvard University Press; London: Loeb Classical Library, W. Heinemann, 1926), 39.

40. Ibid.

## CHAPTER 6. MAYAN ASTRONOMY AND GODS

1. John Van Auken, "Understanding the Prophecy of 2012: A Mayan Age Ends," http://knol.google.com/k/edgar-cayce/understanding-the-prophecy-of-2012/2jpovtg0qy5vm/14.

2. David Stewart, trans., UT Mesoamerica Center Discussion Board, http://groups.google.com/group/utmesoamerica/browse_thread/thread/2ad64b039cb60983/0396cfd4957fd61e?pli=1.

3. Nikolai Grube, Simon Martin, and Martin Zender, "Palenque and its Neighbors," Proceedings of the Maya Hieroglyphic Workshop, March 9–10, 2002, University of Texas at Austin.

4. John Major Jenkins, "Comments on the 2012 text on Tortuguero Monument 6 and Bolon Yokte K'u," May 2006, http://Alignment2012.com.

## CHAPTER 7. THE GREAT WINTER

1. Gregory F. Fegel, "Earth on the Brink of an Ice Age." *Pravda,* http://english.pravda.ru/science/earth/11-01-2009/106922-earth_ice_age-1.

2. Ibid.

3. Ibid.

4. Fegel, "Earth on the Brink of an Ice Age."

5. Peter Harris and John Faraday, "An Urgent Signal for the Coming Ice Age," *Western Institute for Study of the Environment Colloquium,* Western Institute for Study of the Environment (Lebanon, Oregon: 2008), www.westinstenv .org/2008/04/28.

6. Ibid.

7. Edmund Rouse, *A Dictionary of Scientists* (New York: Oxford University Press, 2003).

8. James Croll, *Climate and Time in Their Geological Relations* (London: Trafalgar, 1875).

9. Wikipedia, "Milutin Milanković," http://en.wikipedia.org/wiki/ Milutin_Milanković.

10. "Wallace S. Broecker," www.absoluteastronomy.com/topics/Wallace_S._ Broecker.

11. Harris and Faraday, "An Urgent Signal for the Coming Ice Age."

12. Ibid.

13. John Imbrie, James Hays, and Nicholas Shackleton, "Variations in the Earth's Orbit: Pacemaker of the Ice Ages," *Science,* 238, no. 12 (June 1976).

14. Fegel, "Earth on the Brink of an Ice Age."

15. Daniel Carnahan, "Are We Entering a New Ice Age?" *Time* 91, no. 18 (June 24, 1974): 21–38.

16. Ibid.

17. Nigel Calder, *International Wildlife* 12, no. 15 (July 1975): 11–21.

18. Ken Caldera and F. Kasting, "Susceptibility of the Early Earth to Irreversible Glaciation by Carbon Dioxide Clouds," *Nature* 359 (September 17, 1992): 17–25.

19. Gifford H. Miller and Anne de Vernal, "Will Greenhouse Warming Lead to Northern Hemisphere Ice-sheet Growth?" *Nature* 355 (January 16, 1992): 22–30.

20. Caldera and Kasting, "Susceptibility of the Early Earth to Irreversible Glaciation."

21. Terry Devitt, "Pioneer of Climatology Dies at 88," *University of Wisconsin-Madison News,* June 12, 2008, www.news.wisc.edu/15316.

22. Ibid.

23. Terry Devitt, "About Reid Bryson," *University of Wisconsin Office of News and Public Affairs,* 2011, http://ccr.aos.wisc.edu/about/ReidBrysonScholarship/reidBryson.php.

24. John H. Douglas, "Climate Change: Chilling Possibilities," *Science News* 107, no. 9 (March 1, 1975): www.sciencenews.org/view/feature/id/225547.

25. Ibid.

26. "Scientists Fear Smog Could Cause Ice Age," *Milwaukee Journal,* December 5, 1974, 16.

27. Erin Wayman, "Carbon Dioxide in Atmosphere Reaches Landmark Level," *Science News,* Spring 2013, www.sciencenews.org/view/generic/id/350341/description/News_in_Brief_Carbon_dioxide_in_atmosphere_reaches_landmark_level.

28. Ibid.

29. Ibid.

30. Ibid.

31. "North Pole Now a Lake," Fox News, July 26, 2013, www.foxnews.com/science/2013/07/26/north-pole-now-a-lake/?intcmp=obinsite#ixzz2aUoa6tt2.

32. "Anchorage Breaks Heat Record, in Unusually Warm Summer," The Weather Channel, August 1, 2013, www.weather.com/news/anchorage-breaks-heat-record-unusually-warm-summer-20130731.

33. "Icelights: Your Burning Questions About Ice and Climate," National Snow and Ice Data Center, http://nsidc.org/icelights.

34. "Record Wettest Day in Philadelphia," Wunderground, July 29, 2013, www.wunderground.com/news/record-deluge-philly-and-south-jersey-20130728.

35. Douglas, "Climate Change: Chilling Possibilities."

36. Christopher C. Burt, "Record Hailstorms and Hail Stones," July 9, 2013, www.wunderground.com/blog/weatherhistorian.

37. "National Weather Service: Stormy Weather Brings 'Unprecedented' Hail Storms over Hawaii," Fox News, July 14, 2013, www.foxnews.mobi/quickPage.html?page=24508&content=68029027&pageNum=-1.

38. Robert W. Felix, *Not by Fire, but by Ice* (Bellevue, Wash.: Sugarhouse, 1997), 118.

39. "Science: Another Ice Age?" *Time,* November 13, 1972, www.time.com/time/magazine/article/0,9171,910467,00.html.

40. Victor Cohn, "U.S. Scientist Sees New Ice Age Coming," *The Washington Post,* July 9, 1971, http://pqasb.pqarchiver.com/washingtonpost_historical/

access/144703752.html?dids=144703752:144703752&FMT=ABS&FMTS =ABS:AI&fmac=&date=Ju.

41. Oleg Sorokhtin, "A Cold Spell Soon to Replace Global Warming," Sputnik International, http://sputniknews.com/analysis/20080103/94768732.html.

42. Steven Goddard, "Coolest Summer on Record in the U.S.," *Real Science,* http:// stevengoddard.wordpress.com/2014/07/26/coolest-summer-on-record-in-the-us.

43. Douglas, "Climate Change: Chilling Possibilities," 52.

44. Harold M. Schmeck, "Scientists Warn Predictions Must Be Made Precise to Avoid Catastrophe," *New York Times,* January 19, 1975.

45. Ibid.

46. Felix, *Not by Fire, but by Ice,* 44.

47. David E. Loper, "The Earth's Magnetic Field and Life," Geophyical Fluid Dynamics Institute, Florida State University, July 25 2005, www.iugg.org/ IAGA/iaga_pages/pdf/toulouse2005/david_loper.pdf.

48. Imbrie, Hays, and Shackleton, "Variations in the Earth's Orbit," 22.

49. I. K. Crain, "Possible Direct Causal Relation between Geomagnetic Reversals and Biological Extinctions," *Geology Society of America Bulletin* 82 (1971): 17.

50. C. G. A. Harrison, and J. M. Prospero, "Reversal of the Earth's Magnetic Field and Climate Changes," *Nature* 250 (August 16, 1974): 23.

51. Thomas J. Crowley, *Consequences,* www.gcrio.org/CONSEQUENCES/ winter96/crowley.html.

52. David M. Raup, "Magnetic Reversals and Mass Extinctions," *Nature* 314 (March 25, 1985): 341–43, www.nature.com/nature/journal/v314/n6009/ abs/314341a0.html.

53. Geneviève M. Woillard, "Grand Pile Peat Bog: A Continuous Pollen Record for the Last 140,000 Years," *Quaternary Research* 9 (1978): 1–21.

54. Ibid.

55. W. F. Ruddiman and A. McIntyre, "Severity and Speed of Northern Hemisphere Glaciation Pulses: The Limiting Case?" *Geological Society of America Bulletin* 93, no. 12 (December 1982): 1273–79, http://gsabulletin .gsapubs.org/content/vol93/issue12.

56. Douglas, "Climate Change: Chilling Possibilities."

57. Felix, *Not by Fire, but by Ice,* 143.

58. John C. Ridge, Greg Balco, Robert L. Bayless, Catherine C. Beck, Laura B. Carter, Jody L. Dean, Emily B. Voytek, and Jeremy H. Wei, "The New

North American Varve Chronology: A Precise Record of Southeastern Laurentide Ice Sheet Deglaciation and Climate, 18.2–12.5 kyr BP, and Correlations with Greenland Ice Core Records," *American Journal of Science* 312, no. 7 (September 2012): 685–722.

59. Woillard, "Grand Pile Peat Bog."

## CHAPTER 8.
## A SUPER SOLAR STORM

1. Committee on the Societal and Economic Impacts of Severe Space Weather Events, *Severe Space Weather Events—Understanding Societal and Economic Impacts: A Workshop Report* (Washington, D.C.: National Academies Press, 2009).

2. Michael Brooks, "Space Storm Alert: 90 Seconds from Catastrophe," *New Scientist,* March 23, 2009, www.ntia.doc.gov/legacy/broadbandgrants/comments/7927.pdf.

3. Paul Bedard, "Massive Solar Flare Narrowly Misses Earth, EMP Disaster Barely Avoided," *Washington Examiner,* July 31, 2013.

4. Stuart Clark, *The Sun Kings: The Unexpected Tragedy of Richard Carrington and the Tale of How Modern Astronomy Began* (London: Princeton, 2007), 49.

5. Bruce Tsurutani, "NASA Warns of Super Solar Storm," May 9, 2009, http://socioecohistory.wordpress.com/2009/05/09/nasa-warns-of-super-solar-storm-2012.

6. Ibid.

7. National Academy of Sciences, www.pnas.org/content/105/20.toc.

8. Tony Phillips, "Severe Space Weather: Social and Economic Impacts," January 21, 2009, http://science.nasa.gov/headlines/y2009/21jan_severespaceweather.htm?list5029.

9. John Kappenmann, "Severe Space Weather Events: Understanding Societal and Economic Impacts Workshop Report," http://books.nap.edu/catalog.php?record_id=12507.

10. Ibid.

11. Brooks, "Space Storm Alert."

12. Quoted in Tony Phillips, "Severe Space Weather," NASA Space Place, www.cardiff-astronomical-society.co.uk/nasaspaceplace/nasasp012009-1.html.

13. Federal Bureau of Investigation, "Uniform Crime Reports," 2008, www.fbi .gov/ucr/08aprelim/index.html.

14. Brooks, "Space Storm Alert."

15. Ibid.

16. Ibid.

17. Ibid.

18. Kappenmann, "Severe Space Weather Events."

19. Robert Roy Britt, "The Great Solar Storm of 1859 Revealed," www.rense .com/general43/great.htm.

20. Brooks, "Space Storm Alert."

21. Bedard, "Massive Solar Flare Narrowly Misses Earth."

22. "Timeline: The 1859 Solar Superstorm," *Scientific American,* July 29, 2008, www.sciam.com/article.cfm?id=timeline-the-1859-solar-superstorm.

23. Tsurutani, "NASA Warns of Super Solar Storm."

24. Andrew Fazekas, "Giant Solar Tornado Caught in NASA Video," *National Geographic News,* March 29, 2012, http://news.nationalgeographic.com/ news/2012/03/120329-sun-solar-tornadoes-biggest-nasa-sdo-space-science.

25. Ibid.

26. "Sunspot Credited with Rail Tie-up," *New York Times,* May 16, 1921, 2.

## CHAPTER 9.
## MONSTERS FROM BENEATH THE SEA

1. Terrance Aym, "Doomsday: How BP Gulf Disaster May Have Triggered a World-killing Event," World Issues, July 6, 2010, www.worldissues360 .com/index.php/doomsday-how-bp-gulf-disaster-may-have-triggered-a-world-killing-event-11785.

2. NASA, "The Great Dying," http://science.nasa.gov/science-news/science-at-nasa/2002/28jan_extinction.

3. K. Koeberl, K. A. Farley, B. Peucker-Ehrenbrink, and M. A. Sephton, "Geochemistry of the End-Permian Extinction Event in Austria and Italy: No Evidence for an Extraterrestrial Component," *Geology* 32, no. 12 (2004): 1053–56.

4. James P. Kennett, Kevin G. Cannariato, Ingrid. L. Hendy, and Richard J. Behl, "Carbon Isopotic Evidence for Methane Hydrate Instability during Quaternary Interstadials," *Science* 288, no. 5463 (April 7, 2000): 128–33.

5. Bruce Tsurutani, "NASA Warns of Super Solar Storm," May 9, 2009,

http://socioecohistory.wordpress.com/2009/05/09/nasa-warns-of-super-solar-storm-2012.

6. Aym, "Doomsday."

7. Dan Dorritie, "Killer in Our Midst," 2007, www.killerinourmidst.com.

8. Ibid.

9. Ibid.

10. David Archer, Bruce Buffet, and Victor Brovkin, "Ocean Methane Hydrates as a Slow Tipping Point in the Global Carbon Cycle," *Proceedings of the National Academy of Sciences of the United States of America* 46, no. 49 (January 29, 2008): 31.

## CHAPTER 10.
## EAST-WEST PARALLELISMS

1. Kenneth Caroli, private e-mail correspondence with the author, February 20, 2009.

2. Ibid.

3. Laurie L. Patton, trans., *The Bhagavad Gita* (New York: Penguin Classics, 2008), book 4: 5, 7, 8.

4. Chief Dan Evehema cited in Thomas E. Mails, *The Hopi Survival Kit: The Prophecies, Instructions and Warnings Revealed by the Last Elders* (NY: Penguin Books, 1997), 68.

5. Ibid.

6. Ibid.

7. Allen C. Ross, *Mitakuye Oyasin: We Are All Related* (Bismarck, N.Dak.: Wicóni Wasté Publishers, 1989), 174.

8. Ibid, 173.

9. Frank Waters, *Book of the Hopi* (New York: Viking, 1963), 137.

10. Snorri Sturluson, *The Prose Edda,* trans. Jesse L. Byock (New York: Penguin Classics, 2006), 77.

11. Kevin Crossley-Holland, *The Norse Myths* (New York: Pantheon Books, 1980), stanza 44.

12. Ibid., stanza 49.

13. Padraic Colum, *Nordic Gods and Heroes* (New York: Dover, 1996), 61.

14. Dennis J. McKenna and Terence McKenna, *The Invisible Landscape: Mind, Hallucinogens and the I Ching* (New York: Seabury, 1975), 43.

15. Ibid., 41.

## CHAPTER 11.
## THE INCAN CALENDAR

1. Rand Flem-Ath and Rose Flem-Ath, "The Wayward Sun," http://cyberspaceorbit.com/waysun.html.

2. Ibid.

## CHAPTER 12. DOOM NUMBER

1. Kenneth S. Guthrie, *The Pythagorean Sourcebook and Library: An Anthology of Ancient Writings Which Relate to Pythagoras and Pythagorean Philosophy* (Grand Rapids, Mich.: Phanes Press, 1987), 7.

2. Leonardo Tarán, *Academica: Plato, Philip of Opus, and the Pseudo-Platonic Epinomis* (Philadelphia: American Philosophical Society, 1975), 42.

3. Maria Valla, *The Power of Numbers* (Camarillo, Calif.: DeVorss and Co.), 1971, 35.

4. Erica Vidnjevitch, "Lunatics or Solartics?" *Psychology Today* 7, no. 4 (December 1979): 9–13.

5. Dennis Duda, "Whale Song of the Sun," *Natural History* 53, no. 11 (August 1982): 11–16.

6. Frank Godwin, "Fish Behavior Surprises Marine Biologists," *Chicago Today Magazine* 13, no 10 (December 30, 2006): 22.

7. Burland, *Gods of Mexico.*

8. Edward Turner, "Scientists Warn Time Is Short for Environment," *Columbine Gazette* 2, no. 4 (January 5, 2002): 18.

## CHAPTER 13. HOW COULD
## THEY HAVE POSSIBLY KNOWN?

1. Erich von Däniken, *Chariots of the Gods* (New York: Berkeley Books, 1999), 102.

## CHAPTER 14. PLATO AND CAYCE

1. Herbert M. Vaughan, *The Medici Popes* (New York: G. P. Putnam and Sons, 1908).

2. Edgar Cayce, *Atlantis, the Edgar Cayce Readings,* vol. 22 (Virginia Beach, Va.: Association for Research and Enlightenment, 1987), 1602–3.

3. Ibid.

4. Hugh Lynn Cayce, *Cayce on Atlantis* (Virginia Beach, Va.: Association for Research and Enlightenment, 1980), 173.

5. Ibid, 188.

6. Cayce, *Atlantis,* 1391-1 F.28, 1935.

7. Ibid., 1874-1 F.39, 5/6/39.

8. Alfred North Whitehead, *Process and Reality* (New York: Free Press, 1979), 231.

9. Plato, *The Timaeus and the Kritias,* trans. Desmond Lee (London: Penguin Books, 1977).

10. P. Allen, *Evagrius Scholasticus, the Church Historian* (Leuven, Belgium: Peeters Publishers, 1981), 213.

11. Ibid, 215.

12. J. Barnes, *The Cambridge Companion to Aristotle* (Cambridge, UK: Cambridge University Press, 1995), 172.

13. Aelian, *On the Characteristics of Animals,* vol. 3, books 12–17 (Cambridge, Mass.: Loeb Classical Library, 1958), 99.

14. Auguste Helaine, *Astronomy Across Cultures: The History of Non-Western Astronomy* (Brendt, Netherlands: Kluwer Academic Publishers, 2000), 182.

15. Thomas L. Pangle, *The Laws of Plato* (New York: Basic Books, 1980), 146.

## CHAPTER 15.
## LOST MOTHERLAND, DROWNED FATHERLAND

1. Edgar Cayce, *Atlantis, the Edgar Cayce Readings,* vol. 22 (Virginia Beach, Va.: Association for Research and Enlightenment, 1987), 274-1 M.34, 2/13/33.

2. Ibid., 877-26 M.46, 5/23/38.

3. Ibid., 442-1 M.57, 11/15/33.

4. Ibid., 2713-5 F.43, 9/23/29.

5. Ibid., 257-201 M.45, 9/4/38.

6. Ibid., 2464-2 F.24, 11/13/41.

7. Ibid.

8. Ibid., 618-3 F.61, 3/6/35.

9. Ibid., 2262 F.22, 10/11/40.

10. Ibid., 787-23 M.44, 1/12/37.

11. Ibid., 2750-1 F.44, 3/12/30.

## CHAPTER 16.
## EDGAR CAYCE'S DREAM OF LEMURIA

1. Edgar Cayce, *Atlantis, the Edgar Cayce Readings,* vol. 22 (Virginia Beach, Va.: Association for Research and Enlightenment, 1987), 877-26 M.46, 5/23/38.

2. Ibid., 364-13, 11/17/32.

3. Ibid., 2801-5 F.43, 5/11/25.

4. Vada F. Carlson, *The Great Migration* (Virginia Beach, Va.: Association for Research and Enlightenment, 1970).

5. Cayce, *Atlantis,* 4349-1 M.14, 10/13/24.

6. Carlson, *Great Migration,* 56.

## CHAPTER 17. HE SAW ATLANTIS

1. Benjamin R. Foster, ed. and trans., *The Epic of Gilgamesh* (New York: W. W. Norton, 1997), 68.

2. Edgar Cayce, *Atlantis, the Edgar Cayce Readings,* vol. 22 (Virginia Beach, Va.: Association for Research and Enlightenment, 1987), 1743-1 M.28, 11/11/38.

3. Ibid., 364-3, 2/16/32.

4. Webre, Alfred L. "Earth Changes: A Spiritual Approach," http://exopolitics .blogs.com/earth_changes.

5. Cayce, *Atlantis,* 5748-6, 7/1/32.

6. Ibid., 2688-1 M.2, 1/16/42.

7. Ibid., 797-1.

8. Ibid., 440-5 M.23, 12/20/33.

9. Ibid.

10. Ibid., 2462-2 M.35, 6/19/41.

11. Ibid., 440-5 M.23, 12/20/33.

12. Ibid., 2012-1 M.26, 9/25/39.

13. Ibid.

14. Ibid., 1073-4 F.51, 2/17/36.

15. Ibid., 1210-1 M.54, 6/29/36.

16. Ibid., 1486-1 M.55, 11/26/37.

17. Ibid.

18. Ibid.

19. Ibid., 691-1 F.20, 8/17/34.

20. Ibid., 2688-1 M.2, 1/16/42.

## CHAPTER 18. THE TERRIBLE, MIGHTY CRYSTAL

1. Edgar Cayce, *Atlantis, the Edgar Cayce Readings,* vol. 22 (Virginia Beach, Va.: Association for Research and Enlightenment, 1987), 263-4 F.23, 3/6/35.

2. Ibid., 528-14 F.29, 12/30/34.

3. Ibid., 440-5 M.23, 12/20/33.

4. Ibid., 2072-10 F.32, 7/22/42.

5. Ibid., 440-5 M.23, 12/20/33.

6. Ibid., 3004-1 F.55, 5/15/43.

7. Ibid., 440-5 M.23, 12/20/33.

8. Ibid., 440-5 M.23, 12/20/33.

9. Ibid., 378-16 M.56, 10/29/33.

10. 1989 IBM Stock Holders' Report cited by Cayce, 92.

11. Ibid., 440-5 M.23, 12/20/33.

12. Ibid., 1298-1 F.43, 11/27/36.

13. R. J. Collins, D. F. Nelson, A. L. Schawlow, W. Bong, C. G. Garrett, and W. Kaiser, "Coherence, Narrowing, Directionality, and Relaxation Oscillations in the Light Emission from Ruby," *Physical Review Letters* 5, no. 7, 303–5.

14. Cayce, *Atlantis,* 440-5 M.23, 12/20/33.

15. Plato, *The Timaeus and the Kritias,* trans. Desmond Lee (London: Penguin Books, 1977).

16. Cayce, *Atlantis,* 440-5 M.23, 12/20/33.

## CHAPTER 19. NORTH AMERICA'S ATLANTO-LEMURIAN LEGACY

1. Joseph H. Wherry, *The Totem Pole Indians* (New York: Funk and Wagnalls, 1964), 227.

2. Edgar Cayce, *Atlantis, the Edgar Cayce Readings,* vol. 22 (Virginia Beach, Va.: Association for Research and Enlightenment, 1987), 1215-4 M.17, 6/4/37.

3. Ibid., 5750-1, 11/12/33.

4. Ibid., 3004-1 F.55, 5/15/43.

5. Ibid., 5750-1, 11/12/33.

6. Ibid., 1286-1 F.30, 11/8/36.

7. Flavius Josephus, *The New Complete Works of Josephus,* trans. William Whiston (New York: Kregel Academic and Professional, 1999), 128.

8. Hugh McCulloch, "The Bat Creek Stone," *Tennessee Anthropologist* 18, no. 9 (Spring 1993): 47.

9. Cayce, *Atlantis,* 691-1 F.20, 8/17/34.

10. Cayce, Edgar Evans. *Mysteries of Atlantis Revisited* (New York: Harper & Row Publishers, 1988).

11. Cayce, *Atlantis,* 1219-1 F.40, 7/13/36.

12. Ibid., 509-1 F.54, 2/18/34.

13. Ibid., 851-2 F.44, 8/23/40.

14. Ibid., 691-1 F.20, 8/17/34.

15. Ibid., 812-1 F.48, 2/4/35.

16. Vada F. Carlson, *The Great Migration* (Virginia Beach, Va.: Association for Research and Enlightenment, 1970), 69.

17. Cayce, *Atlantis,* 440-5 M.23, 12/20/33.

18. Ibid., 1252-1 F.2, 4/26/36.

19. Ibid., 470-22 M.48, 7/5/38.

## CHAPTER 20. MIDDLE AMERICAN CRUCIBLE

1. Edgar Cayce, *Atlantis, the Edgar Cayce Readings,* vol. 22 (Virginia Beach, Va.: Association for Research and Enlightenment, 1987), 5750-1, 11/12/33.

2. Vada F. Carlson, *The Great Migration* (Virginia Beach, Va.: Association for Research and Enlightenment, 1970), 104.

3. Cayce, *Atlantis,* 364-3 F.26, 3/30/34.

4. Ibid., 851-2 F.44, 8/23/40.

5. Ibid., 2073-2 F.39, 4/12/40.

6. Ibid., 3384-3 M.22, 12/5/43.

7. Ibid., 2397-1 F.39, 11/11/40.

8. Ibid., 5750-1, 11/12/33.

9. Ibid.

10. Richard N. Luxton, trans., *The (Chilam Balam) Book of Chumayel; The Counsel Book of the Yucatec Maya* (Walnut Creek, Calif.: Aegean Park, 1995), 83.

## CHAPTER 21.
## THE INCA'S ATLANTO-LEMURIAN HERITAGE

1. Edgar Cayce, *Atlantis, the Edgar Cayce Readings,* vol. 22 (Virginia Beach, Va.: Association for Research and Enlightenment, 1987), 470-2 M.35, 5/15/25.

2. Alexander P. Braghine, *The Shadow of Atlantis* (Kempton, Ill.: Adventures Unlimited, 1997), 162.

3. Cayce, *Atlantis,* 3611-1 F.59, 12/31/43.

4. Ibid., 3345-1 F.47, 10/24/43.

5. Ibid., 5252-1 M.29, 6/14/44.

6. Ibid., 1159-1 F.80, 5/5/36.

7. Ibid., 845-1 F.36, 3/5/35.

8. James Churchward, *The Books of the Golden Age—The Sacred and Inspired Writings of Mu* (1927; repr., Albuquerque: Brotherhood of Life Publishing, 1997), 79–81.

9. Cayce, *Atlantis,* 2305-2 M.60, 6/9/29.

10. Ibid., 364-4, 2/16/32.

11. Ibid., 4805-1 F.49, 12/3/25.

12. Ibid., 2887-1 F.57, 5/25/31.

13. Ibid., 2688-1 M.2, 1/16/42.

14. Ibid., 772-2 F.42, 8/5/36.

## CHAPTER 22. EDGAR CAYCE'S
## ATLANTEANS AND LEMURIANS

1. Vincent Scramuzza, *The Emperor Claudius* (Cambridge, Mass.: Harvard University Press, 1940), 231.

2. Peter Hulme. *Wild Majesty: Encounters with Caribs from Columbus to the Present Day, An Anthology* (London: Oxford University Press, 1992), 168.

3. Edgar Cayce, *Atlantis, the Edgar Cayce Readings,* vol. 22 (Virginia Beach, Va.: Association for Research and Enlightenment, 1987), 813-1.

4. Ibid., 470-2 M.35, 5/15/25.

5. Ibid., 1219-1 F.40, 7/13/36.

6. Ibid., 2537-1.

7. Ibid., 615-1, 487-17, 961-15, 1007-3, 1035-1, 1217-1, 1574-1.

8. Ibid., 440-5 M.23, 12/20/33.

9. Ibid., 5750-1 11/12/33.

10. Ibid., 3004-1 F.55, 5/15/43.

11. Ignatius Donnelly, *Atlantis, the Antediluvian World* (New York: Harpers, 1882), 218.

12. W. B. Emery, *Archaic Egypt* (New York: Penguin, 1974).

13. Donnelly, *Atlantis, the Antediluvian World,* 238.

14. Veronica Ions, *Egyptian Mythology* (London: Hamlyn, 1968).

15. Cayce, *Atlantis,* 38-1.

16. Ibid., 5750-1.

17. Ibid., 1523-4.

18. Elena Maria Whishaw, *Atlantis in Spain* (Kempton, Ill.: Adventures Unlimited, 1994).

19. Cayce, Atlantis, 5232-1.

20. Ibid., 303-1.

21. Ibid., 2545-1.

22. Ibid., 1219-1.

23. Ibid., 1743-1.

24. Ibid., 5750-1.

25. Ibid.

26. Ibid., 1690-1.

27. Ibid., 966-1.

28. Ibid., 1523-4.

29. Ibid.

30. Ibid., 3004-1.

31. Ibid., 500-1.

32. Ibid., 5252-1.

33. Ibid., 5232-1.

34. Ibid.

35. Ibid.

36. Ibid., 2725-1, 364-6.

37. Ibid., 2887-1.

38. Ibid., 2464-2.

39. Ibid., 2886-1.

40. Ibid.

41. Ibid.

42. Ibid., 2655-1.

43. Ibid., 1827-1.

44. Ibid.

45. Ibid., 1610-2.

46. Ibid., 1681-1.

47. Ibid., 3344-1

48. Ibid., 2988-2.

49. Ibid., 1827-1.

50. Ibid., 2690-1.

51. Ibid., 1695-1.

52. Ibid.

53. Ibid., 2856-1.

54. Ibid., 3004-1.

55. Ibid., 2986-1.

56. Ibid., 5252-1.

57. Ibid., 2655-1.

58. Ibid.

59. Ibid., 1610-2.

60. Ibid., 3344-1.

61. Ibid.

62. Ibid., 2988-2.

63. Ibid.

## CONCLUSION. FIREBALLS AND POISONED BEES

1. Clara Moscowitz, "Asteroid headed toward Earth?" Fox News, March 20 2013, www.foxnews.com/science/2013/03/20/asteroid-threat-earthly-budgets.

2. Ibid.

3. Alicia Fowler, "Einstein on Bees," Global Climate Change, http://globalclimatechange.wordpress.com/2007/04/20/einstein-on-bees.

4. William Stockwin, "Colony Collapse Disorder Threatens a Future without Honeybees," Examiner, January 31, 2011, www.examiner.com/article/colony-collapse-disorder-threatens-a-future-without-honeybees.

5. "EFSA Identifies Risk to Bees from Neonicotinoids," European Food Safety Authority, January 16 2013, www.efsa.europa.eu/en/press/news/130116.htm.

6. Plato, *The Timaeus and the Kritias,* trans. Desmond Lee (London: Penguin Books, 1977).

7. Serge Hutin, *History of Astrology: Science or Superstition?* (London: Pyramid, 1972), 94.

8. Plato, *The Timaeus and the Kritias.*

9. Edgar Cayce, *Atlantis, the Edgar Cayce Readings,* vol. 22 (Virginia Beach, Va.: Association for Research and Enlightenment, 1987), 364-4, 2/16/32.

10. Ibid., 1416-1 M.34, 7/27/37.

11. Ibid.

12. W. Pitezel, *Missionary Life* (Cincinnati: Walden and Stowe, 1857).

13. Cayce, *Atlantis,* 1417-1 M.8, 7/30/37.

14. Ibid., 3345-1 F.47, 10/24/43.

15. Ibid., 1688-6 F.30, 2/14/41.

16. Ibid., 1859-1 M.26, 4/7/39.

17. Ibid., 640-1, 8/22/34.

18. Ibid., 256-1 M.23, 7/20/35.

19. Ibid., 440-1 M.23, 11/14/33.

20. Hugh Lynn Cayce, *Cayce on Atlantis* (Virginia Beach, Va.: Association for Research and Enlightenment, 1980), 173.

21. Cayce, *Atlantis,* 440-1 M.23, 11/14/33.

22. Samuel Warren Carey, *Expanding Earth: Developments in Geotectonics,* (Amsterdam: Elsevier Scientific Publications Company, 1976).

23. John Imbrie, James Hays, and Nicholas Shackleton, "Variations in the Earth's Orbit: Pacemaker of the Ice Ages," *Science,* 238, no.12 (June 1976), 7.

24. Brooks, "Space Storm Alert," 33.

25. Craig B. Hatfield and Mark J. Camp, "Mass Extinctions Correlated with Periodic Galactic Events," *Geological Society of America Bulletin* 18 (March 1970): 85.

26. Richard D. Schwartz, and Philip B. James, "Periodic Mass Extinctions and the Sun's Oscillation about the Galactic Plane," *Nature* 308 (April 19, 1984): 27.

27. George E. Williams, "Possible Relation between Periodic Glaciation and the Flexure of the Galaxy," *Earth and Planet Science Letter* 26 (1975): 17.

28. U.S. Census Bureau, May 30, 2009, www.census.gov/ipc/www/popclockworld .html.

29. Amitabh Avasthi, "After Near Extinction, Humans Split into Isolated Groups," *National Geographic News,* April 24, 2008, http://news .nationalgeographic.com/news/2008/04/080424-humans-extinct.html.

# Bibliography

Aldred, Cyril. *The Egyptians*. New York: Praeger, 1962.

Alexander, William. *North American Mythology*. New York: Harcourt Brace, 1935.

Anklin, M. "Climate Instability during the Last Interglacial Period Recorded in the GRIP Ice Core." *Nature* 364 (July 15, 1993): 203–7.

Arribas, A. *The Iberians*. New York: Praeger, 1950.

Baines, John, and Jaromir Malek. *Atlas of Ancient Egypt*. New York: Oxford University Press, 1980.

Banincourt, Michael. *Five Letters of Cortez to the Emperor*. New York: W. W. Norton, 1962.

Baran, Michael. *Atlantis Reconsidered*. New York: Exposition, 1981.

Boylan, Patrick. *Thoth, the Hermes of Egypt*. Oxford University Press, 1922.

Braghine, Col. A. *The Shadow of Atlantis*. Kempton, Ill.: Adventures Unlimited, 1997. First published in 1940.

Brestead, James. *A History of Egypt*. New York: Scribner's and Sons, 1909.

Briggs, Cabot. *The Stone Age Races of Northwest Africa*. London: Oxford Press, 1973.

Brinton, Daniel G. *The Books of Chilan Balam*. Philadelphia: Stern, 1882.

Broecker, Wallace S., D. L. Thurber, J. Goddard, Te-lung Ku, R. K. Matthews, and K. L. Mesolella. "Milankovitch Hypothesis Supported by Precise Dating of Coral Reefs and Deep-Sea Sediments." *Science* 159 (January 19, 1968): 297–300.

Brown, George. "Illiterate Man Becomes a Doctor When Hypnotized, Strange Power Shown by Edgar Cayce Puzzles Physicians." *New York Times* 22, no. 13 (March 3, 1910).

Bryant, Alice. *The Message of the Crystal Skull*. Woodbury, Minn.: Llewellyn, 1989.

Budge, E. A. Wallis. *Ancient Egyptian Amulets and Talismans*. New York: University Books, 1968.

Burland, C. A. *The Gods of Mexico*. London: Eyre and Spottiswoode, 1970.

Burland, C. A., and Werner Foreman. *Feathered Serpent and Smoking Mirror*. New York: G. P. Putnam and Sons, 1975.

Bushnell, G. H. S. *Peru*. New York: Praeger, 1967.

Carey, S. Warren. *The Expanding Earth*. Developments in Geotectonics. New York: Elsevier, 1976.

Carlson, Vada F. *The Great Migration*. Virginia Beach, Va.: Association for Research and Enlightenment, 1970.

Caso, Alfonso. *The Civilizations of Ancient Mexico*. New York: Prescott, 1960.

Catlin, George. *Illustrations of the Manners, Customs, and Conditions of the North American Indians*. New York: Dover, 1970.

Cayce, Edgar. *Atlantis: The Edgar Cayce Readings*. Vol. 22. Virginia Beach, Va.: Association for Research and Enlightenment, 1987.

Cayce, Hugh Lynn. *Cayce on Atlantis*. Virginia Beach, Va.: Association for Research and Enlightenment,1980.

Cerve, W. S. *Lemuria: The Lost Continent of the Pacific*. San Jose, Calif.: AMORC, 1942.

Childress, David Hatcher. *Lost Cities and Ancient Mysteries of South America*. Kempton, Ill.: Adventures Unlimited, 1986.

———. *Lost Cities of Ancient Lemuria and the Pacific*. Kempton, Ill.: Adventures Unlimited, 1988.

———. *Lost Cities of China, Central Asia and India*. Kempton, Ill.: Adventures Unlimited, 1985.

Christenson, Allen J., trans. *Popol Vuh: The Sacred Book of the Maya*. Norman: University of Oklahoma Press, 2003.

Churchward, James. *The Children of Mu*. Albuquerque: BE Books, 1988. First published in 1928.

———. *Cosmic Forces of Mu*. Vol. 1. Albuquerque: BE Books, 1998. First published in 1933.

———. *Cosmic Forces of Mu*. Vol. 2. Albuquerque: BE Books, 1998. First published in 1935.

Clark, R. T. Rundle. *Myth and Symbol in Ancient Egypt*. London: Thames and Hudson, 1959.

Coe, Michael D. *Mexico*. New York: Praeger, 1966.

Colum, Padraic. *Nordic Gods and Heroes*. New York: Dover, 1996.

"Computer Models Predict Magnetic Pole Reversal in Earth and Sun Can Bring End to Human Civilization in 2012." March 1, 2005. http://en.minghui .org/html/articles/2005/3/6/58186.html.

Cooper, C. W. *Crystal Magic*. London: Faber and Faber, 1986.

Corliss, William R. *Ancient Structures*. Glen Arm, Md.: Sourcebook Project, 2001.

Crossley-Holland, Kevin. *The Norse Myths*. New York: Pantheon Books, 1980.

Crow, Robert. *Crystal Handbook*. Somerset, MA: Hathaway, 1984.

Daniel, Glyn. *The Illustrated Encyclopedia of Archaeology*. New York: Thomas Y. Crowell, 1970.

Dansgaard, W., and J. Duplessey. "The Eemian Interglacial and Its Termination." *Boreas* 10 (1981), 13.

Davies, Nigel. *The Ancient Kingdoms of Mexico*. London: Penguin Books, 1982.

De Ayala, Felipe Guaman Poma. *Nueva corónica y buen gobierno* [*New Chronicle and Good Government*]. Translated by David I. Frye. New York: Hackett, 2006.

De Camp, L. Sprague. *Lost Continents: The Atlantis Theme in History, Science and Literature*. New York: Gnome, 1954.

De Onis, Harriet, trans. *The Incas of Pedro de Cieza de Leon*. Norman: University of Oklahoma Press, 1959.

Devitt, Terry. "Pioneer of Climatology Dies at 88." University of Wisconsin–Madison. www.news.wisc.edu/15316.

Doake, Christopher S. M. "Climate Change and Geomagnetic Field Reversals: A Statistical Correlation." *Earth and Planetary Science Letters* 38 (1978): 313–18.

Donnelly, Ignatius. *Atlantis, the Antediluvian World*. New York: Harpers, 1882.

Dorland, Frank. *Holy Ice*. Lakeville, Minn.: Galde, 1995.

Duran, Fray Diego. *Book of the Gods and the Rites of the Ancient Calendar*. Translated by Fernando Horcasitas and Doris Heyden. Norman: University of Oklahoma Press, 1971.

Ebon, Martin. *Atlantis: The New Evidence*. New York: New American Library, 1977.

Ellis Davidson, H. R. *Gods and Myths of Northern Europe*. New York: Penguin Books, 1982.

Ellis, Ralph. *Thoth, Architect of the Universe*. Kempton, Ill.: Adventures Unlimited, 2001.

Emery, Walter B. *Archaic Egypt, Culture and Civilization in Egypt Five Thousand Years Ago*. London: Penguin Books, 1961.

Engl, Lieselotte, and Theo Engl. *Twilight of Ancient Peru*. New York: MacGraw Hill, 1969.

Erman, Adolf. *Life in Ancient Egypt*. New York: Dover, 1966.

Fegel, Gregory F. "Earth on the Brink of an Ice Age." *Pravda,* November 1, 2009. http://english.pravda.ru/science/earth/106922-earth_ice_age-0.

Felix, Robert W. *Not by Fire, but by Ice*. Bellevue, Wash.: Sugarhouse, 1997.

Fiedel, Stuart J. "Onset of the Younger Dryas Chronozone in the American West and Its Temporal Relationship to Clovis Expansion." http://gsa .confex.com/gsa/inqu/finalprogram/abstract_53841.htm.

Gaddis, Vincent H. *Native American Myths and Mysteries*. New York: McDonald, 1972.

Gallenkamp, Charles. *Maya*. London: Frederick Muller, 1960.

Garvin, Richard. *The Crystal Skull*. New York: Doubleday, 1971.

Giovannini, A. "Peut-on démythifier l'Atlantide?" *Museum Helveticum* (Paris) 42 (1985): 151–56.

Graves, Robert. *The Greek Myths*. Vols. 1 and 2. Harmondsworth, UK: Penguin Books, 1984.

Greenland Ice-core Project (GRIP) Members. "Climate Instability during the Last Interglacial Period Recorded in the GRIP Ice-core." *Nature* 364 (July 15, 1993): 203–7.

Hennes, D. *The American Aborigines: Their Origins and Antiquity*. New York: Cooper Square, 1963.

Hodge. F. W. *The Handbook of the American Indians North of Mexico*. 30 vols. Washington, D.C.: Bulletins of the Bureau of American Ethnology, 1907.

Hunter, Bruce C. *A Guide to Ancient Mexican Ruins*. Norman: University of Oklahoma Press, 1978.

Imbrie, John, James Hays, and Nicholas Shackleton. "Variations in the Earth's Orbit: Pacemaker of the Ice Ages." *Science* 238, no.12 (June 1976).

Imel, Martha Ann, and Dorothy Myers. *Goddesses in World Mythology, A Biographical Dictionary*. New York: Oxford University Press, 1993.

Ions, Veronica. *Egyptian Mythology*. London: Hamlyn, 1968.

Jakeman, M. Wells. *The Origin and History of the Mayas*. Los Angeles: Research Publishing, 1957. First published in 1945.

Jenkins, John Major. "The How and Why of the Mayan End Date in 2012 A.D." *The Mountain Astrologer* (December 1994): 14–26.

Jimenez, Randall C., and Richard B. Graeber. *The Aztec Calendar Handbook*. Santa Clara, Calif.: Historical Science Publishing, 2001.

Johnson, Charles William. "The Aztec Calendar: The Spatial Divisions," *Science in Ancient Artwork Series,* 4, http://earthmatrix.com/aztec/spatial/introduc.htm.

Joseph, Frank. *Atlantis and Other Lost Worlds*. London: Arcturus, 2008.

———. *The Destruction of Atlantis*. Rochester, Vt.: Inner Traditions, 2002.

———. *Discovering the Mysteries of Ancient America*. Franklin Lakes, N.J.: New Page Books, 2005.

———. *Edgar Cayce's Atlantis and Lemuria*. Virginia Beach, Va.: Association for Research and Enlightenment, 2001.

———. *The Last Civilization of Lemuria*. Rochester, Vt.: Bear and Co., 2006.

———. *The Lost Pyramids of Rock Lake*. Rev. ed. Lakeville, Minn.: Galde, 2003.

———. *Opening the Ark of the Covenant*. Franklin Lakes, N.J.: New Page Books, 2007.

Josephus, Flavius. *The New Complete Works of Josephus*. Translated by William Whiston. New York: Kregel Academic and Professional, 1999.

Katsonopoulou, Dora. "Helike and Her Territory in Historical Times." *Pallas* 58 (2002): 175–82.

Kenny, Andrew. "The Ice Age Cometh." *The Sunday Mail,* July 14, 2002. www.ourcivilisation.com/aginatur/iceage.htm.

Knappert, Jan. *Indian Mythology: An Encyclopedia of Myth and Legend*. London: Diamond Books, 1995.

Kohlmann, Robert, trans. *The Edfu Texts*. Dallas: University of Texas Press, 1968.

Kramer, Noah. *A Sumerian Lexicon*. New York: University of New York Press, 1975.

———. *The Sumerians*. Chicago: University of Chicago Press, 1969.

Kronkheit, C. A. *A Dictionary of Ancient Egyptian Terms*. Chicago: University of Chicago Press, 1929.

Krupp, Edwin C. *Echoes of the Ancient Skies: The Astronomy of Lost Civilizations*. New York: Harper and Row, 1983.

Lanning, Edward P. *Peru before the Incas.* Englewood Cliffs, N.J.: Prentice-Hall, 1967.

Leicht, Hermann. *Pre-Inca Art and Culture.* New York: Orion, 1960.

Le Plongeon, Augustus. *Sacred Mysteries among the Mayas and the Quiches.* New York: Cosimo Classics, 2007. First published in 1909.

Lomas, Victor. *The Magdalenians.* Toronto: MacPherson, 1971.

MacCana, Prosinas. *Celtic Mythology.* London: Hamlyn, 1970.

Malkowsky, Edward. *Egypt before the Pharaohs.* Rochester, Vt.: Bear and Co., 2006.

Malkus, W. V. R. "Precession of the Earth as the Cause of Geomagnetism." *Science* 160, no. 3825 (April 19, 1968): 259–64.

Maloney, Evan Coyne. "Fear the Coming Ice Age." http://brain-terminal.com/posts/2008/10/01/fear-the-coming-ice-age.

Marriott, Alice, and Carol K. Rachlin. *American Indian Mythology.* New York: New American Library, 1968.

Massa, Aldo. *The World of the Etruscans.* Geneva: Editions Minerva, 1973.

Matthew, William Diller. "Plato's Atlantis in Paleogeography." *Procedures of the National Academy of Sciences* 6 (1920): 17f.

McKenna, Dennis J., and Terence McKenna. *The Invisible Landscape: Mind, Hallucinogens, and the I Ching.* New York: Seabury, 1975.

McMoneagle, Joseph. *Memoirs of a Psychic Spy: The Remarkable Life of U.S. Government Remote Viewer 001.* Charlottesville, Va.: Hampton Roads, 2006.

Men, Hunbatz. *Secrets of Mayan Science/Religion.* Rochester, Vt.: Bear and Co., 1990.

Mercatante, Anthony S. *Who's Who in Egyptian Mythology.* New York: Clarkson N. Potter, 1978.

Mercer. A. B. Samuel. *Horus, Royal God of Egypt.* Cambridge, UK: Society of Oriental Research, 1960.

Metraux, Alfred. *The History of the Incas.* New York: Penteon Books, 1969.

Milewski, J. V., and V. L. Harford, eds. *The Crystal Sourcebook.* Sedona, Ariz.: First Editions, 1987.

Miller, Mary, and Karl Taube. *The Gods and Symbols of Ancient Mexico and the Maya.* London: Thames and Hudson, 1993.

Morehouse, David. *Psychic Warrior: The True Story of America's Foremost Psychic Spy and the Cover-up of the CIA's Top-secret Stargate Program.* New York: St. Martin's, 1998.

Morley, Sylvanus. *The Ancient Maya*. Palo Alto, Calif.: Stanford University Press, 1946.

Moseley, Michael E. *The Incas and Their Ancestors*. London: Thames and Hudson, 1994.

Namkhai Norbu. *Drung, Deu and Bön: Narrations, Symbolic Languages and the Bön Tradition in Ancient Tibet*. Translated by Adriano Clemente and Andrew Lukianowicz. New York: Library of Tibetan Works and Archives, 1988. Reprint, 1995.

Nicholson, I. *Mexican and Central American Mythology*. London: Hamlyn, 1967.

Nuttall, Zelia. *The Fundamental Principles of Old and New World Civilizations*. Vol. 2. Cambridge, Mass.: Peabody Museum of American Archaeology and Ethnology, 1901.

O'Brien, Henry. *The Round Towers of Atlantis*. Kempton, Ill.: Adventures Unlimited, 2002. First published in 1834 as *The Round Towers of Ireland*.

Olivier, Guilhem. *Mockeries and Metamorphoses of an Aztec God Tezcatlipoca, "Lord of the Smoking Mirror."* Boulder: University Press of Colorado, 2003.

Olson, Carl. *The Theology and Philosophy of Eliade: A Search for the Centre*. New York: St. Martin's, 1992.

Osborne, Harold. *South American Mythology*. London: Hamlyn, 1970.

Pallottino, M. *The Etruscans*. New York: Harper and Row, 1978.

Panov, Alexander. "Chelyabinsk Meteorite: Mystery Revealed." *Russia behind the Headlines,* March 19, 2013. http://rbth.ru/society/2013/03/19/chelyabinsk_meteorite_mystery_revealed_24039.html.

Patton, Laurie L., trans. *The Bhagavad Gita*. New York: Penguin Classics, 2008.

Peithmar, Irwin M. *Echoes of the Red Man*. New York: Expectation, 1955.

Petrie, W. M. Flinders. *A History of Egypt*. Vol. 3, *The IX and XX Dynasties*. London: Methuen, 1896.

Plato. *The Timaeus and the Kritias*. Translated by Desmond Lee. London: Penguin Books, 1977.

Porch, Douglas. *The Conquest of the Sahara*. New York: Alfred Knopf, 1984.

Powell, T. G. E. *The Celts*. New York: Praeger, 1959.

Prescott, William H. *The Conquest of Mexico*. New York: Julian Messner, 1950.

———. *The Conquest of Peru*. New York: New American Library, 1961. First published in 1847.

Radin, Paul. *The Winnebago Tribe*. The Thirty-Seventh Annual Report of the Bureau of American Ethnology. Washington, D.C.: Smithsonian Institution, 1923. Reprint, Lincoln: University of Nebraska Press, 1970.

Ramoino, Michael R. "Possible Relationships between Changes in Global Ice Volume, Geomagnetic Excursions, and the Eccentricity of the Earth's Orbit." *Geology* 7 (December 1979): 584–87.

Sahagún, Bernardino de. *Florentine Codex: General History of the Things of New Spain.* Translated by A. J. O. Anderson and C. E. Dibble. Santa Fe, N.M.: Worther,1963.

Santesson, Hans. *Understanding Mu.* New York: Paperback Library, 1970.

Savoy, Gene. *On the Trail of the Feathered Serpent.* New York: Bobbs-Merrill, 1974.

Schnell, Howard, trans. *The Oera Linda Bok.* London: Truebner, 1876.

Scofield, Bruce. *Day Signs.* Amherst, Mass.: One Reed Publications, 1996.

Seleem, Ramses. *The Illustrated Egyptian Book of the Dead: A New Translation with Commentary.* New York: Sterling, 2001.

Sharkey, John. *Celtic Mysteries: The Ancient Religion.* London: Thames and Hudson, 1970.

Sitchin, Zechariah. "Olmec Civilization Older Than Believed." *Ancient American* 9, no. 6 (April 2001).

Smith, Richard J. *Fathoming the Cosmos and Ordering the World: The Yijing (I Ching or Classic of Changes) and Its Evolution in China.* Charlottesville: University of Virginia Press, 2008.

Smithsonian Institution. *The Aztec "Sun Stone."* Washington, D.C.: Smithsonian Institution, National Museum of Natural History, Department of Anthropology, Public Information Office, 1987.

Spence, Lewis. *The Problem of Lemuria.* London: Rider, 1930.

Steinhoff, George, and Kenneth Seele. *When Egypt Ruled the East.* Chicago: University of Chicago Press, 1957.

Sturluson, Snorri. *The Prose Edda.* Translated by Jesse L. Byock. New York: Penguin Classics, 2006.

Swanson, Claude. *The Synchronized Universe.* Tucson, Ariz: Poseidia, 2003.

Sykes, Edgerton. *Lemuria Reconsidered.* London: Markham House, 1968.

———. *Who's Who in Non-Classical Mythology.* New York: Oxford University Press, 1993.

Thunderhorse, Iron. "The Calendar Stone: Myths and Facts." *Ancient American* 7, no. 44 (March–April 2002): 7–11.

Thompson, Gunnar. *American Discovery: The Real Story*. Seattle: Misty Isles, 1995.

Tozzer, Alfred M. *A Maya Grammar*. New York: Dover, 1978.

Tyler, H. A. *Pueblo Gods and Myths*. Norman: University of Oklahoma Press, 1964.

University of Vermont. "When Did the Last Glacial Age End?" www.uvm.edu/whale/GlaciersAgeEnd.html.

Vaillant, George C. *Aztecs of Mexico*. New York: Doubleday, 1962.

Van Over, R. *Sun Songs: Creation Myths from Around the World*. New York: New American Library, 1980.

Von Hagen, Victor. *The Ancient Sun Kingdoms of the Americas*. Cleveland: World Publishing, 1957.

Xu, H. Mike. *Origin of the Olmec Civilization*. Norman: University of Central Oklahoma Press, 1996.

Wasilewski, Krzys. "Computer Software Says Armageddon Will Arrive in 2012." *The Student Operated Press*, May 1, 2008. http://thesop.org/index.php?article=11011.

Wasson, R. Gordon, Stella Kramrisch, Jonathan Ott, and Carl A. P. Ruck. *Persephone's Quest: Entheogens and the Origins of Religion*. New Haven, Conn.: Yale University Press, 1986.

Waters, Frank. *Book of the Hopi*. New York: Viking, 1963.

Watts, Anthony. "The 1970's Global Cooling Compilation—Looks Much Like Today." Watts Up with That? March 1, 2013. http://wattsupwiththat.com/2013/03/01/global-cooling-compilation.

Whishaw, Elena Maria. *Atlantis in Spain*. Kempton, Ill.: Adventures Unlimited, 1994. First published as Atlantis in Andalusia, London: Rider, 1924.

Wikipedia. "Solar Storm of 1859." http://en.wikipedia.org/wiki/Solar_storm_of_1859.

Wikipedia. "Yuga." http://en.wikipedia.org/wiki/Yuga.

Wilkins, Harold T. *Mysteries of Ancient South America*. Kempton, Ill.: Adventures Unlimited, 2000. First published in 1947.

Williams, Mark R. *In Search of Lemuria*. San Mateo, Calif.: Golden Era Books, 2001.

Zimmerman, J. E. *Dictionary of Classical Mythology*. New York: Bantam Books, 1971.

# Index

Page numbers in *italic* refer to illustrations.